D1596526

Clare Abbott

HORNED DEATH

The author with "Spots", a favorite pet.

Horned DEATH

By *John F.* BURGER

SAFARI PRESS, INC

P.O. Box 3095, Long Beach, CA 90803, U.S.A.

Burger, John F.

ISBN 0-940143-66-6

10 9 8 7 6 5 4 3 2

FOREWORD

Even though there is an introduction elsewhere, we would still like to give a small foreword on John F. Burger, which we think will be of interest to the reader. The author was born in South Africa on the Great Karoo in the Prieska District. He lived there until 1905 on the family farm where his father reared sheep and ostriches. During those years John Burger saw the last of the great springbok migrations, which by some estimates contained millions of animals.

Later he took part in that infamous South African historical event: the great trek — a journey of Afrikaners traveling from the Orange River to Southern Rhodesia, now Zimbabwe, through the Kalahari Desert. The journey lasted five months during which much hardship was suffered by all.

After settling in the city of Bulawayao, he started work with the local newspaper as a typesetter. In those days he met and hunted with many famous hunters such as Selous, van Rooyen, v.d. Westhuizen and Cooper. During the First World War, he enlisted with the Rhodesian military and served as a scout and meat supplier for the ever-hungry troops. It was during this time that he gained much of his experience with all types of game, but especially the notorious African buffalo. During the East African conflict, he was wounded and relieved from his duties. He settled back in South Africa in Durban. Here he became owner of a boxing school.

However, the lure of the bush and its game would not leave him alone. He returned to the Belgium Congo, now Zaire, where he had been before. He tried his luck with mining for uranium and gold. While prospecting for metals, he hunted profusely in the Ituri Forest, Kivu, Ubangi, Sudan, Uganda, and Kenya. Many of his adventures in these places are retold in this book. After fifteen years in the Congo, he settled in Tanzania in order to hunt the omni-present buffaloes as well as mine. Here he also worked to control the locust plagues. In 1947 he returned to Southern Rhodesia. Burger started writing about his adventures after World War II, which resulted in this fine book.

The Publisher.

Introducing:

JOHN F. BURGER, Afrikander

The African Cape buffalo (Syncerus caffer) is a notoriously bad actor. In fact, he is no actor at all, in the Thespian meaning of the word. Many wild animals—lions, tigers, and other beasts whose names are synonyms for ferocity—can be half-tamed and then expertly controlled to provide thrills for movie-goers and circus crowds. But not so with the African bull buffalo; he is one wild animal who intends to remain wild. In Hollywood's celluloid world of genuine roaring lions, snarling tigers and trumpeting elephants the surly, unpredictable buffalo is never on the roster of living, four-footed deviltry. On those rare occasions when the bull buffalo is scheduled to demonstrate his terrifying specialty—the charge—the net result on the screen is a furious waving of tall grass and glimpses of a rapidly moving head-and-horns, of papier maché. With that quaint deception accomplished, the mummers' representation of horned death is again deposited in the property room to gather dust with the bloodless guillotine and the shockless electric chair.

John F. Burger, Afrikander and author of this book, would heartily endorse any theatrical effort to simulate the charge of an African bull buffalo—if no human life is to be risked. This notable professional hunter, who is here being introduced to the American public, has miraculously survived to live and tell of many last-ditch encounters with the powerful and crafty buffalo. Mr. Burger's experiences in the game fields of his native continent cover a period of forty years, and in that time more than one thousand of the massive brutes have fallen to his rifles. As he takes care to explain, only a small number of the animals in that record bag have actually charged; but in that temperate statement there rests proof of his usual success in placing a first, effective hit—the shot that renders a charge improbable. Failure of that first shot, or the effect of factors beyond the hunter's control, constitutes the explosive cap that can set this specimen of black dynamite into action. Once the buffalo's charge is actually under way his only objective is to produce a dead hunter. The animal has accomplished his grim purpose in many instances. Too frequently the gored and trampled victim has been a veteran of the trails, not a novice hunter or a defenseless native. In s o m e vitally unaccountable way the buffalo had gained advantages at a rate faster than was allowed the hunter. The man was then denied that last precious asset for survival, luck. Our author lives to tell of his close encounters with the horned death simply because luck never failed to tip the scales in his favor.

Americans must read the history books of their country to know of men whose mode of life and deeds can stamp them with the romantic designation "pioneer." Nowadays, we depend on centennial celebrations for ox-teams, covered wagons and temporarily bearded citizens to remind us of the vanished frontier and its people. But Africa is newer in the matter of frontiers, and there we must turn if we would find living Caucasians who have known frontier life and all that the term implies. John F. Burger is one such person, and he is as indigenous to the Dark Continent as the rugged baobab tree and the Cape buffalo itself.

Our author was born in the Prieska district, a dozen years before the Boer War (1899-1901). At that war's conclusion his parents joined their neighbors in a great trek to the north, into Rhodesia. Traveling with donkey wagons, they set out over the Kalahari Desert, the forbidding land obstacle that lay between them and their goal. Once well into the desert the caravan lost direction and before long the finding of water became a matter of life or death. As a last resort, scouts fanned out in search of a pool. One of those scouts was young John Burger; he went alone and unarmed. On that day luck twice tipped the balance in his favor. At one time only a few yards lay between him and a hungry lion. He had come upon the brute without warning as it was in the act of taking a native. The badly frightened lad fully expected to be the lion's next victim, but for a reason known only to the lion he was allowed to escape unharmed. Escape —to what? The answer came late that afternoon, when the thirst- tortured, stumbling boy discovered the headquarters of Khama, the Bechuana king. Khama's people guided the caravan from the desert.

It was while on this historic trek, which lasted four months, that Burger made his first acquaintance with the African buffalo. It was a gruesome introduction but one without threat of harm from the buffalo. Thousands of their carcasses littered the open plains, in mute reminder of the great rinderpest epidemic which had swept the land only a short while before.

The trek toughened this boy, and it was well, because his father died shortly after the family reached Rhodesia. Burger now believes that part of his life to have been the hardest; he could earn little money and he was hungry much of the time. In this period he was apprenticed to a printer, but the lure of better earnings and adventure caused him to run away and join a safari. And that is how, at the age of seventeen, he had already met and hunted with every notable hunter then in Rhodesia. He was only twenty when he joined with the famous Vander Westhuizen for the trip through the Kivu, and a year later—feeling, as he expresses it, "qualified to take any safari on my own bat"—he made his very dangerous passage through the country of the Ubangi cannibals. A natural linguist, he was then able to converse in seven languages and to that ability he attributes much of his success in dealing with natives. And when talk failed, he could oblige with a brief display of rifle marksmanship, which seldom failed to restore the conversation to a sensible level.

By 1914 Burger was a veteran of many safaris and entirely familiar with every aspect of life in the bush. In that year the sound of war drums in civilized Europe caused the hunter to enlist in his King's service. The military column to which he became attached moved from Victoria Falls to Abercorn, and early in the march he was assigned the special duty of supplying game meat for the troops and porters. The animals to be shot included buffalo, and it was then that the "Burger buffalo campaign" got well under way. The problems of transport during that time were the same as had always existed in Africa; the motor car had not yet appeared in hinterland military operations and black men toted as they did in the days of Livingstone. The hardships of the hunting field were aggravated further by relentless military necessity and it was small wonder that hunter Burger's health broke in 1917, during the East African Campaign. He was invalided South and discharged shortly after.

He lived for a time in Durban, where he revived an earlier interest in boxing and established his own boxing school. His training produced three South African ring champions. But life in Durban was not for him; back to the bush he went, this time to the Belgian Congo.

The promising occupations in the Congo were prospecting and mining for rare minerals. Burger had an early part in the activity, being closely associated with the discovery of uranium deposits at Tantara and Chinklobwe. He was the first person to sample and prepare ore for export to Hoboken, in Belgium. The finding of those deposits permitted the Belgians to market precious radium at almost half the price that prevailed at that time. The Congo's deposits of radioactive ore continue to be the largest known in the world.

The Great Depression of the 1930's, which many Americans have cause to remember, reached into the heart of Africa, too. When the commercial paralysis crept into the Congo, Burger migrated to Tanganyika. There he spent the next fifteen years at alluvial and reef mining—and hunting. Finally, towards the end of 1946, he returned to the scenes of his early life, to Southern Rhodesia. At that time nearly thirty years had elapsed since he left Durban for the Congo—three decades spent in the bush, with never a trip south of the Zambesi River.

As this is written, Burger is engaged in a mining enterprise in his native Rhodesia; Lonely Mine is his post office, and Bulawayo (18,200 white people and 27,000 non-Europeans) is hundreds of miles distant. John F. Burger, veteran of the bush, has returned to civilization!

*   *   *   *   *

A few words regarding Mr. Burger's text and the means of securing it for publication would not be amiss. As is generally recognized, the game hunters of the world comprise a great, if unofficial, brotherhood. From the far corners of the earth they communicate with each other, and it was through the good offices of the American hunter and firearms author Elmer Keith that the present publisher was first made aware of the Burger collection of true adventure stories. In the hunter-talk letters that passed between them Burger mentioned his habit of recording his more notable adventures and that it was a form of literary relaxation in which he had indulged for many years and wherever he happened to be. He also wondered if the American reading public would be interested in the life of which he wrote.

So began the chain of circumstances which brought the manuscript to Elmer Keith, at North Fork, Idaho, and thence to the publisher's office for editorial appraisal. A short session of reading left no doubt that the Burger manuscript was the kind of offering a publisher hopes for but seldom receives. Those tissue-thin foolscap pages, neatly typed and held together by tiny rusted pins, carried text as authentic as elephant ivory or the precious pebbles of Kimberley. The prospective publisher's next task was to get into direct communication with the author. This was done, distance and time notwithstanding, and the relationship immediately became a happy one.

Reader, the book is yours, and we are certain that you will shortly know John F. Burger as a modest gentleman, a fascinating raconteur, and an African hunter from the mould that is now broken.

The Publisher

CONTENTS

CONTENTS

ILLUSTRATIONS

ILLUSTRATIONS

1: THE POINT OF VIEW

How many agonizing hours I have spent on the trail of the Cape buffalo, the "bad boy" of the African Bush! It is nearly forty years since I first accompanied a famous hunter on the trail of the buffalo and from that day I have hunted him assiduously, with only a few breaks. Not only have I devoted most of my hunting to that animal, but never have I let an opportunity pass without discussing him with others who, like myself, have followed the buffalo trail. Among those hunters I count Selous, van Rooyen, V. D. Westhuizen, Norton, Bacon, Sutherland, Barnes, Downing, Bishop, von Roelen, and Michardt. Also there were Booysen and Joubert, both of them killed while hunting the buffalo. They all followed that trail, but to them the buffalo was only incidental; to me he is an obsession. I must, perforce, have learned something about the buffalo, and it was inevitable that I should have many exciting adventures with him.

For a good many years past the buffalo has claimed the doubtful honour of being "Hunter's Enemy No. 1," and he has been described variously as "the most dangerous," "the most vindictive," "the most cunning," and "the most aggressive" animal in Africa. Perhaps, in the view of some writers, he richly merits such an unsavoury reputation. But for myself, I cannot agree with them entirely and I must dissociate myself from his long list of calumniators, that is, in so far as his natural and inherent instincts are concerned. I will not dispute that in the matters of retaliation and rendering evil-for-evil he has acquired, and richly deserves, his present wicked reputation. But I do maintain that under *normal* conditions he is no more dangerous than any of the numerous antelopes which are considered harmless. Look over the long list of accidents and you will find that every one of them was due to provocation. In many cases the victims themselves were guilty of no provocation whatever, but provocation of some sort, at some other time, undoubtedly was responsible for the aggression.

In parts of the country where buffaloes had not previously been hunted or molested I have often encountered herds and solitary animals, and I cannot remember a single occasion on which such animals have shown the least sign of aggressiveness. As a rule, they will look at one in wonder and surprise, and only when they are approached very closely will they make a move. Then they will trot off in an opposite direction and often they will turn around to have another look in order to satisfy their curiosity. This they will do under *normal* conditions. But the trouble with buffaloes is that one can never tell whether they are normal or not! A lone old bull may have left the herd because the inevitable bickerings and squabbles had become distasteful to him. He finds happiness in solitude. He has no particular grievance to settle, and if he should be encountered in the bush he will probably try to escape in the quickest possible time. Another bull may have suffered violence and wounds in fights with other herd bulls and have left the herd, not by choice, but because he was forced to do so. Such a bull has a grievance and, as likely as not, will resent the approach of a human being; he may quite possibly show his resentment by charging without direct provocation. Another may be suffering from gun wounds, and yet another from infirmity or disease. In such cases the animals are not normal and are almost certain to act in an abnormal manner. It is easy to understand, therefore, that the conduct of either a solitary or herd bull is governed to a large extent by conditions, even as is human conduct.

The numerous adventures and narrow escapes I have had with buffaloes were due entirely to the fact that provocations of some sort were directly responsible, and in describing those unpleasant incidents it must not be forgotten that they represent only a few isolated cases out of thousands of encounters I have had with them. On several occasions I have hunted a year or more without a single untoward incident, and then, by contrast, I have had as many as three hair-raising adventures in the course of one week.

That a buffalo with a grievance to settle is one of the most dangerous animals on earth, if not the most dangerous, cannot be disputed, and it is well for those who hunt him to bear this in mind. The cunningness of a wounded buffalo, bent on revenge, cannot be exaggerated and would appear to give the lie to the contention that animals do not reason, for in order to attain his ends the buffalo will often resort to strategy that would do credit to a human being under similar circumstances. Certainly, in his attempts to catch up with a tormentor he will generally follow a well thought-out plan, and it is at such moments that he will qualify for the distinction of being the most dangerous of animals. His vindictiveness then knows no bounds and often he will carry the feud beyond death. I have known of several cases where buffaloes have returned to a corpse in order to exact further vengeance. Compare this with the elephant, who will frequently bury his victim!

I have often been asked, "Which is the more dangerous, the lion or the buffalo?" One cannot give a straight answer to such a question. Conditions alone determine each case. There are no statistics available, and if there were, they would prove nothing. Buffaloes are far more numerous than lions, and are hunted far more frequently. It is only natural, therefore, that there should be more accidents with the former than with the latter. But far and away the largest number of accidents with lion have been due to inexperience and foolishness. I am, however, convinced that many more experienced hunters have been killed by buffaloes than by lions. This fact, of course, does not necessarily make the buffalo the more dangerous of the two. My own view is that, given the choice, I would very much sooner shoot it out with an enraged lion than with an enraged buffalo. In the matter of speed the lion has the advantage, but in natural cunning, resistance, and tenaciousness of life, the buffalo has it all his own way. A well-placed shot from a

Wounded, this enormous bull charged a gun-bearer and was brought down at uncomfortably close range.

A water buck bull, a soft-skinned animal which is noted for its resistance to bullet shock.

comparatively light rifle will, as often as not, prove sufficient in the case of lion, whereas a shot from a heavy-calibre, .375 and upwards, is almost certain to break down his charge. A double-barrel shotgun, at close quarters, is as effective a weapon as one could wish for against a charging lion, and I have known of several cases where a lion has been put "hors de combat" in hand-to-hand encounters with man. By contrast, there are several cases on record where the heaviest calibre rifles have failed to stop a charging buffalo in time; I have experienced similar cases myself. A shotgun would be utterly useless, and as for tackling a buffalo in a hand-to-hand fight . . . well, has anyone ever heard of it?

Before closing this homily on the respective merits of the lion and the buffalo I would raise the question of courage. The lion is frequently called the "King of Beasts." "King of Carnivora" would be more correct, and even here his superiority is not unchallenged. My own contention is that deep down in the makeup of every adult male lion there runs a broad yellow streak. One has but to dig deep enough in order to find it. Frequently, when the going gets really tough, the lion will seek safety in flight. He is a believer in the adage that discretion is the better part of valour. This cannot be said of the buffalo, who, to my mind, is the most courageous of animals, and once his animosity has been aroused sufficiently to provoke a charge, no odds are too great for him. In such cases he gives, or asks, for no quarter, but will fight it out silently and courageously to the bitter end. The observations I have made are, of course, based on my own experience. By far the greater part of my hunting has been devoted to the buffalo, and I have no doubt that those who have hunted the lion more assiduously than I have done will not agree with my views. But then, is there a subject on earth on which men will not disagree?

And now, having said so much in favour of the buffalo in his natural state, I quite expect those who are opposed to hunting in any form to ask, "Why, then, hunt and persecute him so persistently?" The answers are: First: For the same reason that thousands of animals, most of which are completely harmless, are hunted daily everywhere. Man has been a hunter ever and will be always. In hunting the buffalo there is always the element of danger. He is worthy of the hunter's steel, and to hunt him successfully requires skill, endurance and courage. Second: He is a most potent medium for carrying diseases that are harmful to man and other beasts. Third: There are very few, if any, places where the buffalo lives a natural and normal life. Native hunters all over Central and East Africa have increased tremendously, especially during the war years when food was scarce. As the hunting has increased, so has the wounding. In many and large tracts in Africa today the buffalo is a positive danger and menace, and frequently innocent persons pay for the misdeeds of the guilty. I am convinced that many hundreds of people are killed yearly in accidents with buffaloes. The true figures will never be known, as a great many such accidents are never reported. During the three months preceding this writing, I can vouch for at least a dozen fatal accidents in an area fifty miles square, and twice as many narrow escapes. There is no doubt that the buffalo, with his inherent inoffensive nature, has declared war on man, and has become Africa's greatest killer. That he has been driven to this I freely admit. But that he is incapable of exercising discretion is also true. We do not permit disgruntled human beings to exact vengeance indiscriminately—whatever the provocation. Is there any reason why the buffalo should be allowed to do so?

2: DEATH TOUCHES, LIGHTLY

"THIS IS the end. This time his good luck did not save him. It happened just as we always said it would happen, but he would not listen to us. It is a bad business for all of us . . ." This, and a description of virtues and compliments usually reserved for the dead, made strange listening. Ndege*, my head tracker, was the speaker.

The foregoing soliloquy, over what was supposed to be my dead body, was somewhat premature but quite understandable. For the last Ndege and the retinue of trackers and spotters had seen of me was when an enraged buffalo bull was charging down on me, only a few feet separating us. Now I was lying flat on my stomach, face and hands covered with blood. No wonder they thought I was dead and that the bull had deposited me in my present unenviable position! As usual, Ndege was giving play to a rather lively imagination. I was far from dead, but I had had my closest call with buffalo. And bad as it was, this was but the opening scene of as adventurous a day of hunting as one could ever have the good, or bad, fortune to experience and survive. Of course, at the time we did not know what was still in store for us. Perhaps it was as well.

---

* NDEGE (properly 'Mtu Ndege) means "the bird man" in the Sawhili language, and is pronounced Un-deggie, with a slight emphasis on the "un." The tracker, Ndege, received his name from fellow natives because they respected his uncanny ability to find and follow game.

DEATH TOUCHES, LIGHTLY

This was to have been my last day of hunting on the present trip. All camp kit had been packed since the previous day and in the morning I had left camp with the intention of finding a small buck to provide food for the porters while en route to my next camp, about fifty miles away to the north. Anything in the way of a reedbuck, kongoni or some such small fry would have been sufficient for our present requirements. In view of the unpretentious nature of this hunt I had taken only a half-gallon of water, a bottle of coffee and a couple of mangoes, expecting as I did to be back in camp before midday. Only nine natives, including the trackers, accompanied me, and for the immediate need that number was ample.

I expected to find the game I needed near a water hole in a swamp about five miles from my camp, and by 8 a.m. we arrived at the spot. But once there, we found a tremendous grass fire raging and, of course, no game of any description. Under the circumstances there was nothing else to do but strike out for another swamp a few miles away where, in the distance, we could see zebra, kongoni and topi grazing. This area had apparently been well hunted previously, for although game was plentiful, it was extremely timid, and try as I would I could not approach closer than 300 yards to any of the various herds. This range is by no means excessive, but visibility was bad, due to considerable heat mirage and the settling of smoke from nearby grass fires.

I finally selected a kongoni bull, and was pleased to see him go down to my first shot. The natives rushed up immediately to secure the kill. That animal was all I needed, and as I started to prepare for the return journey my attention was drawn to shouting in the direction where the kongoni had gone down. As the natives approached him, he had suddenly recovered from the shock and was already running at a moderate speed across the plain, with the natives close on his heels. As the natives were in the direct line of fire I dared not attempt another shot and all I could do was to stand and look on helplessly at their wild race. Soon the kongoni and his pursuers disappeared from sight and, knowing how tenacious of life these animals can be, I realised that it might take a long time to track down the wounded animal. As I had two of the finest trackers one could find anywhere I had not for a moment anticipated failure, but it soon became evident that no tracker living could hold that trail. The conditions were completely against them and after an hour or more of futile effort we were compelled to call off the trail.

It was now 10 o'clock in the morning, already the heat was intense, and the herds of game we had seen earlier had completely disappeared. Reluctant as I was to return to camp empty-handed, there was nothing else to do, and soon we were on our way back. We were taking a short-cut back home and behind me I could hear the natives grumbling about our bad luck. I was listening to the different points of view when suddenly I noticed the fresh tracks of a buffalo herd. They had been to water during the night and in the early hours of the morning they had made for the somewhat distant wooded country. The natives were all in favour of trailing down this herd, explaining that, in view of the intense heat, we might expect to find them under shelter in the forest. Although I had not come out to hunt buffalo, I felt that there was a good chance of trailing down this herd, and any meat in excess of my own requirements would be very acceptable to the villagers near my camp.

The trail was on, and hopes were running high—prematurely, as usual. The herd must have got into forest country very early and walked for several hours before they were put out by the heat. For three hours we followed their trail through difficult country before we finally spotted them. They had gone to the far end of the forest and were evidently about to enter another open plain when the heat proved too much for them, and here at the edge of the open plain, under a cluster of big trees, they had come to rest. They were quite unaware of our presence, and I was able to approach within 150 yards before a cow at the head of the herd suddenly looked in my direction. I kept dead still whilst for fully five minutes she stared in my direction. Finally she must have decided that all was well and started to look in the opposite direction. I was now able to observe the herd at some leisure, for I had made up my mind to shoot from where I was.

The herd consisted mainly of cows, two very young bulls, and two big bulls. The latter were of a light bluish-grey colour and differed so much from the usual colouring that I was completely puzzled. However, they were both full grown bulls and I decided to get the one nearest me. There was a heavy heat mirage, and visibility, even at such short range, was extremely bad. I was using a heavy .404-calibre rifle and took careful aim for the shoulder, hoping to bring off a heart shot. As the shot rang out there was a great rush and in the ensuing confusion I lost sight of the bull I had fired at, but I knew the bullet had struck home, as I had heard its resounding thud. The next instant the herd was off at top speed, making for the open plain. Both of the blue bulls were well up with the herd as they came out in the open, and it was impossible for me to tell which one I had hit. Then, one bull began to lag behind and I felt certain he was the one that had received the bullet. As he offered a broadside target I gave him another shot and this time he slumped to the ground. But now an astonishing thing happened; suddenly, a few yards ahead, the other blue bull collapsed in a cloud of dust. I realized at once that this second bull to fall was the one I had fired on first. He had evidently received the slug in the heart, where it was intended, and then had run some distance, as they frequently do, before the shot took effect. The other bull had apparently received a brain shot, to bring him down so suddenly. He was still lying motionless and to all intents and purposes he had died on the spot. The other bull, on the contrary, was still alive and making desperate efforts to regain his feet. As I was not very far from him, I took a light rifle from one of the gun bearers and finished him off with a shot in the brain. No sooner had I fired this shot when the other bull, which I believed to be dead, suddenly jumped up and started to run across the plain at a fast trot. So unexpected was this move that before I could exchange rifles and try another shot, he was several hundred yards from me and I missed him completely.

This was an extraordinary thing to happen. For the second time in one day an animal which I had believed dead was trying to make a get-away. I determined that this bull would not escape. Before starting to trail him, I went over to the place where he had gone down and a big pool of blood there convinced me that this bull also had received a bullet in the chest. I immediately got the trackers on the blood trail; the bull was bleeding rapidly, and I felt certain he could not last long. A little more than a mile across the open plain was more dense bush, and that was the place the bull had made for. Following the blood trail was easy work for the trackers and we fully expected to come up with the bull at the edge of the forest. This, in any case, was to be hoped for, because during the long trail earlier in the day I had very nearly exhausted my water supply. The heat at this time of the day on the open plain was terrific, and even if we were to catch up with the wounded animal at the edge of the forest it would be necessary for us to lay up until later in the afternoon, when it would be cooler. At a pinch, I could make my water supply last if we remained inactive during the hottest part of the day. Even so I would be forced to walk several miles without water. The natives, as usual, had indulged more freely than they should have done, and their water supply was completely exhausted. For 500 yards from where the bull had first gone down he left an easy trail, which the trackers followed at a fast pace. But shortly the tracks merged with other fresh tracks and trailing became extremely difficult. It was fully an hour and a half before we finally emerged on the trail at the far end of the plain. By now we were all suffering from acute thirst. My supply of water had dwindled to little more than a pint. We had hoped to find the buffalo dead long before now, but that bull had not died in the long grass and the trail now led into thick forest. Although I expected to find the bull dead near by, I warned the trackers to proceed very slowly and keep a sharp lookout on all sides. For another 200 yards we followed the tracks in close bush. The visibility was limited, but not nearly as bad as we had experienced on previous occasions. I was very surprised, therefore, when the natives suddenly called a halt. They were not prepared to follow that trail any farther in close country. The bull might have doubled back on his tracks, and the trees were all of a thorny variety which would make them difficult to climb in case of an emergency. This, and several other excuses, made it obvious that the natives were calling it a day. Ndege, also, had decided to take no further part in the proceedings. He is an old and experienced buffalo hunter, and the fact of his refusing to go further should have placed me on my guard. But in this mass refusal I saw nothing but a planned scheme to get back in order to quench their thirst. The manner in which it was done enraged me so that I threatened to fire the lot. I bandied no compliments, and after telling them they could go back home whilst I hunted the buffalo on my own, I took over my heavy-calibre rifle from the gun bearer. I was determined to see the business through. This was no bravado on my part; I firmly believed that no animal living could survive such a loss of blood for long. By all standards of judgment this bull should have died before he entered the forest country; at the very worst, he could have very little fight left in him at this stage.

There was now a distinct break in the close bush and for several yards I could see clearly on all sides. A bit farther ahead was a cluster of heavy thorn bush, and there I expected to find the buffalo. It was a comparatively easy position even were he still alive, which I doubted. After I had checked up on my rifle carefully I followed the trail on my own, taking no heed of protests from Ndege and the other natives. I had not gone more than fifty yards before I spotted the outline of the buffalo under a big thorn tree. He was standing with his head well down and offered an easy broadside target. He was barely a hundred yards from me and had not seen me. In order to make quite sure of my shot I moved up a bit closer and, after I had lined him up well in my sights, I fired for his head. But once again things went all wrong, for just as I pressed the trigger the bull lifted his head and the bullet grazed his neck. I was now in full view and in the next instant the bull came out in full charge. At the moment he took off there could not have been more than 75 yards between us, and before I could place my next shot he had reduced this distance to less than 50 yards. I could hear the second bullet strike distinctly and fully expected to see him go down, but the only effect the bullet seemed to have on him was to accelerate the charge. Now only 20 yards separated us, and once again I fired for the shoulder. Once again I could hear the bullet strike, but that bull seemed to be immune to punishment and came straight for me. There was no more time left now to try another shot. I was face to face with an enraged buffalo carrying out a last determined charge. At such moments one either thinks very quickly, or one does not think at all. Luckily for me, in my younger days I once made a precarious living as a professional boxer; in that sport one learns to think and act quickly, and I have retained the habit. In a flash my bygone training told me there was no point in standing erect to meet that deadly charge. Then I made, I am sure, the most spectacular dive in all history. Headlong I flew into the grass at my left and before I could touch the ground I felt a violent blow on my right leg, the impact thereof helping me on in my momentary flight through space. By a miracle I had escaped the head-on rush, but one of the hoofs had actually struck my extended leg. So far, I had escaped the most imminent and terrible danger, but I fully expected the bull to wheel around on me and lift me on one of his horns. To avoid this immediate danger I went down flat on my stomach, a position in which it would be very difficult for the buffalo to impale me. It was one of the tensest moments of my life—lying there waiting for the bull

[16]

to turn on me. But that bull did not turn around. He was beyond the stage of thinking or exacting vengeance. In a straight line he carried on his charge for another 20 yards and then he suddenly collapsed, for the second and last time in that day.

Both bullets aimed at the charging buffalo had entered the chest. One had pierced the heart, an injury from which he could not possibly recover. Although animals shot through the heart will often run long distances before they finally collapse, I believe that they do so only in a semi-conscious, if not an entirely unconscious state. I doubt whether that bull ever saw me after he had received the bullet in the heart, but he stuck to his course and had I remained erect in his path I would not be writing this now.

It was certainly a close call, and it all happened in very quick time. As I lay there, the usual nervous reaction had not set in. When I saw the natives approaching me I felt quite normal and feigned death. From where they were watching the proceedings they could not tell that I had voluntarily taken that plunge. They believed that the bull had killed me, and then were overjoyed to see me revive in much the same manner that they had seen the kongoni and buffalo revive earlier in the day. Apart from cuts and bruises on my hands and face I was none the worse for this terrifying experience. But long before we had traversed the plain on the trail of the buffalo I was suffering from an acute thirst, and now after the ordeal I had gone through, my lips were parched, my throat was burning and my tongue felt as though it had swollen to twice its normal size. Gallons of water could not quench such a thirst and in my bottle there was only a pint left. But even that was better than none at all.

"Water, water," I shouted at the native who was carrying the bottle. He did not seem to be in a great hurry to come to the rescue, but now he was within reach. Madly I grabbed for the bottle; to quench my thirst was all I could think of. It was only after I had withdrawn the cork that I realized the horror of the position I was in. That bottle was as dry as the parched ground I stood on! The full realization of this awful fact turned me speechless. If murder could have improved the situation in any way I would have sent a heavy slug through the brain of that native. When finally I had calmed down sufficiently to ask for an explanation he was quite equal to the occasion.

"We all thought you were dead, Bwana; dead men do not drink water. There was only a little left and I drank it before the others could grab it from me." This was a perfectly logical explanation and there was not much I could say to it.

The position now was desperate; we were at least twelve miles away from the nearest water, and with natives in the state of fatigue these porters were in the return journey would take at least six hours. They were all from the local village and had no interest in me. My trackers, both elderly men, had reached their limit and could not contemplate such a walk. Besides, they insisted that it was up to the man who had stolen my water to remedy the situation. After a great deal of discussion I finally persuaded two porters to go for water. They agreed to do the return trip, in return for all the meat of one buffalo. It was after 2 p.m. when they finally set out on their journey. If all went well they could be back by 8 o'clock that night. This meant suffering an agonizing thirst for another eight hours in that sun-baked plain.

The buffalo was lying dead on his side where he had dropped and there we left him whilst we took shelter under the trees nearby. By 5 o'clock the intense heat had subsided and then we had to face the task of dissecting the animal and carrying the meat to the spot where the other buffalo had fallen. This task was finally accomplished under the greatest of difficulties, and by 6:30 p.m. the carcasses of the two blue bulls were heaped together under a small tree in the open plain. All we had to do thereafter was to nurse our feelings and try to master the craving for water. That, at least, was how it appeared at the moment. In reality we had only got over the first stage of this memorable day. For the rest of that night we were subjected to an ordeal that taxed our nerves and powers of endurance to the extreme.

Our improvised camp for the night could not be moved to the big trees at the edge of the plain, as it would take time and the natives were too exhausted and thirsty. At the spot where we were camped, some 400 yards inside the open plain, we could find only a few sticks of firewood. With the greatest of difficulty I had managed to persuade the natives to bring in a few loads of this firewood for the night. The amount of meat on hand caused me to feel certain we would have trouble with lions and hyenas in the dark. As I had not expected to be out that night, I had brought no lamps or lighting equipment of any sort. The camp-fire would be our only means of providing light in case of an emergency, and the amount of wood we had gathered was barely sufficient to keep a fire glimmering for the night. Any demand of importance would exhaust the supply of firewood in an hour or less. But there is a limit to everything, and the natives were too tired and thirsty to do more. They admitted all I had to say on the subject, but they had reached the limit. Further discussion was quite useless.

By 7 p.m. it was quite dark. We were thirsty and hungry—hungry, in spite of the fact that we had more than a ton of meat on hand. But when one suffers thirst such as we were then suffering the best food in all the world is unpalatable. By 8 p.m. there was still no sign of the natives we had sent for water and I had small hopes of seeing them back that night. In a sense, I could not blame them should they fail to return. It was a pitch-black night without moon; the country they had to traverse was extremely rough and consisted for the greater part of thorn bush with intermittent swamps in which there were thousands of elephant-track holes. It is an ordeal to traverse such ground in daytime and infinitely worse at night. They were even more exhausted than ourselves. At the best, they would find it extremely difficult to fix their bearings in the dark as there were no landmarks to guide them. The more I thought of it the more I became reconciled to the idea of spending a night out in the open without water, food or cover.

I was still explaining my views to the natives when suddenly there was a loud rustle in the grass quite close to us. The campfire amounted to a mere flicker, but luckily I had earlier persuaded the natives to prepare grass flares to be lit in case of emergency. We all listened intently to the rustling in the grass, and quite clearly we could hear footsteps approaching us. Fortunately, I had brought my shotgun along and it was loaded with buckshot. I grabbed for the gun and ordered the flares to be lit at once. In a few seconds two flares were alight and there, not more than ten yards away, was the cause of the alarm—a huge male lion. As the flames from the flares mounted he gave vent to a menacing snarl, and before I could get him in my sights properly he had disappeared.

This lion had evidently followed the trail along which we had carried the second buffalo that afternoon. After we had dissected the buffalo and removed the last piece of meat, the vultures had settled down and cleared up all the debris. When the lion arrived at that place he had found nothing to eat and had then proceeded to follow the trail of the meat. As the meat had been carried right across our camp, there was the distinct danger that he would stick to the trail until he got to the meat. We were right in his path, and I have no doubt that but for the timely lighting of the flares he would have removed or carried off the first obstacle in his path—myself.

I am accustomed to lions and their ways, and I

had no doubt whatever that our visitor was in desperate need of food and would stand for no interference. The meat had all been put into one big heap and covered with thorny branches, and I felt relieved to have put the brute off his course, for as he ran off after the flares had been lit I could hear him trampling down the grass in the direction of the meat. Now he would find the meat without having to pass through our camp. To this extent at least our danger was lessened. I made up my mind that if matters came to a point I would let him satisfy his hunger at the expense of the dead buffaloes. But at the same time, I did not feel disposed to hand him this royal feast on a platter. If he wanted it he would have to fight for it the same as I did, and only if he made things too uncomfortable for us would I allow him to get away with it.

By now, the natives had miraculously recovered from their fatigue! They were all anxious to help in any way I might direct. The first thing I called for was more flares. Luckily, there was an abundance of dry grass from which flares could be made easily and quickly. In order to augment the supply of firewood I ordered the natives to cut down three young thorn trees which stood close by. These trees were green and in bloom, but I knew they would dry and burn if exposed to fire long enough. They were quickly cut down to await further developments. We had not long to wait before the natives, now all on the *qui vive,* again detected the sound of footsteps approaching in the dark, the heavy dry grass helping to make each step clearly audible. The lion was now approaching the meat from the opposite side, as I had hoped he would do, and there was no immediate danger of his attacking any of us, but there was always the possibility that he would resent our presence and take steps to rid himself of any interference whilst he was on the kill.

The fire had again been revived and all eight of us now stood in line with rifles and spears waiting for the next move. Suddenly there was a loud grunt followed by a leap in the grass, then two more loud grunts. Although the lion's attitude was distinctly menacing and aggressive, he kept well out of the light provided by the fire and it was impossible to fix his exact whereabouts. A chance shot under such circumstances would be much too dangerous, for to wound him now would be a sure way of inviting a charge. Once again I withheld my fire and depended on lighted flares to scare him away. This time he moved off at his leisure and I knew he would return as soon as the flares were burnt out. The second flare had hardly died down when we could hear him coming back again. This time he adopted different tactics to frighten us away, for as he approached the meat he kept up a continuous and vicious snarling. There was menace in those snarls and if they were intended to frighten us away from the scene they very nearly succeeded in doing so, as the natives now were in a state of abject terror and it took me all my time to prevent them from lighting and burning up all the flares at once. Two more flares were lit and thrown in the direction of the snarling animal, but again it was impossible for me to sight him properly, and once again he moved off slowly.

It was quite obvious that there would be no peace for us that night until the lion was shot dead or had appeased his hunger. I was in favour of the former and determined that I would get him the next time he came. To this end I instructed the natives to wait until the lion was actually on the kill and feeding and then to light four flares, instead of two. I felt certain that once the lion had started to feed he would not leave the kill so quickly and the light of the two additional torches would help me to sight him properly. It all seemed very easy and I was looking forward to the next visit, feeling certain that it would be the last one. But the next time he came the snarling had increased in intensity and so menacing had he become that long before he was anywhere near the meat all four flares were burning brightly. The natives were taking no chances! The extra light from the flares and the shouting of the natives completely upset my plans and once again the lion retreated, this time grunting loudly as he disappeared in the dark. There was no doubt about it, things were coming to a head. This last visit had been the most determined he had made so far, and the tone of his grunting as he walked off was a clear warning that his temper had been ruffled.

The natives were now scared completely out of their wits and I feared that the next visit would scatter the lot of them in all directions. I was still busy explaining to them what the results of such a foolish act would be when, once again, there came a series of grunts and snarls and rapidly moving footsteps in the dark. So menacing had the lion become now that I expected to see him land in our midst in the very next instant. There was no time to lose, and before the flares were fully alight I fired in the direction of the sounds. Wounded or not, I felt certain the brute would not be put off any longer. As my shot rang out there was a violent rustle in the grass and then all was silent. For five minutes we listened intently. There was no sound of any description. I was beginning to hope that I had succeeded with my chance shot when again we could hear the grass being trampled down. This time the steps were receding. For fully thirty minutes after that there was silence. Either the lion had got off with a helping of meat, or I had wounded him so badly that he had decided to abandon further attempts. After a few more minutes of silence I managed to persuade the natives to light more flares and accompany me to the pile of meat to see if it was still intact.

We had hardly advanced five yards when there was a violent rustle in the grass right next to me. I am not of a very nervous disposition, but I will admit that this sudden rustle in the grass on my blind side, coming at a time when my nerves had been subjected to intense strain for many hours, gave me one of the grandest shocks of my life. Luckily, it was all very harmless and the brute was merely making a quick get-away. But he did not stay away for very long after that. Twice more during the night I was compelled to fire at an imaginary target in the dark in order to keep the brute away. That fellow had a charmed life and certainly was not destined to die from lead poisoning on this occasion. With the help of flares and occasional flames as the green leaves became ignited, we managed to keep him away until daybreak. Then, as a gesture of contempt, or respect, I do not know which, he stood up and roared loudly. Twice more the performance was repeated for our special benefit, but on the last occasion the sound was receding in the distance. Our night of terror was over. As a farewell to this persistent creature I fired a shot in the direction from where the last sound had come and, respectfully raising my hat to him, I sank down, utterly fatigued.

We had not slept a wink that night, and the urgency of the work in hand had kept us from thinking too much about the terrible thirst we were suffering. A bitter cold wind swept that sun-baked plain all night long, but in spite of the cold our tongues remained swollen and parched. As the sun rose we looked longingly across the plain for the porters with the water, but there was no sign of any living being. I was beginning to think that the two men had gone on to their village some twenty miles away and would return at their leisure late in the afternoon—when we heard a call in the distance. In a few seconds my natives made off in that direction and by shouting and whistling they soon established our exact whereabouts. By 8 a.m. water arrived in camp.

The two porters had walked until darkness overtook them and then they had completely lost their way and spent the night in a tree. During their long walk and their enforced stay in the bush overnight they had helped themselves freely to the water they were carrying for us, but what they brought was sufficient to help us through until we ourselves could reach the water hole. The water there, crystal clear, issues from a spring in a mountain. Only once before did water taste so good to me and that was when I was lost in the Kalahari Desert for three days. But that had nothing to do with hunting the buffalo.

We got back to camp at 2 o'clock that afternoon utterly fatigued. The long walk in the tropical sun after the exposure of the previous day and night had helped to sap the last ounce of energy we had left in us. I had hardly crawled into bed before I was fast asleep. At 4 p.m. I was awakened by my cook, who announced that a native from the village nearby wanted to speak to me urgently. I had no particular desire to speak to anyone at that moment; rest was what I wanted. But not knowing what this urgent visit might be about I called for the native to enter. In response to my inquiry as to what he wanted he excitedly informed me that a big herd of buffaloes had just left the water hole near by, and did I want to hunt them? Well—if any reader is on the lookout for promising material for the 100 yards in the next Olympiad I can recommend an excellent prospect!

Earlier in this account I mentioned the peculiar colouring of the two buffalo bulls. When finally they were accounted for I found that this was due to their having wallowed in mud during the night and the mud had dried on their hides, giving them a bluish appearance. Those bulls certainly helped to give me as exciting a time as ever I have had on the buffalo trail. On this trail I had the unusual experience of facing the two great killers, buffalo and lion, within a period of twenty-four hours. The lion made things extremely unpleasant throughout the night; but he had the advantage of the darkness. I still maintain that of the two, I would much sooner shoot it out with the "King of Beasts" than with the "Bovine Monarch."

3: THE GENTLEMEN POACHERS OF LADO

NORTHEAST of Lake George, and to the east of Lake Albert Nyanza, lies a stretch of country which the modern map of Africa shows as belonging to Uganda. This allocation was made by the Anglo-Belgian Border Commission of 1910. Previous to the sitting of this Commission, that particular stretch of country was known as the Lado Enclave. In other words, the frontiers of Uganda, Sudan and the Belgian Congo were then not defined, and the Lado Enclave was No Man's Land. In that place there was no government and no law.

The Lado, at that time, was the Utopia of ivory hunters, for no licence was required to hunt the elephant, and even ivory hunted in the adjoining licenced areas was smuggled into the Enclave from where it was sold as a Lado product. Since there was no law in Lado to restrict the operations of the hunters there, no one ever queried the legitimacy of this trade, nor was there any attempt made to limit these activities. In spite of the favourable conditions, the Lado was never exactly overcrowded, but most of the men who congregated there were the pick of African elephant hunters. I was one of the lesser lights who operated in the area at that time.

After the Commission had completed its work and the borders were defined, an official circular was sent to the hunters in the Enclave; this circular was addressed to "The Gentlemen Poachers of Lado," and advised those gentlemen that in future that territory would come under the Uganda administration and that all who wanted to hunt the elephant on British soil would be required to procure licences for the purpose. Those who failed to comply with the new regulations would render themselves liable to the penalties of the Game Laws.

Those of us who represented the law-abiding section of Lado immediately proceeded to Hoima and conformed to the new regulation by procuring our licences. But there were others who were not of a particularly law-abiding nature, and to them the new regulations were of no significance whatever.

To this community belonged Bill Lang, one of the most notorious adventurers in Central Africa. Bill, at that time, was quite a power in Lado. He had his own regiment of trained askari soldiers and his own canoes, and had even arrogated to himself the right to dispense of land in the Enclave. It was on Enclave land granted by Bill that an important Mission station was built at Koba. He was no longer plain Bill Lang but Captain Lang. All of us who knew Bill were convinced that sooner or later there would be a showdown between him and the Government.

It was not long before the District Commissioner from Hoima arrived and called on Bill to surrender himself within twenty-four hours, or suffer the consequences. But the D.C. underestimated his man. Far from surrendering, Bill in turn presented an ultimatum to the official, ordering him to quit in just half that time or otherwise face Captain Lang's regiment of askari. Not being prepared for such an eventuality, and realizing that Bill was quite capable of carrying out his threat, the official decided that discretion was the better part of valour, and gracefully retired within the stipulated time.

It was quite obvious that the matter would not be allowed to rest at that, and for a fortnight we all lived in an atmosphere of expectation. At the end of that time Inspector X arrived on the scene with an armed squad and ordered Bill to surrender. Bill would not entertain the idea of surrendering, but declared that he was prepared to meet the Inspector in a stand-up fight and abide by the result. To this the Inspector promptly agreed, and that night saw Bill safe under lock and key, awaiting his removal the next day to the Masindi prison.

At the subsequent trial he got off on a point of law and after that he returned and joined forces with a Greek named Karamojo George, ostensibly for the purpose of hunting buffalo, for which no licence was required. But Bill would not keep off elephant and, less than a month later, he was sentenced to six months' hard labour for contravention of the Game Laws. The Government confiscated his property, part of which consisted of an enormous canoe which was transported overland on rollers to Port Bell on Lake Victoria Nyanza, an undertaking which required the services of two hundred natives for a month.

On his release, Bill was deported and during the

great war he joined a labour battalion for service in France. After the war he went to Tanganyika Territory, where he discovered a rich mica field which he sold for a small fortune. But he never lived to enjoy the benefits of that wealth, for he died a few weeks later.

Of the same type as Bill Lang, but less aggressive, was Jack Pickering. Jack was not prepared to flout the law, but neither did he like the idea of paying for a licence. He therefore resorted to the simple expedient of transferring his activities to the Belgian side of Lake Albert. It was not long before he was in trouble with the Belgian authorities, who confiscated all his guns, ammunition, and other belongings; in addition, they made him pay for a licence. Before long Pickering was again equipped for the field and decided to operate the licence he was forced to buy from the Belgian Government. He installed himself on the western side of Lake Albert and soon was on terms of friendship with the Belgian officials.

One night Pickering decided to go over to the Belgian post, where two officials were stationed, and show them a few points in the art of poker. As it happened, these officials knew a lot of things about poker that Pickering himself did not know. So pronounced was their superiority that by midnight they had won all his available cash as well as a consignment of ivory that he had brought along for registration. He did not have the good sense to take this reverse in a sporting sense, and immediately started to shoot up the post. Before any serious damage was done, the officials returned his money and ivory to him, and provided him with an escort of askaris to see him home. So anxious were they to be rid of him that they even supplied him with porters to remove his ivory.

The next morning, Pickering's natives came in to report some elephant in the vicinity. Jack was still under the influence of the liquor of the previous evening, but that did not deter him from setting out on the trail of the elephant. Somewhat later he came up to the herd and fired at a big bull, which he brought down. He did not trouble to make sure that the animal was dead, but went forward and sat down on its trunk. The elephant was only stunned and when it revived Pickering never had a chance to leave his seat, for the infuriated beast promptly set about him and, by way of commencing hostilities, tore his head from his body.

To Pickering's friends of the previous evening fell the unpleasant duty of interring what was left of him after the elephant had completed its work. These unfortunate men had been fated continually to suffer unpleasantness on Pickering's account. During his activities in Belgian territory he had given them endless trouble, and in making his final exit he provided them with the greatest unpleasantness of all, for the elephant has a peculiar manner of settling his grievances, and to carry on from where the huge beast left off was a gruesome task indeed. One may forgive them if they did, as we were afterwards told, spend that evening in celebration.

One more anecdote about a Gentleman Poacher

of Lado, before drawing the curtain. "Bish,"* as he was commonly known to his friends, was a true pioneer; he was on the Rand during its early history, and after that he migrated to Rhodesia when that country was but little known. He also walked up to the Belgian Congo before the railroad was constructed. The Sudan, Uganda, Kenya and Tanganyika Territory all knew Bish during their various stages of development.

It is small wonder then that Bish was also a "gentleman poacher" of Lado, and smaller wonder still that he did not take well to the new scheme of things in that area. Bish decided to have no trouble with the authorities, and like his friend Pickering, he transferred his activities to the Belgian Congo, paying special attention to the auriferous area of Kilo-Moto. In this area, for some time, he hunted ivory without falling foul of the law, but presently his interests were transferred solely to the gold industry.

There were various ways of smuggling gold in those days, and Bish selected the best and safest method of all. He opened a trading store in the vicinity, where all those who were possessed of the precious metal would find suitable wares in exchange on the shelves of his store. As most of his customers had only a slight idea of the value of gold, it is no wonder that Bish soon prospered beyond all expectations. Ere long, he had a motor boat operating on the Lake; he became the proud possessor of a farm and considerable property, and was generally known as a prosperous merchant.

---

* The late Ernest Bishop. His picture, with a prize tusker, is shown on the opposite page.

The end of a successful safari in the Lado Enclave.

Ernest Bishop seated upon his notable elephant. The animal's near-record tusks proved to be 9 feet 3 inches long, and weighed 195 and 197 pounds, respectively.

THE GENTLEMEN POACHERS OF LADO

If Bish had taken the trouble to learn how to control an irritable temper, all would have gone well, but a difference of opinion with a Belgian official led him into the indiscretion of emulating the example of his friend Pickering. Bish successfully shot up the nearest post and made himself disagreeable in various ways. This offence got him into serious trouble with the long-suffering authorities and prompted them to make further investigations into his past activities. These investigations were distinctly unfortunate for him, for they resulted in the confiscation of all his property, and made him a compulsory guest in one of King Albert's homes of correction for a period of three months.

When I met Bish on his way to Lake Albert, he was making the journey on a bicycle, accompanied by a few porters who carried his blankets and foodstuffs. It was quite obvious that he was quitting the neighbourhood. On my asking him how things were with him, he described the misfortune related above. It appeared that, in all, there were fourteen charges formulated against him; he did not know exactly what the details were, nor did he know on which one, or on how many, he was convicted, for he spoke or understood no French and there was no interpreter available at his trial. But he hastened to assure me that no injustice had been done to him and that the contrary was the case. In fact he was quite happy and content. I was better able to appreciate his mood a minute later—when he asked me to feel the weight of his bicycle. It was only with difficulty that I could lift it from the ground. Nor was this surprising, for, carefully hidden in the frame of the bike, Bish had no less than twenty-eight kilos of gold, the value of which at that time was about £3,000.

When the trouble had started, Bish had had a good idea as to what was going to happen, and he had then taken the necessary precautions. The machine had been carefully hidden away and on his release he had again taken possession of it. On the Lake, he had to wait for a boat for more than a month. Most of this time he spent in the company of the Belgian officials, but no one ever thought of examining his bicycle which, of all places, he had left in the police storeroom!

In my subsequent wanderings I have met several of the ex-gentlemen poachers of Lado. It must not be thought that all those who settled down in the Lado Enclave at that time were outlaws and brigands. They were simply men who had chosen hunting as a profession, and under the existing conditions the Lado was a profitable field, which they operated to advantage. Many of the best hunters in Africa were to be found there, and most of the adventures related in W. D. M. Bell's "Wanderings of an Elephant Hunter," a classic on elephant hunting, were based upon experiences in or near the Lado Enclave. In that locality Bell was known to his friends as "Karamojo" Bell.

It is doubtful if, in the history of African hunting, such a large number of notorious hunters ever congregated in such a small area. Of most of them it could be truthfully said that almost every round of ammunition in their belts would secure a trophy, and never before, or after, was the elephant hunted with such a small average of accidents. But with so many expert hunters operating a limited field, the area was soon reduced in fertility, and with the application of the Game Laws the district became unprofitable.

The Lado Enclave and its many expert elephant hunters belong to history. It is well that the height of the hunters' killing was of fairly short duration, otherwise the elephant would have become an extinct species in a few years.

4: THE SACRED BULL OF KAFUVU

THAT ONE was a devil! Ndege declared, with solemn conviction. He continued, "There is murder in those eyes, even though he is dead. Yes, it makes me afraid to look at him. Perhaps, Bwana, you had better shoot him in the brain and make quite sure. Who knows, in a moment he may jump up again and kill one of us."

"That fellow is as dead as all day yesterday, Ndege. He will do no more jumping. It is true, he had murder in his soul before he went down, and those eyes bear witness to it, even though he is dead. He surely gave us a tough time but I do not think he was any worse than any other of his tribe. He was just lucky—perhaps luckier than dozens of others, and the longer he lasted the worse he became. Had he gone down to that first slug we would have collected him just as we have collected many others, and without fuss."

Ndege persisted, "No, Bwana, this one was different. He refused to die. See there, five shots from that big gun of yours, and that one shot went clean through his heart. Still he came for me, and I was very lucky that he did not get me before the good Lord helped me to get up in the tree. I thought he was going to climb the tree to get me. Yes, Bwana, he was a devil, he was different from all the others. You don't believe that these people are right after all and that the spirit of the dead Sultan perhaps did live in this black devil?"

"Ndege, you are suffering from a bad attack of nerves, as you may well do after this experience. But buffaloes do not climb trees, nor do they harbor departed spirits. As for the good Lord helping you to climb that tree, I do not think He would waste much time on the likes of you. This fellow took a lot of punishment, and it is true he lived longer with a slug in the heart than they usually do. But if you believe in the foolish stories that these people tell you will end up in the same way the Sultan did—with a buffalo horn in your side. Come, forget all this nonsense; you see now that this black devil is really dead. Try to persuade those men to leave the trees and help us to get the meat back to camp. See that the neck is cut off at the shoulders, so that I may prepare the mask. It is an excellent trophy."

With finality in his voice, Ndege said, "Those men will not touch this animal, Bwana. You have done well to kill a dangerous beast, but they believe that the departed spirits of their dead Sultans lived in this black devil's body, and by killing him you have made enemies. It will be well for us to leave this place as soon as possible, and since the head is too heavy for three of us to carry, we had better leave it where it is."

Ndege was right. The natives who had taken refuge in the trees when the trouble started were now assured that the buffalo was really dead. But nothing that I could say would induce any of them to touch the dead animal.

Perhaps I had better explain all that happened prior to this conversation between Ndege and myself. I had arrived at my present camp some six weeks earlier on a two months' holiday which I intended to spend hunting buffaloes. For a long time I had heard about the large herds that frequented this area, and before coming out here I had sent Ndege to investigate. He had brought back an excellent report; there were many buffaloes, and never before had he seen so many big bulls in such a small area. The buffaloes were "kali" (dangerous) and there had been several accidents during the past two years. But this, he explained, was due to the fact that natives were hunting on a larger scale than before, and that the powder they were using in their muzzle-loaders was not very good, being of local manufacture.

Ndege had been with me for many years. Together we had hunted hundreds of buffaloes and other big game. During those years of hunting there had been many incidents and narrow escapes. Buffalo hunting had become a specialty with us and Ndege favored this area. That was good enough for me. I arrived on a Monday night and the news of my arrival spread quickly to several native villages in the neighborhood. Owing to war conditions, there had been a great shortage of foodstuffs, especially meat, and the advent of a European hunter caused quite a stir amongst the native population. In spite of the late hour of my arrival,

[40]

The Sacred Bull of Kafuvu

I was soon surrounded by a motley crowd of native hunters, all anxious to take a share in the hunting. I was naturally pleased to have the assistance of these men as I could count on their knowledge of the district, which is always of great help to a stranger.

After listening to a great many tales about the abundance of game in the area, I explained to the Jumbe that my interest in game, other than buffalo, extended only to the necessary supply of meat for myself and my natives. Buffalo was what I had come to hunt, and buffalo was what I wanted them to show me. At this, the old man became very effusive and promised me all the help I might require the next day.

Early the next morning a dozen or so men of the local community turned out at my camp and agreed to take me to buffalo country. That day I was given the "run-around" for fully thirty miles. I saw zebra, kongoni, roan, topi, and several other kinds of game, but apart from a few old tracks, there was no sign of buffalo. Ndege explained that he had seen plenty of buffaloes on the Kafuvu River, which was south of my camp, but the local guides had brought us to the north. In order to supply the immediate requirements of the camp I shot a zebra, the meat of which was distributed equally between my own natives and the guides who had taken me out on the futile hunt.

On my return to camp that night I felt that, for some reason, I had been taken to the wrong place deliberately. Under normal conditions this would not be surprising, as native hunters do not like Europeans to trespass on their favourite preserves. But conditions here were not normal, as on all sides I had been assured that the local villagers had seen no meat for several weeks. Under such circumstances there could be no objection to my hunting buffaloes in a district where everyone admitted there were plenty. But all my questioning was of no avail and produced only evasive answers. I was told that I was just unlucky on my first outing; I would certainly have better luck in good time; buffaloes do not always remain in the same place, etc. I was not at all impressed with these explanations.

After the villagers had left camp that night I called for Ndege. "Ndege," I said, "those men are lying to us. For some reason they do not wish to help us hunt buffaloes. Tomorrow you will take me to the place where you saw the buffaloes. Now you go to the Jumbe and tell him I do not require any more of his guides—only porters to carry in any meat we may shoot. Tomorrow we go south and, unless you also have lied to me, we shall find what we are looking for." Ndege once again affirmed his previous report and with that he left for the Jumbe's hut.

Later that night Ndege returned, accompanied by the Jumbe. The latter had come to see me personally. I was just finishing my dinner and after the table had been cleared I called for the Jumbe. "Now then, Jumbe, what is it that worries you?" I asked. "I have come to tell you, Bwana, that only a few men are willing to accompany you tomorrow. They are mostly all new arrivals, but they are strong men and will be able to carry much meat. My own men refuse to follow you where you are going." This was a strange turn of events which I was quite unable to understand. I countered, "Do your people think then that I am not competent to hunt the buffalo? They saw me kill an animal at a very great distance this morning. A gun that will kill a zebra at such a distance will surely kill a buffalo at close range. One does not shoot at buffaloes when they are many hundreds of yards away. My head-man will tell you that in many years he has seen me shoot lots of buffaloes. He has been with me for many years and is still alive, and so, also, am I." For a while the old man sat thinking things over, then quietly he left the seat he had occupied and moved nearer to the fire. "If the Bwana can spare a little of the tobacco he is smoking and has the patience to listen to me I will explain why my people refuse to go on the hunt tomorrow."

I have walked and hunted in almost every part of Central and East Africa, and in many years of wandering I have learned about all that is worth knowing about the African native. The story that followed, therefore, did not surprise me at all, and in no way interfered with my intention to hunt buffaloes on the Kafuvu River the next day.

"You see, Bwana," began the old man, "in the hospital across the road there is a 'toto,' and he has been there for several weeks. Tomorrow he leaves for his home on the Kafuvu River. That he has healed up and is able to return home is not only a miracle, but it is a warning for us all to respect the spirits of the dead. That young man's father was the Sultan of this district. A good and brave man, but not always very intelligent and sometimes very hard of head. For a long time the stream near his village was honoured daily by a great buffalo bull. This animal harmed no one, but came only to drink at the stream and then returned to the forest. Often he came close to where the women and children were fishing but, as I have said, he harmed no one and they were not afraid of him. We soon realized that this animal was not the same as other buffaloes who think of nothing else but to cause trouble to peaceful folks. The 'Mgana' (witch doctor) soon discovered that the reason why this animal was so different from the others was because the spirits of the dead Sultans had gone to rest in his great body. If this were not so, why is it then that even when the river is in flood and water is plentiful everywhere this animal drinks only at the village of the Sultans? We all know this and we all believe it. The last Sultan, the father of the young man in hospital, also knew it. But one day the evil spirit entered into the Sultan and he decided to kill the buffalo. When the buffalo came to drink that day the Sultan hid behind a bush and fired at this harmless beast. It was only natural that he did not succeed in this evil attempt, and whilst he was preparing to fire another shot the buffalo descended on him. He was killed instantly and it was a sad day for us when we buried his poor mangled remains. This happened only ten moons ago. From that time onward the villagers met every week to pray for forgiveness. But the buffalo did not appear again and everyone knew that until the buffalo appeared again the Sultan's misdeed would not be forgiven. You may laugh at this, Bwana, but I will soon prove to you that this is all true.

"Soon after the Sultan was killed his son returned to the school at the Mission, where he remained for six months. During all this time the villagers frequented the river regularly. No harm came to any of them, but none of them ever saw the buffalo during that time. Two months ago the Sultan's son returned from school; he is a youth of fifteen. He returned to the village on a Saturday evening, and early on Sunday morning he went to pray at the spot where his father was killed. It was whilst he was kneeling at the spot where his father was killed that the buffalo descended on him. The son was tossed two times and suffered terrible injuries, but by the Grace of God no limbs were broken and his wounds have now healed completely. You will understand now why my men will not accompany you on this hunt tomorrow. If it should so happen that, with their assistance, you should harm this sacred beast they would be responsible for the retribution which is sure to follow. It is true, there are many other buffaloes that you may safely hunt in that area and everyone will be pleased to see them killed. But, who knows, if the evil spirit should guide you to this one animal and harm should befall him, we will all suffer as a result."

So, that was that! A typical African superstitious tale, and, whereas I fully believed that a buffalo had killed a Sultan who had enraged him, and that subsequently his son had been attacked by a buffalo—not necessarily the same animal that had killed the father

—I was not going to let this stupid story interfere with my programme for the next day. On the contrary, I felt that this buffalo, assuming he was the same one in both cases, was a dangerous beast and should be destroyed before he could do more damage. The fact that he was described as an enormous animal was further inducement for me to collect a good trophy. But there it was; this Jumbe, who came under the direct authority of the Sultan at Kafuvu, had no intention of tempting the gods. And I could quite easily understand that should there be an accident, which can happen at any time when buffalo is the quarry, this unfortunate man would have to bear the brunt of it. African domestic squabbles can reach major proportions, especially when actuated by superstition.

In view of the story I had listened to I informed the old man that, under the circumstances, I did not expect him to persuade any of his people to participate in the hunt. At the same time I assured him that I was going out with the definite intention of finding, and killing, this buffalo. I would take my own trackers and would welcome any assistance of the natives in the village who did not owe allegiance to the Sultan at Kafuvu.

No sooner had I told him this when I realized how foolishly I had spoken, for superstition is, and always will be, the predominant trait in the African's life, and to flout this superstition is not the best method of enlisting his support. In view of my avowed intention to hunt the sacred buffalo I did not expect to get any help from any of the Jumbe's men, but I hoped that the strangers in the village would turn out to accompany me on the hunt. But the news of my intention had spread; the next morning only four natives turned out and they made it quite clear that, apart from carrying my kit to the Kafuvu, they had no intention whatever of accompanying me on the hunt. As I had intended to spend at least a week on the Kafuvu I had a considerable amount of camp kit to carry, and four porters were not of much use to me. But, talk as I would, I could persuade none of the local community to give a hand. Finally, I decided to take only the most essential equipment and by 10 a.m. we were on our way to Kafuvu, ten miles from my camp.

On arriving at the Sultan's village I found that the African bush telegraph had done itself full justice and the entire village knew that I had come to hunt the "Sacred Buffalo." The new Sultan himself was on the scene early and I was treated to a recapitulation of the story I had heard the previous night. It all boiled down to the fact that if I intended to interfere with the big bull I must look for no assistance from his quarter. Other buffaloes, yes, I could shoot as many as I liked. They would be pleased to see them all dead, and would help me to kill them. All the natives knew the big bull and would keep me informed so as to avoid any possible mistake. This was a good deal better than I had expected. I pointed out to the Sultan that I had come to hunt buffaloes, and to me, at any rate, the one was as good, or bad, as the other. I agreed that if I should encounter the big bull and be informed in good time I would not molest it—a straight promise,

which I intended to adhere to textually. But mentally
I made the reservation that, should I meet the big bull,
I would make it my business to have the cards stacked
so he would be dead long before I was warned! In
entering into an agreement which I had no intention
of carrying out, I was not unduly worried by my
conscience, for from what I had heard from the Sultan's own lips, I was convinced that this legendary
buffalo was a nasty job of work and the sooner he was
accounted for the better it would be for everybody in
the vicinity. The agreement made, I went to bed feeling more hopeful for the success of the hunt.

Early next morning, some thirty natives rolled
up at my camp; they had come to take me to buffalo
country and would carry in any meat I might shoot.
The leader of this gang was in a hurry to get started
as early as possible, so that we could find the big herd
near water and avoid trailing in the heat of the day.
He at once set off in a northern direction and I knew
well that he was taking me away from the direction
where the big bull might be found. I let him have his
own way for some distance and then called on him to
halt. I pointed out that there were no tracks to indicate
the presence of large herds, and also informed him that
Ndege had seen several herds in the south. I insisted
that he should turn to the south and assured him, as I
had the Sultan, that no harm would come to the big
bull if they kept me informed. This appeared to satisfy
him, and then we swung back south.

Things were working out according to plan; the
porters were keeping up a loud conversation all the

way and this was exactly the excuse I had hoped for. We were now in pretty rough country, dense forest and thorn trees, the kind of country buffaloes generally frequent. I had previously explained my scheme to Ndege, which, in short, was that as soon as we struck buffalo country the porters should be ordered to remain well behind us for fear their noise and movement would interfere with our chances of trailing the animals. By keeping the porters well behind us I figured that, should we be lucky enough to catch up with the bull, I would be able to attend to him long before the porters could be aware of the fact. Ndege now entered into a heated argument with the leader of the gang and said that unless he and his men were prepared to stop talking and keep well back the hunt would be called off immediately. Also, buffalo trailing was dangerous work and we did not wish to have any accidents; a charge from close quarters with so many men packed in a close group would surely end in tragedy before we could do anything to save the situation, etc. Whilst this argument was in progress the other tracker came up to report that he had picked up a fresh herd trail. Natives are always afraid of buffaloes in close country, and with the prospect of catching up with a herd at any moment the porters were quite satisfied to remain in the background.

We examined the tracks carefully and it was quite obvious that there was no outstanding bull amongst that herd. For more than a mile we stuck to the trail and then the herd was spotted taking shelter under a large tree, where I examined them closely. They consisted mainly of cows and calves and a few young bulls. I did not expect to find the big bull in this or any other herd. He was, I believed, an old bull that had been turned out of the herd and, at best, he would be accompanied by one or two others in a similar plight; but more than likely he would be on his own. Feeling quite certain that our quarry would not be amongst the herd, I now beckoned for the head porter to come on. We were under perfect cover; the wind sat in our favour and the herd was peacefully settled, quite unaware of our presence. After the porter had looked them over carefully he assured me that the big bull was not amongst them. No sooner was I given this assurance than I brought down a young bull nearest to me with a slug in the neck. The herd ran for a short distance and then turned round to see what the trouble was about. On all sides the porters were begging me to shoot again, but this I refused to do as I realized that a surfeit of meat would interfere with the subsequent hunting. "Tomorrow," I said, "Tomorrow we will come again. First, let us get this meat back to camp." The meat was duly carried in, with the usual rejoicings. The Sultan himself was handed a generous portion and expressed himself as being very satisfied with the manner in which I had stuck to my promise. Things were going well—better than I had expected.

Later that afternoon I discussed matters with my trackers and it was decided that I would not go out the next day, but the two trackers would go down to the river early and check up on the drinking pools. Any likely-looking solitary track was to be followed, and if they should happen to trail down the big bull we would have an idea as to the direction he took after he had been to water. If unmolested, buffaloes generally frequent one area for long periods until they are forced by local conditions to migrate. As there was plenty of food and water, and no molestation from the natives, the chances were that this bull would remain in this vicinity, hence I was not surprised when my trackers returned before noon to report that they had trailed the big bull to his lair that morning. When Ndege and Abeli, both experienced buffalo trackers, assured me that this was one of the biggest bulls they had ever seen, with a pair of magnificent horns to boot, I began to look forward with keenness to the prospect of catching up with this big fellow the next day.

In view of the smooth manner in which the hunting had been conducted the previous day, I had allayed all suspicions, and early the next morning the porters were again at my disposal. Ndege had instructions to find the big bull and to waste no time on any other tracks. During the morning we crossed two herd-tracks which the porters insisted we should follow, but they were overruled by Ndege, who maintained that the tracks were several hours old and not worth following. Soon, he maintained, we would find fresher tracks and those we would follow. Soon after that I heard the familiar whistle. Ndege was on the trail and, according to arrangements, I immediately widened the distance between us. The porters were told to remain well behind, as they had done on the previous occasion, and to follow me and keep well away from the trackers.

This time there was no difficulty in persuading them to fall in with the scheme. In this manner the trackers were left freedom of movement without observation from the porters. I was watching Ndege closely all the time, and as the sun was now well up I expected at any moment that we would find the quarry under shelter. In this I was disappointed, as it was fully an hour before I next heard the warning whistle and saw both trackers go down flat on their stomachs. The porters were 100 yards behind me and I immediately signalled to them to go to cover.

Up to now I had seen no sign of the buffalo, but Ndege pointed persistently at one spot, a sure sign that the bull was at rest and not moving. I could see only one likely-looking tree where the bull might have gone to shelter and on this tree I fixed my attention. But for fully two minutes I could see no sign of the bull. Then suddenly a movement caught my eyes. The bull was lying under the tree where I had expected to find him, but he was completely covered by grass and short scrub, and the heavy shade made visibility extremely difficult. But now that I had discovered his exact whereabouts it was not so difficult to identify him. He was lying down but was not asleep, and so far he was still unaware of our presence. In the position he occupied he was quite safe from the observation of the porters, but he offered a most difficult target from my station. With the possibility of arousing the suspicions of the porters who, I felt certain, would shout out as soon as they identified the bull, I realized that there was no time to waste in maneuvering for a better position. Without further ado I fired for the head, hoping to bring off a brain shot. But as my shot rang out the big bull jumped to his feet. Somewhere on that big carcass the bullet had made contact, but it could not have done much damage, as he now stood up and glared in my direction. There was a vicious scowl on his face and I realized that the slightest movement to betray my presence would result in a charge, and this I was anxious to avoid.

In reloading slowly whilst at the same time avoiding a fast movement that might attract his attention, I had lost more time than I would have done normally, but I felt quite safe, as I was under perfect cover and did not expect the bull to move before I could fire the next shot. The animal's truculent attitude had apparently scared the other tracker, who was quite close to Ndege, and as I was reloading that man took off for the nearest tree on his left. In the next instant the bull came out in full charge. Ndege's position now was desperate, for although the bull had not seen him, he was almost in the direct line of charge. Abeli was then quite safe, as the tree he was making for was close by and he could get out of reach before the bull could catch up with him. For Ndege it was not so easy, as he had got a later start, and the tree he was making for was farther away. The bull was gaining rapidly on him. This sudden turn of events had placed me at a complete disadvantage. Had the bull remained stationary I could easily have placed a second shot on an exposed target. But in rushing towards Ndege he had got behind a cluster of bushes some twenty yards in front of me. With this obstruction, and a rapidly moving target, there was no hope of placing a shot. All I could do was to run at top speed in order to clear the obstruction. In doing this I considerably endangered my own position, for as I emerged on the far side of the cluster of bush the distance that separated me from the bull was no greater than that between him and Ndege, who still had fifty yards to run before he could reach the tree, a distance he would be hard put to cover in time. Now I had a clear field of fire, and although I was shaking from the effects of the sprint I had made, I realized there was no time to lose and, aiming as well as I could, I fired for the shoulder. As the bullet struck, the bull bellowed loudly and there and then he changed his course and came straight for me. In a second I reloaded and the brute was brought well into my sights. Only then did I realize what a tremendous pair of horns the animal carried. Normally, in a head-on charge, the best place to fire at is the left shoulder, but as the bull came for me with his head down, both shoulders were almost completely covered by the immense horns. In this critical situation the bull himself solved the problem, for as I was about to try for a shoulder shot, the great skull rushed into my sights. In the next second I witnessed one of the most spectacular sights I have ever seen in buffalo hunting, for as the bullet struck his forehead his knees seemed to give way and he turned a complete somersault. Any elation I may have felt on this account was short-lived, however, for in a little more than a second he was back again on all fours. But now he was completely dazed and started running away from me—in the direction

The sacred bull of the Kafuvu River. A magnificent
trophy, with a 44-inch spread of horns.

This bull took two heavy-calibre bullets in the heart and
dropped only five paces from the guns.

where Ndege was still struggling to get up the tree. This was no longer a charge—just an aimless trot. Once more I fired as he presented a broadside view, but still he kept moving forward aimlessly. Now he was only a few yards from the tree where Ndege had at last managed to reach safety and here he started to totter like a drunken man. Finally he came to a stop and stood glaring at the tree where Ndege was. The "Sacred Bull" was definitely on his way out, and my next bullet brought proceedings to an end.

For some time now the porters up in the trees had been shouting at me at the top of their voices. There was no doubt about it—they had recognized the bull; but I was far too busy with the job in hand to worry about anything else. Now that it was all over I walked up to the carcass. But before I got up to it I took the precaution to reload, as my magazine was empty. This precaution was quite unnecessary; the big bull was, as I said to Ndege in the conversation recorded at the beginning, "as dead as all day yesterday." But Ndege was not quite convinced and it was several minutes before I could persuade him to leave the tree. In spite of the reverence in which this bull was held by the local natives, he was a vindictive brute, a killer of the first order, with a grievance to settle. This was clear from the manner in which he came out in full charge at the only moving object he could see after being hit by my first shot—a flesh wound in the neck. The second bullet, which turned him in my direction, had lodged in the stomach, whilst the head shot that brought him down a few yards from me had passed over the brain. (Such failure to reach the brain is the reason buffalo hunters seldom try for a brain-shot at a buffalo in a head-on charge; the head then is held at such an angle that it is difficult to reach the brain. But in this particular case it paid dividends.) The fourth shot, as he was trotting away from me in a dazed condition, was placed in the heart, and although he survived this injury much longer than they usually do, this was the shot that really brought him down.

As a trophy, the "Sacred Bull" was a superb specimen; but as Ndege said in the beginning, if I wanted to collect him we should have to carry him home ourselves, which was quite out of the question. The local natives remained in their respective hide-outs for a long time and when finally they were persuaded to come to earth, terror was written all over their faces. They refused to touch any part of that carcass; so, at the spot where this legendary brute fell, he remained —at the mercy of the vulture and the hyena.

The reception I got on my return to the village that afternoon made it quite clear that I was an unwelcome guest and that same evening I returned to my main camp.

If the killing of the Sultan and the attack on his son at the same spot by the same buffalo, is at all likely to induce any reader to invoke the supernatural, I would hasten to explain that this was a perfectly logical sequence of events. Buffaloes have regular habits and soon settle down in a locality where they are unmolested and where food and water are to their taste. This bull had formed regular habits and had no reason to fear the villagers. He naturally resented the attack the Sultan made on him and settled the score without ceremony. That he was not seen by the natives again was due to the fact that they probably never again went near the scene of the accident. The son was the first to do so, and it was an unfortunate coincidence that the buffalo happened to be on the spot at that moment. The bull saw the son in a kneeling position similar to that assumed by the Sultan at the time of his unsuccessful attack and the sight caused unpleasant memories to stir in the brute brain. But to persuade a simple-minded and superstitious native to accept this explanation would be quite another matter!

This incident is an excellent illustration of what I have said before. Under normal conditions that bull was quite harmless, and for the attack he made on the Sultan one can hardly blame him. But was the attack on the son justified? Had the bull not been overtaken by Nemesis in the form of a heavy-calibre .404 rifle, I am persuaded that many more of the unfortunate natives of that village would have fallen victim to him. In this particular case the bull had an ally in the form of fear of the supernatural and it is unlikely that any of the villagers would have made any serious effort to curb his activities.

5: TERROR STALKS THE SIRA

It WAS a cloudless, blistering hot day in the Sira Valley. By 11 a.m., as I got back to camp, the heat had become quite unbearable. I had been out since daybreak, looking for buffalo, but today, as on previous days, I had drawn a complete blank. The Sira Valley is ideal buffalo country, and when I came out ten days earlier the natives in the Valley assured me that the blank spell, which had lasted for fully twelve months, would come to an end. I was assured on all sides that buffalo could be had for the asking.

Each day I had gone hopefully on the trail, but always the result was the same, and today's terrific heat had put the final touches to it. I would waste no more time in the area. After lunch I would pack up my truck and look for pastures new. Instructions were given to my cook to pack up the camp kit and after lunch we would be on our way.

But whilst I was sitting down to food one of the local natives came in to report that he had just seen a troup of four buffaloes not far from my camp. They were making for a cluster of trees in the immediate vicinity and in view of the terrific heat it was certain that we would find them not far from the spot where he had seen them.

I had reached the limit of my patience and endurance, and was not greatly interested in the story

at first. But now the trackers argued that, as the buffaloes had been seen close to the camp only a short
while before, it was more than likely that we would
catch up with them if we followed the guide, who was
quite willing to take us to the spot he spoke of. Their
argument held a certain amount of logic. We had
wasted ten full days without success; why not a last
attempt which promised to give results in a few hours?
Finally I decided to give it another trial, and at 3 p.m.
we set out on the trail. The guide immediately struck
out in the direction which we had covered that morning. I was not at all impressed, as I had then noticed
no fresh tracks or other indications which suggested
the presence of buffaloes. The guide, however, was
quite emphatic, and before we had gone much farther
he brought us to the fresh tracks of a troup of four
bulls. Apparently we had just missed them earlier in
the day. Following the tracks was quite an easy matter;
the bulls had made for the dense trees near by. Nearer
and nearer we came to the trees, until we were within
fifty yards of the outside cluster, but still there were
no signs of buffaloes. Then I felt a tap on my shoulder;
it was the guide next to me. Pointing ahead, he whispered, "There they are, Bwana, all four of them." He
was quite right. They were walking away from us
in single file, and the best target I could select was the
one at the back. I decided to try for a spine shot, as
a bullet at the base of the tail would have immediate
results. This shot should have been fired from a kneeling position, so that the bullet could follow an upward
course, but the long grass rendered such a shot im-

possible. As they were walking at a fast pace and were soon to enter still longer grass. I took a standing shot and, as I feared, I failed to hit the spine. However, the bull was badly hurt and immediately started sagging to the ground, but just as he was about to go down he recovered and trotted off for about twenty yards, and there he suddenly collapsed.

The three other bulls had taken off at top speed, but after they had run for about 100 yards the leader stopped and turned around to make sure what the trouble was about. I was behind cover, and as he stood looking around, head well up and sniffing the air, I placed a bullet in his forehead. The effect was instantaneous, and he went down without another move.

The bull first shot was still lying down, but he had turned around and was now facing me, head well down on the ground. I did not fancy a frontal shot, as the grass was rather long and the position of the head was not satisfactory. Should my shot result in a ricochet it might easily provoke a charge, which I was anxious to avoid. The rest of the "gang*" was behind me and they would have difficulty in reaching the trees in case of trouble. My own position was secure, as I was next to a suitable tree. The best way to deal with the situation would be to walk well out to the side and try for a neck shot. As I walked around in a half-circle, I kept my eyes fixed on the bull all the time; he, in turn, was watching me intently. Only a few more

---

* *Editor's Note:* Actually, the author's "gang" included Mrs. Burger and her sister, and in private correspondence which accompanied the book manuscript the author stated that the ladies' presence at such a critical time gave him a "bad moment." His stated reason for not identifying the ladies was that he feared that by so doing he would appear to be striving to inject "dramatic effect" into his narrative. He also added that Mrs. Burger "is an old stager at the game," and has been an active participant in many of his longer expeditions.

yards and I would be in the right position for a final shot. Suddenly, a shot rang out behind me on the left! In an instant the buffalo was up on all fours and with a vicious snort he took off in full charge, heading straight towards the spot where the rest of the gang were standing. The animal's charge was directed at a native who was screaming at the top of his voice and running for life. For a moment I was so taken aback by this unexpected development that I was unable to grasp the situation. Instinctively I stepped back, and in the next moment I was lying flat on my back. I had backed into an old elephant track fully two feet deep. As quickly as possible I regained a standing position, and by the time I again had the bull in my sights he was actually lowering his head to toss the fleeing native. This was a desperate position, with no time to lose in aiming for a vital spot. The report of my shot had hardly ceased before the huge mass was sprawling on the ground. The native, in his panic, was still screaming and running at top speed, unaware that the danger was over. His wild dash came to a stop only when one of the watching gang caught hold of him. That lucky shot, fired from an Express at seventy yards, had struck the spine high up on the shoulder, and although it did not kill outright, it served to bring the bull down immediately.

The native in question was one of the local villagers and I had not been aware that he had followed us, as he had kept in the background throughout the trail. On seeing the bull lying down, he had taken it for granted that the animal was incapable of rising and, in spirit of bravado, he was going to put the final touch to the proceedings. The old muzzle-loader he was using did not prove equal to the situation; the bullet landed low and splashed sand all over the buffalo's face, an indignity he strongly resented and which provoked an immediate charge. That native had experienced the greatest shock of his life, but in view of the fool trick he had played I doubt whether I should have been unduly upset had he come to grief.

It was late that night before we got all the meat into camp and the best part of the following morning was devoted to cutting it up and sharing it amongst the porters. Whilst waiting for the meat to be distributed, some natives from a nearby village came to ask me to destroy a hippo who was making himself unpleasant in many ways. By routing up their plantations he had practically reduced the villagers to starvation, and now he had taken possession of the pool from which they drew their water supplies. On several occasions he had forced the women to run for their lives when they approached the pool for water. I readily agreed to help these people out of their difficulty and set out for the village, which was about three miles away. I had hardly settled down at the pool before the hippo broke water and began to snort loudly. The snorting ceased when a .404 slug made contact with the brain.

It was several hours before the hippo carcass came to the pool's surface, and by the time the meat was cut up for the porters to carry back to camp, the afternoon was well advanced. Whilst the distribution of meat was being attended to I noticed a party of women coming down the footpath leading to my camp. They were crying and wailing as they do when they are afflicted by sorrow. Behind them moved a party of men who carried a heavy object; at first it was impossible to tell what their load consisted of, but as they came nearer I could see part of a buffalo head. One horn was exposed, but the other appeared to be draped with cloth, at the end of which a pair of legs was dangling. I was completely puzzled at first, but when they deposited their load in front of me it was not difficult to understand what it was all about. The buffalo's neck had been severed at the shoulders and impaled on one of the horns was the corpse of an old man. The natives were on their way to the District Officer's office where they would present this mute evidence of one more ghastly buffalo tragedy.

I was informed that the old man, accompanied by his son, had set out that morning on the trail of a lone bull. After careful stalking they had caught up with him. The son was the first to fire, but no sooner had his bullet found the mark than he found himself at the end of a charge. The old man had promptly rushed forward and fired at the infuriated beast, but in doing so had only diverted the danger from his son and had himself become the object of the charge. There was no time to reload their old muzzle-loaders, and in this desperate position the old man ran for the nearest tree. But long before he could reach safety the buffalo had caught up with him and hooked him from the back. The horn had penetrated the body and several

[63]

inches of it protruded through the chest. But the old man's last shot had been well placed, and almost immediately after he had been impaled the buffalo had collapsed—with the victim transfixed on his horn. Those grieving natives had then severed the neck from the carcass, keeping the unnatural assembly intact, in order to present the evidence at court. It was ghastly evidence indeed!

Later that afternoon I received an invitation from the Jumbe of the district to attend a native hunt which was due to take place in two days' time. The Jumbe's village was about six miles from my camp, and out of curiosity I decided to accept his invitation. The hunt which I attended subsequently was the most barbarous and cruel exhibition I have ever witnessed.

(By way of explanation: The Sira Valley at this point is hemmed in for some twelve miles by two mountain ranges. The average width of the valley would be about six miles, and the entire area is overgrown with elephant grass, from ten to twelve feet high. At this time of the year (September) the grass is completely dried out. Through the valley runs the Sira River and two of its tributaries. With plenty of food and water available throughout the year, the area attracts thousands of animals of all species; but owing to the long grass, hunting is extremely difficult, if not impossible. The absence of molestation for long periods is a further inducement for the animals to frequent the locality.)

At the time of my arrival at the Jumbe's village some two thousand natives had already congregated

The author and Mrs. Burger with a buffalo which fell
to his rifle during a hunt in Tanganyika.

there, as the hunt had been widely advertised for some weeks previously. The natives were armed with every imaginable implement that could be turned to use in hunting, ranging from muzzle-loaders to mongrel dogs. An atmosphere of intense excitement prevailed throughout the village, and the old Jumbe himself was eaten up with excitement and expectation. I was informed that the hunt would start early the next morning and by the time I left my bed before sunrise the village was completely deserted, the hunters having left at daybreak in order to take up their respective positions.

Shortly before 7 a.m. I could see palls of smoke rising from the south end of the valley—the direction from which the wind was blowing. Within half an hour the entire south end of the valley was ringed by fire, the object obviously being to drive the game to the narrow exit at the north end of the valley. But now, suddenly, palls of smoke began rising from the north end also. The animals' only exit had been effectively cut off by fire! By 10 a. m. the entire valley was a seething mass of flames and smoke, surrounded by native hunters and dogs. Any unfortunate animal who tried to effect an escape was promptly shot down, speared, or run down by dogs. How many animals perished in this barbaric hunt I am unable to judge. On a narrow footpath where I stood, I counted seven half-baked carcasses being carried past in less than an hour. Farther along the valley I saw two elephants; they had been driven to the steep embankment of the Sira River which they were unable to descend, and around them a circle of fire was slowly closing in. Elephants are mortally afraid of fire, and as the flames came nearer and nearer I saw them drawing water from their stomachs with their trunks to spray the flames. In sheer panic they finally rushed through the cordon of fire as the flames began to lick against their bodies.

In addition to the fire and the hunters, the valley was strewn with every imaginable kind of trap and snare. The barbaric affair continued until late in the afternoon, by which time the hunters were too fatigued to carry on. After seeing this, I was convinced that if man's inhumanity to man will make the angels weep, his barbarity towards the dumb animals of the veld should move Satan himself to tears.

This revolting affair happened in September, 1942, and immediately on our return home, a few days later, I sent a report to the nearest competent authority, informing him that this native hunt was an annual event. I did not receive a reply to my communication. As recently as September, 1945, I was reliably informed that this barbaric hunt was staged again— according to schedule, and without interference. In a similar manner, in 1944, a herd of buffaloes was driven into the gap below the mountain range at old Cherida Village in the Rungwa district. No sooner had they entered the gap than a ring of fire was lit around them. Only thirteen buffaloes were burned alive on this occasion!

That same year, in the same area, a native hunter, on the verge of starvation, was sent to prison for thirty days. The crime? He had killed a buffalo without licence in order to provide food for himself and his starving family.

6: JIMMY AND THE FRIENDLY TREE

My BUMPTIOUS young hunting companion, Jimmy, was again giving robust expression to his opinion, in this vein: "I wonder what amusement you old-timers get out of telling these cock-and-bull stories about the buffalo being such a tough guy to hunt? Why, those fellows have only one ambition, and that is to run away as soon as someone gets near them, as fast as their legs can go. Look at that lot— 500 yards away, and all one can see is a cloud of dust! Why, they're not dangerous, they're just dead-scared, and unless one can knock them over at a thousand yards you may as well call it a day. How about stalking that lot and trying to get a shot at them?"

Jimmy had recently returned from England, where he had finished his engineer's course and subsequently joined the local African firm which was doing war work. His father was the managing director of the property where I was also doing contract work and, during my spare time, helping to implement meat supplies for the native labourers. Jimmy had come out with me on several occasions during the preceding four months, and on his first outing, a day on which I was notoriously off form, I had fired at a buffalo, not more than 100 yards away, and missed. Hardly had the report of my shot died down when there was a second report and I saw the buffalo collapse in his tracks. Jimmy had enjoyed beginner's luck, and with a light .256 rifle he had placed a perfect kidney shot. It remained only to finish off the bull with a brain shot and collect the meat. That initial success went completely to his head and since then he had adopted an air of superiority that was difficult to endure. For weeks he talked of nothing but buffalo and the way to "knock 'em over."

Jimmy senior, however, did not approve of all this, and promptly read the young man a lecture on the subject, finishing the advice by telling him he was on no account to go buffalo hunting on his own and, moreover, when hunting in the company of more experienced men, he would have to follow their advice or otherwise leave the business alone. Jimmy senior was an individual who could impose his will on others, and although the young fellow was itching to get out after buffalo he did not dare to do so on his own. As a result, I had this packet of "bounce" wished on to me every time I went hunting. What was worse, I had also received instructions to see that no untoward incident should happen when Jimmy senior's headstrong offspring accompanied me. On several occasions I had my hunting spoiled completely in order to carry out the old man's injunctions. On those occasions I had to take Jimmy's chivvying with a smile. His ill-chosen remarks that I was "scared stiff," and many other tantalising observations, had been getting under my skin for some time, and now he brought me to boiling point with this last uncalled-for outburst.

"Say, young fellow," I retorted, "you seem to think that, along with others, I have cooked up a pack of lies and exaggerations for your special benefit. I'm not scared stiff of buffaloes, but I have sense enough to know when to leave them alone. Since you appear to know better, I have decided to leave the game to you. The last fellow I heard talking the way you did a minute ago is lying six feet underground. A buffalo did that for him, and he was just as clever as you are. I only hope you don't come to the same end before you are able to learn a bit more." I had had enough, and I further stated that if Jimmy was determined to look for trouble it was to be his own affair. The lame excuse that his remarks were not intended for me did not carry much conviction.

I was all set to strike out in a different direction. The buffaloes had entered wooded country and under the circumstances I did not wish to look for trouble and unpleasantness. With a final warning to watch his step, I left Jimmy and walked off. But it did not work out as easily as all that, for as I walked away the trackers and spotters all lined up behind me and started to follow me. I explained to them that, for this occasion, I was going to leave the buffaloes to Jimmy whilst I looked out for something else. I did not require more than two natives to follow me; the rest were to remain with Jimmy and help him. But they would have none of it; if there was going to be any buffalo hunting I would have to go along, as they were not prepared to follow a greenhorn in difficult country. Finally I had to give in to them.

JIMMY AND THE FRIENDLY TREE

I explained to Jimmy what it was all about and told him that I would come along merely in the role of spectator.

We were soon on the trail of the herd, and before long we again put them up. We were in close, wooded country and near the high banks of a small but deep river. As soon as the buffaloes spotted us they made for the river, and by the time we came to the near bank the leader of the troup was making his way up the steep embankment on the far side. The animals became perfect targets as, one by one, they followed the leader and slowly mounted the embankment. I was quite close to Jimmy and watched him carefully. He raised his rifle, and as a big bull came into full view he fired. There was no doubt that he had registered a hit; the thud of the bullet and the spasmodic jerk as the bull jumped forward made it obvious that he had "taken it." As he cleared the embankment, and before he could move out of sight, a second shot rang out. But this time Jimmy missed and the bullet sprayed sand in front of the bull; in a second the animal had disappeared from view. The hunt was either over, or it was just beginning!

"Well, old-timer," I said, "you didn't do so well *this* time. What's the next move? That buffalo is wounded and cannot be left at large; the way he turned and looked at you before you fired the second shot makes me think he is a nasty customer. This is where we novices consider buffalo bad medicine. Perhaps you would like to show me how the fundis (experts) go about it?"

Jimmy's exasperating utterances had come home to roost! I could see from his expression that he had no heart for the business, but he had committed himself so far with his wild talk that he could not retire from the situation without losing face. So, with an air of bravado, he assured me that he was "going to see the business through." To this I readily agreed, and without further ado we looked for a suitable spot to cross the river. The stream was narrow and deep, and the banks were so steep that we had to walk a mile before we could find a suitable crossing. By the time we got back to the spot where the buffaloes had crossed nearly an hour had elapsed, and it was some time before we finally picked up the blood trail. Although the blood had dried, I could see that neither the heart nor the lungs had been attained. "A flesh wound," I remarked, as together we examined the blood. The bull was losing very little blood externally and had joined up with the others; this made it difficult to single out his tracks. Several of the natives had mounted tall trees in the vicinity in order to get a better view of the surrounding country, but there was no sign of the buffaloes.

There was nothing else to do but follow the blood trail and look out on all sides for a single set of tracks in case the bull had left the herd, as they usually do when they are too hard-pressed to keep up. Every now and again the trackers would come across blood on the grass and for a mile, at least, the bull had stuck to the herd. Obviously, his wound was not worrying him very much up to this time. But a few hundred yards ahead the trackers picked up a lone trail; the bull had left the herd, and it was not long before more fresh blood was discovered on the trail. This was dangerous business and I at once warned the natives not to remain in a group, but to separate and leave the head tracker on the trail. Jimmy was to stick to one end of the extended line whilst I covered the other end. Fortunately, it was comparatively easy country; visibility was fair and there were several trees on every side. In this kind of country the bull would have to charge from very close quarters to make a man's escape impossible—should we fail to drop the animal at once. The grass was quite short, and with so many trained eyes on the lookout the danger was reduced to a minimum.

I had told Jimmy that I would shoot only in case of emergency; for the rest, he would have to settle the business on his own. Trailing was slow work, as all of the natives were nervous and there was very little blood on the trail. The hard ground made it difficult to stick to the tracks at more than a crawling pace. We were coming now to more open country and only a mile or so ahead lay the open plain. I felt certain the bull was hiding in that intervening space, behind one of the numerous clusters of thick bush which were dotted at intervals of fifty to a hundred yards in our line of advance. The nearest cluster, in front of Jimmy, was not more than a hundred yards away. I felt it was time to call a halt and try to make sure of the whereabouts of the bull. One of the natives had mounted a tree and given the country around a thorough going-

over, but he could see no sign of the buffalo. I did not
like the idea of going farther ahead in a straight line
towards the cluster, for although the observer had
failed to detect the bull, there was always a possibility
that he might be hiding under the branches on the far
side, which would make detection from our position
impossible. We now decided to encircle the cluster and
not approach closer than seventy yards. Jimmy would
stick at the left side whilst I circled round the right
side. In this way it would be impossible to miss seeing
the bull in good time, should he be hiding on the far
side of the cluster.

For some seconds we advanced slowly; I was
keeping a sharp lookout on my side and every now and
again I would look towards Jimmy to make sure that
all was well. We went a few yards and then I lost
sight of him as he disappeared behind the cluster.
As I had seen no sign of the bull, I started to walk at
a fast pace so as to be lined up with Jimmy when he
would emerge at the far end of the bush. Then, it
happened! From the other side of the cluster I could
hear the natives shouting loudly, and within a few
seconds I could see the first of them running at top
speed towards the nearest tree. As I doubled back on
my tracks I saw more natives making for trees. At last,
Jimmy came into view and then—the buffalo!

(In walking around the cluster of bush, Jimmy
had got well ahead of the natives and when the bull
decided to take off Jimmy was the man nearest to him,
and this, of course, made him the immediate object
of the charge. No sooner had he realised what had

happened than he set off at full speed for the nearest tree. Unfortunately for him, this tree proved to be little more than a thorny sapling. There were no branches strong enough to support his weight, but the trunk was large enough to enable him to climb out of the bull's reach.)

Now, as I caught sight of him, Jimmy was hanging on grimly for life, his legs and arms entwined around the trunk of the tree, whilst, below, the buffalo menaced him. The bull was so engrossed in Jimmy that he did not notice my approach and this allowed me to come quite close and take careful aim. I placed a shot in the animal's neck and without further move he slumped to the ground. But even though the bull went down in a heap at the foot of the tree, Jimmy kept hanging on for dear life until I came up and assured him that all danger had passed. When finally he came down to earth he presented a sorry spectacle, as he had thorns embedded in almost every part of his body. He told me that the bull had rushed headlong into the tree trunk and that the resulting impact had all but pitched him out of the tree. When I asked him why he had not fired at the bull, he explained that the sudden shock of natives shouting and running in all directions had deprived him of his thinking powers; also, seeing the bull coming for him, head down had so aggravated matters that he promptly discarded his rifle and followed the example set by the natives.

I did not think it would be "cricket" to pile on the agony at this stage, but I could not resist saying to him, "I wonder why you old-timers will persist in telling these cock-and-bull stories about the buffalo being dangerous to hunt. Why, this fellow fell down dead with fright as soon as I looked at him!"

Jimmy's career as a buffalo hunter had come to an abrupt ending, and for the next few weeks he talked of nothing else but the terrifying experience he had been through. He certainly had a lot of the bounce taken out of him and if it were not for the fact that I had lived through several such experiences I should have appealed to him to write me a chapter on "What it feels like to be charged by a buffalo from close quarters."

7: LIONS, ON OCCASION

Unlike the buffalo, who is hunted mainly for food, and frequently in order to curb his aggressiveness, the lion is hunted for sport and also to curb his predatory activities. It is natural, therefore, that those who hunt the lion are ever on the lookout for a prize trophy, and even amongst the most experienced of hunters the bagging of a good specimen is always the subject of excitement and discussion. Around the campfire at night the imagination is frequently given full play and often I have listened to "lion stories"—some true and others untrue—that strained credulity to the breaking point. To the brotherhood of the wilds there is a strange fascination about the lion and, rightly or wrongly, when the King of Beasts is the subject of discussion, the imagination is liable to run riot.

I have watched from the banks of a stream which ran between two mountain ranges, whilst high on the peaks of one range a lion played havoc with the peace of a large family of baboons. Majestically he strode in the wake of the fleeing apes, and before him were scenes of the greatest disorder and confusion. The tree tops had sprung to life and from these sanctuaries there issued forth discordant shrieks of terror. The opposite mountain furnished echoes of the din, which added much to the awe-inspiring spectacle. When seen thus, the lion at once commands respect and admiration. He is the unchallenged monarch of all he surveys, and immune from attack by any other beast of the forest.

It is man alone who will divert the lion's step and turn him from his purpose. I have hunted him and tended to the wounds of those who have been hunted by him; I have seen him making his kill, and I have narrowly escaped being killed by him. But as I have said before, I cannot subscribe to the claim that, under normal conditions, the lion is the most dangerous and courageous of animals. Under abnormal conditions he presents a strong claim, for it is only in extreme cases of hunger, provocation or illness that he will attack man. At other times, and even when hungry and at his kill, he will often abandon his feast at the approach of man. This does not stamp him as a very aggressive animal.

I once had the unpleasant duty to attend to the wounds of a man who, after being attacked unawares, had the best of an argument with a man-eating lion. A pocket knife had been his only weapon of defence. He escaped with a severe mauling, but the lion did not escape. Warriors of several of the African tribes, armed with a spear and a shield of hippo or rhino hide, will cheerfully enter into single combat with any lion, and will generally prove more than a match for the King of Beasts. This establishes that he is not unassailable in a hand-to-hand encounter.

I know of cases where a daring lion had tried conclusions with an adult buffalo bull, and in quick time has beaten a hasty retreat. A buffalo, fighting for his life, is a somewhat uncompromising animal, and the lion knows it. This is not very flattering to his courage. The vaunted nobility of the lion is not altogether without stain, for all the denizens of the forest he is one of the very few who will resort to cannibalism. The vulture and the hyena—prime scavengers of the veld—disdain such practice. Nor is the lion altogether beyond reproach in the matter of personal habits; I have yet to encounter a dirtier feeder.

The foregoing observations, although somewhat detrimental to the lion, do not imply that he is not a dangerous beast to hunt. Once he has been thoroughly aroused, and given country where conditions are favourable to him, he can be the most deadly, dangerous animal to be encountered anywhere. I once had an adventure with a big male that left me in no doubt at all on the subject. This incident happened some years ago in the Belgian Congo. I was out with a big safari in the Lualaba country and had to rely almost entirely on my rifles to provide food for the porters. In this part of the country, as everywhere else, game is plentiful in parts and then, without any apparent reason, there are blank spots where no game can be found.

We had been without meat for several days when one afternoon a herd of roan antelope was spotted in the vicinity of the camp. I lost no time in following this herd, as it was getting late and they were a thousand yards from camp and on the move. Before coming up with the herd we had to cross a small creek on the far side of which were several patches of dry grass.

By the time we had crossed the creek the roan had disappeared from sight and this meant that we had to follow their tracks. I was walking at ease, watching the tracks, when suddenly a native next to me shouted, "Simba, Bwana—Simba!"* There was no doubt about it; about 150 yards in front of us, and apparently following the same trail we were on, was a big black-maned lion. By now he had spotted us and was running towards one of the patches of dry grass ahead of him. He was moving at a moderate speed and presented an easy broadside target. I had run out of ammunition for my light rifle and had only a heavy .425 Express, which was loaded with soft-nose ammunition. As this was an exceptionally large lion, I wasted some seconds to make sure of my shot, and then, with only fifty yards remaining before he would enter the grass, I fired for the shoulder. As the shot rang out the lion rolled over on his side, apparently dead to the world. For fully a minute I stood watching him, but there was no move and, feeling quite satisfied that he was dead, I slung the rifle around my shoulder and walked up to collect my trophy. I had walked hardly twenty paces when suddenly the lion jumped up and made for the patch of grass. Before I was able to fire again he had entered the grass and disappeared from sight.

I fully realised the danger of approaching too near the grass, but as the lion had entered on the far side I determined to remain on the near side, and when I had approached within fifty yards I came to a stop. I had reloaded and was prepared for emergencies.

---

* Simba—the Swahili word for lion.

For some minutes I stood looking over the grass ahead of me, but could detect no movement or sign of the lion. The shock of a .425 Express is something enormous; at 100 yards it has a striking power of over 5,000 pounds to the square foot. The lion had taken that shock broadside and I had no doubt that he had gone into the grass to die. But in order to make quite sure I thought I would throw a stone or stick into the grass and if he was still alive and able to move he would betray his whereabouts. A few yards to my right was some rubble and, turning my back on the grass, I walked over to pick up a stone. The only suitable one I could find was wedged firmly into the ground. Laying down my rifle at my side, I started to maneuver the stone with both hands. Suddenly I was aware of a rustling sound and as I turned to look around I saw the lion coming for me. He was coming so fast and was then so close that there was no time to grab my rifle and prepare to shoot. There was only one thing for it and that was to run for the nearest tree, fully 150 yards away.

The slightest reflection on the situation I was in should have convinced me that there was not the faintest hope of my outrunning the lion over that distance, badly wounded though he was. But at such moments one does not pause to reason; instinct dictated that I should run, and I lost no further time. By now the natives were all up in the trees shouting at the tops of their voices. Whether this was intended to divert the lion from the pursuit or whether they were shouting advice to me, I could not determine. Their vocal efforts certainly meant nothing to me. I was running for my life and already the strain was beginning to tell. I soon realised that I could never make the tree in time, and even were I to do so, I would still have to climb out of reach before I would be safe. Thoughts now flashed through my mind at incredible speed . . . a wounded lion had been known to cover one hundred yards in less than six seconds . . . how could I possibly better such a speed? How long could I maintain even my present pace? Why had the lion not overtaken me ere now? And now, I had come to the end of my tether—I was completely winded. I had best turn around and see what was happening, for if the lion was as close as I expected him to be, he would shortly be on top of me. It seemed better to face him and do my utmost than to be taken unprepared from the back. I decided to compromise; I would keep on running and look back over my shoulder. But as I turned my head, I stumbed and sprawled to the ground. Terror gripped me as I scrambled frantically to my feet. The lion *should* be on top of me any moment now . . . but, miracle of miracles, there was no sign of him!

This could not be a dream from which I had suddenly awakened; I was gasping for breath, and the natives were still up in the trees, shouting as loudly as ever. I started to look to them for an explanation, for I could see no sign of the lion. The native nearest me was pointing towards the spot from where I had taken off in my desperate race, some seventy yards away— for that was as far as I had run in the seconds that had seemed hours to me. I signaled for the native to approach, but this he would not do. He kept waving for me to come to the tree. I made for the tree as quickly as I could, and there I discovered that the lion had collapsed only a few yards from where I had taken off. He was still alive and trying to get to his feet, but seemed unable to do so. Close by him was my rifle, but with the brute still capable of movement I had no intention of tempting fate for a second time that day. With difficulty I got a runner off to camp to bring a shotgun and ammunition to me. The camp was not very far and in a short time he returned. Now, armed with adequate means to defend myself, I set out to finish the unpleasant business. I do not think I am of a very nervous disposition, nor am I one of those "iceberg" characters—to whose stories I have listened so often. A double-barrel shotgun with the right ammunition is, to my mind the best weapon one can possibly have against a lion at close quarters; in fact it is 100 per cent safe. But in spite of such potent protection, my nerves started "playing up" as I approached the struggling lion. When I had come to within ten yards of him I took careful aim, and in order to make quite sure, I pulled both triggers simultaneously. The hectic affair was ended.

On examining the carcass, I found that my bullet had missed the shoulder and had entered the side, passing through the stomach; bone was then encountered and the soft-nose bullet had "mushroomed," creating a gaping wound six inches in diameter. Through this wound the lion's entrails had protruded and were dragging on the ground beside him. At the spot where he collapsed one hind foot had become entangled in the entrails, and this had brought him down within a few yards after the pursuit had started. Of course, I did not know this at the time, although the natives in the trees had done their best to inform me of the lion's collapse.

Shortly after I got back to camp the inevitable nervous reaction set in. That night I slept fitfully and had plenty of time to reflect on the quaint stories I had listened to so often. One that I recalled was told by the heroic Nimrod who showed me a withered hand and explained that it was due to the fangs of a lion. As he told it, he had thrust his hand between the lion's open jaws and held on to the tongue until his gunbearer had shot the lion. My subsequent inquiries revealed that this was a self-inflicted wound, created in order to escape conscription into military service. Then there was another hero who stood resolutely and faced a charging lion because his dignity would not permit him to climb a nearby tree. He ducked just as the infuriated lion made his spring, and then turned round and split its skull in two with a light axe. There was the other ... oh, I could write a volume on the strange stories I have listened to around the camp fire. When the King of Beasts is the subject of discussion, imagination often runs riot and truth is crucified.

My next worthwhile adventure with lion took place several years later. (The big cats have never interested me in the way that buffaloes do, and I have never troubled much to go out and look for adventures with them. When lions have been troublesome and I happened to be on the scene I have taken them in as part of a day's work.) As a prelude to this particular encounter, I had arrived at a small village where a man-eater had taken five natives in a matter of a few days. There was a job of work to do, and I decided to sit up and wait for the marauder. Two days before my arrival this lion had forced his way through the roof of a native hut and taken a native, one of four who were sleeping in the hut. The survivors told of a hectic struggle in which they used spears and clubs, but without avail. The roof had been re-thatched immediately, and the night before my arrival the villagers had had a difficult time to prevent further accidents. As the lion had failed to effect a kill during the previous night, it was fairly certain that he would return again this night, and with more determination. After examining the hut from where he had taken his last kill, I decided to remove a section of the roof-thatch and re-create the hole that had been there. I also directed that the door be reinforced and all other huts in the village be secured in the best manner possible. With great difficulty I persuaded the three survivors of the second last raid to take up the vigil with me. They were each handed a rifle, whilst I stuck to the shotgun. At 8 p. m. all fires in the village were extinguished and we took up our position in the hut. By midnight there was as yet no sign or sound of the lion, and I was beginning to wonder whether that inexplicable instinct which seems to warn animals of danger at the crucial moment was responsible for his nonappearance, when we heard a movement outside the hut. We were at once on the alert, listening carefully and watching the opening in the roof. Now we could distinctly hear the lion sniffing at the door; the next moment he had jumped on the roof. There was a half-moon which provided sufficient light for us to see the outline of the lion clearly as he came to the opening. The natives had received strict instructions that they were not to shoot under any consideration until after I had fired. Now, as the lion started to force his head through the opening, only a few inches from me, I served him both barrels; immediately thereafter three more shots rang out, almost simultaneously. I had omitted to tell the natives to shoot only if it was necessary! The opportunity of "having a crack" at their enemy certainly pleased those natives. Upon examining the carcass I found the skull to be a complete pulp; that lion had shipped a double-barrel load of SSG, two heavy-calibre Express bullets, and a .318 Express slug—all at a range of less than six feet!

8: THE ALBINO BUFFALO

TOWARDS the end of December, 1945, I was sitting in my tent one afternoon, writing, when Ndege came in and started to fidget around with the rifles and safari kit. I could see from the manner in which he handled the different articles that he was not in the tent to attend to the daily clean-up, but that he was waiting for an opportunity to open a conversation.

"You are scratching around like a hen, Ndege," I said. "If you want to lay an egg, of which I am in great need, you will find a suitable place at the far end of the tent."

"No, Bwana, I am not going to lay eggs, but I have just heard a funny story. There are some Wembas outside and, surely, they are the greatest liars one can ever meet. The trouble with these people is that they think all other people are so stupid as to believe their stories."

"Yes, Ndege, perhaps you are right. I know the Wembas are not very truthful people, but they are not the only ones who tell lies. I have heard you doing likewise on a good many occasions. But what is this story that amuses you so much?"

"Sometimes one has to tell lies, Bwana. There can be no harm in it if it helps one to get a bit of meat when one is hungry, or if it prevents one from getting into trouble. But these people tell lies for no reason at all. Just now they were telling us a story about a strange buffalo that their Bwana had shot in Rhodesia. A very strange buffalo that was."

"Buffaloes are always strange creatures, Ndege. One never knows what they are up to. I have shot many strange ones myself and no one has called you a liar when you told of what happened."

"But this one was white, Bwana, *a white buffalo,* so they say. Did you ever hear of such a thing? They must have been frightened so badly when the buffalo charged that they saw the whites of their own eyes. Buffaloes are black, Bwana. Perhaps these people saw a white sheep?"

"If they say that they saw a white buffalo, Ndege, I think you will find that it is really so. It is true, they often tell lies—perhaps more often than you do—but they have not the brains to think up a white buffalo story. If these men are still here I would like you to bring them along so that I may have a talk with them."

The two Wembas were still in camp and Ndege lost no time in bringing them to my tent. In listening to Ndege's story, I had immediately realised that the subject of the discussion was an albino—one of the rarest specimens, if not the only one ever recorded—and if the story was really true, it would prove of great interest to get the details. The Wembas are a great hunting tribe and prone to exaggeration when recounting hunting adventures, but no one could credit them with sufficient imagination to create an albino buffalo.

THE ALBINO BUFFALO

In a short while Ndege had returned with the two men and we soon got onto the subject. They had just arrived from the Saisi plains, in Northern Rhodesia, where they had taken part in a hunting safari with two Europeans. The party had come across a large herd of buffaloes and amongst this herd they had found a very young bull, snow white, and with "red" eyes, nostrils and lips. This young bull they estimated to be about two years old; it still followed its mother. There had been some shooting, the mother was wounded first and subsequently the albino had also received a bullet in the front leg. In the ensuing excitement the mother had charged one of the Europeans, who escaped with his life but had a new rifle smashed to pieces. Also, the albino had charged the other European and inflicted a minor injury before he was finally captured with the aid of long ropes and sticks. The last the Wembas had seen of this albino was when he had been safely tied up in a lorry and was being taken to the Europeans' main camp—alive.

Ndege was quick to draw their attention to the discrepancy in their story, for they had told him that the Europeans had shot a white buffalo. This discrepancy, they explained, was intentional, for as they had already been laughed at when they spoke about a white buffalo they felt certain that if they stretched credulity further by describing the capture of the animal, their story would be discredited by the other natives. However, this pair assured me, "white people have more understanding," and for that reason they were not afraid to add the additional details in relating the story to me.

I was much interested in the narrative and forthwith tried to get further information as to the identity of the Europeans who had succeeded in capturing so rare a trophy. But here I drew a complete blank. Both Europeans were known as "Bwana John." The native nickname for the elder of these men was "Bwana Pika Mbali" (he who shoots at long distances), and the other was just plain "Bwana John." It was the latter man who had wounded the albino and who was subsequently charged and hooked by the young bull. This was all the information I could gather as to the identity of the two hunters. But just before the discussion terminated one of the Wembas informed me that the young "Bwana John" had already left Northern Rhodesia and that he was coming down to the Rift Valley. Just what part of the Rift Valley he was making for they did not know, but they had no doubt that if I kept my ears open I would hear more about him.

I was anxious to obtain a full and more reliable account of the bagging of this rare albino specimen, and would certainly "keep my ears open." My natives were instructed to let me know immediately should they happen to hear of any stranger arriving in our neighbourhood who answered to the description of the young "Bwana John."

Fully a month passed, but none of us heard any more about "Bwana John." Then late one afternoon, one of my gun-bearers, a Wemba, came to report that a stranger from Northern Rhodesia had arrived in the Valley and was camped at Kalumbaleza, a small

A pair of Angolan belles.

village about 100 miles from where I was camped. But this man's name was not Bwana John—the local natives had already given him another name. (Natives generally bestow a nickname to describe the European's profession, or any personal peculiarity they may notice. Thus: a surveyor is generally "Bwana Pima" —he who measures; a paymaster, "Bwana Pesa"—the money man.) The man who had arrived in the Valley was known as "Bwana Pima"—obviously, a surveyor.

The Wembas who had previously told me about the albino did not mention anything about the profession of either man, but I decided to contact this stranger as soon as possible. Early next morning the gun-bearer left with my note, addressed to "Bwana John," in which I explained that I was anxious to contact a hunter who had bagged an albino buffalo in Northern Rhodesia, and that I would be grateful for any information that would help me make this contact. Eight days later the gun-bearer returned with a letter from a Mr. John Combrinck. He had indeed captured an albino buffalo on the Saisi plains in Northern Rhodesia during a hunt with a Mr. Johan Peacock, a well-known hunter. The hunt had taken place in September; the albino had since died, and if there was any further information I required on the subject the writer suggested that I should visit him at his camp, as he was on an assignment which made it impossible for him to leave. At the time, I was in a similar predicament and could not proceed to Kalumbaleza. I managed however, to obtain a written account from Mr. Combrinck and am grateful to him for allowing me to publish his story. The text which follows is translated from the Afrikaans language, in which it was written:

"It was easy to follow the tracks through the long grass and matted weeds, where they left well-defined streaks, but over the burnt patches and hard ground it was quite a different story. In the dim light of the early September morning our footsteps fell with a slosh-slosh as we hurried on through the vast Saisi plains. Last night's shots had put the herd on the run, and to catch up with it again called for a determined effort; there was no time to rest or slacken our speed. We were hot on their trail and, to me, a newcomer to the game of buffalo hunting, this tracking of a large herd was an exciting adventure. My rifle hung firmly over my shoulder, and as I touched the cold butt a tingling feeling ran down my spine. This would be my first encounter with these dangerous customers of the African bush, and I was not at all certain as to what my reactions would be when the time came for me to shoot it out, perhaps at close quarters. Like everyone else who takes to the hunting game, I had heard a great many stories about the buffalo; his vindictiveness, his cunning, his ferociousness in attack, and the many other stories that stamp him as Africa's most dangerous beast. The time had now come for me to verify these stories; I was about to fill the role of hunter.

"With these thoughts passing through my mind, and with eyes fixed on the ground, following the trail, I was all but unbalanced by a sudden jerk on the

[92]

shoulder. Whilst I was watching the tracks intently Johan, my half-section, had spotted the herd. His trained eyes would make no mistake, and when he whispered, 'Buffalo, a large herd!' I knew that we had caught up with our quarry. I could distinguish them only as buffaloes, when the solid black mass some five hundred yards ahead of us suddenly came to life and started moving off. An amateur at hunting, such as I was, could never have picked out a stationary herd at such a distance in such poor light. But I was in good company, for Johan is an old stager at the game. When I suddenly realised that the moment for action had come, I began to shake violently. It was not exactly fear, but I was shaking just the same. I did not want Johan to see how shaky I was, so I quickly went down on my knees. After a while I regained my natural calm and asked Johan what we were supposed to do next. He had been watching the herd closely and decided that we should cut across the spur of open plain and get ahead of them in close wooded country, where we could take cover and wait for them to come close to us before we opened fire. With heads down and backs bent, we ran through the long grass—rough country, where elephant-track holes barred every second yard of our progress. I found this one of the worst forms of exercise I have ever experienced, and when finally we reached the far end of the open plain I thanked Heaven for the opportunity to stretch my back for a moment. I was shaking so violently from this effort that if an elephant had appeared at fifty yards I should have missed the target!

"We took position on a high ant-heap, and from here, unobserved, we could watch the herd and hear the grunting as they approached us. Nearer and nearer they came, and occasionally a massive head would be lifted high in order to make sure there was no danger ahead. Then again, the herd would come to a stop and sniff the air; the sides, as well as the front, must be protected. They were on the alert, these bronze statues, but unaware of the danger that lurked ahead. As I sat there watching them approach us slowly, I found it hard to believe that they were buffaloes indeed. The bull in the lead now turned off to the right, and slowly the herd followed him as they walked past us, not more than thirty yards away. A grumpy old bull, in forcing his way to the front, viciously hooked a young calf who barred his way, and with a warning 'Boo' passed the erring youngster. Peacefully they grazed past us, this immense herd of over 300 animals. Their hoofs fell with a dull, rumbling sound as they moved on slowly. We were looking out for a prize trophy for each of us, but so far only one outstanding bull had passed us and was still within easy range.

"Suddenly, Johan grabbed me by the shoulder. 'Look at that—a white buffalo!' he whispered. And there it was! Coming out into the open, barely thirty yards away, was a perfect specimen of an albino game animal—one of the rarest trophies to be found any-where in the world. A splendid young bull, weighing perhaps 500 to 600 pounds, he was walking close behind his mother. Johan was beside himself with ex-

citement. 'Look, look,' he kept saying, 'Did you ever
see a thing like that?' The time for action had come!
Quickly we decided that Johan would shoot the
mother, whilst I would crease the neck of the albino.
If my shot was well placed over the hump, the bull
would be stunned and before he could recover we
would be able to tie him up securely. No sooner had
we arrived at this decision than two shots rang out
almost simultaneously. Johan was the first to make
contact, and I could hear his bullet strike before my
own bullet found its mark. A violent snorting rent
the air; for a moment the herd whirled round in utter
confusion, but immediately thereafter the moving mass
was lost in a cloud of dust. With the herd went a monster bull I had selected before the albino took pride of
place.

"As the dust cleared, we started to look around
for the two animals we had fired at, but there was no
sign of either of them. The herd had rushed back into
long grass and now we started to follow their trail,
which led towards a large ant-heap deep inside the
patch of long grass. We decided to make for the ant-
heap in order to obtain a better view of the surrounding country. Johan, with his eighteen stone* of flesh,
was in the lead, running as only an eighteen-stoner can
do, whilst only a few feet behind him I followed with
rifle at the ready. This precaution was just as well,
for Johan had all but reached the ant-heap—when it
happened. In a flash, without warning, and moving
at an incredible speed, a black mass of solid bone and
muscle came crashing through the long grass, giving

* Johan weighed 225 lbs.; one stone-weight (British) is 14 lbs.

Johan barely sufficient time to raise his rifle. Before he could get into a shooting position there was a sickening crash, and in the next instant I saw splinters of the gun-butt and the barrel flying in all directions. The impact had sent Johan sprawling to the ground, and as the cow closed in on him my shot rang out. Without a further move she slumped to the ground with a broken neck.

"For a moment, I believed that Johan had been killed, but now a bewildered face, white as a ghost, slowly emerged from the long grass. When finally he regained his feet he started to stutter. Whatever it was that he wanted to say to me I still do not know, for the shock had deprived him of all power of speech. Stuttering and mumbling to himself, Johan now began to collect the remnants of his rifle, a beautiful Express which he had only recently acquired. I remembered that I had seen the barrel tossed off towards my right and started to walk in that direction to retrieve it. With my eyes fixed on the ground, I took no notice of the immediate surroundings, but now I suddenly became aware of a movement ahead of me. I raised my head and looked straight into the face of the albino —barely five yards in front of me! Perhaps his lack of experience in dealing with human beings was responsible for the delayed charge. But now, as he took off in my direction, I saw him stumble and with an effort manage to save himself from falling forward. A front leg was fractured just below the knee. I managed to evade the charge and, running round in a circle, joined up with Johan who had also sprinted to

one side. The albino had come to the end of his charge
and now stood watching us with a scowling face, some
twenty yards away. It was altogether too unpleasant
a position for my liking and Johan agreed that the
ant-heap was a much safer place from which to consider what to do next. Without further loss of time we
made off to the ant-heap.

"Johan's eighteen stone was beginning to weigh
heavily on him as a result of the violent exertions of
the past few moments, and as I ran behind him I
could not help comparing his gait with that of an
overfed duck in deep distress! Finally we reached the
ant-heap and promptly started deliberations as to how
we could capture the albino alive. We had no doubt
the leg could be re-set and that the animal would
survive the injury. The difficulty was to find an
effective method of roping and tying the beast. Neither
of us had had any experience in the art of lassoing,
and the natives, scared to death by what they had
seen earlier, were only now beginning to descend from
the trees where they had taken refuge. There was
small likelihood of any of them coming to our aid.
Finally, we decided to return to camp for ropes and
poles and in some way or other find a means of roping
in the albino.

"After a hurried breakfast we called for volun-
teers to help us lasso the bull. A prize of Shs.50/-
would be paid to any native who would succeed in
bringing the animal down so that we could close in on
him and tie him up. Native courage, where a wounded
buffalo is concerned, is one of the rarest commodities

[97]

on earth, but Shs.50/- to a native in these parts represents an affluence that exists only in dreams—and wild dreams at that. Before we started off in our Chevrolet truck, fully twenty natives, attracted by the cash prize, had found their way aboard. Each one of them was certain that, as far as he was concerned, the prize was already in the bag. My cook, a staid old fellow of fifty or more summers, could not resist the temptation, and along with the others had armed himself with ropes, poles and other odds-and-ends which he described as 'lassoing tackle.' He, also, was certain of a rapid improvement in his financial situation.

"Johan had now armed himself with a heavy .404 rifle and a few moments later the expedition was on its way. We were soon back at the spot where we had left the buffalo, and for some minutes we could find no trace of him, but a little later I spotted him about a mile from where he was last seen. I had approached within twenty yards of him before I became aware of his presence, and no sooner did he spot me than he challenged me with a violent snorting and swinging of the head. With his blood-shot eyes and quivering pink nostrils he looked every inch as dangerous as he really was at that moment. Normally, his ferocious attitude would have sent the natives scattering all over Rhodesia, but the cash prize proved a powerful deterrent and had a steadying influence on their nerves. Now they started to encircle the bull stealthily, according to plan. Johan and I had withdrawn a short distance so as to be ready to close in immediately the bull was brought down. With scowling menace the albino stood watching the natives as they closed in on him, and when at last one of the blacks had approached too close for his liking he came out in full charge. He did not select any particular objective, but simply charged in a half-circle which appeared to embrace the entire retinue of natives. He ran, snorting, in pursuit of the terrified blacks, who were now scattering in all directions and shouting for help at the tops of their voices. This was one of the most comical scenes I have ever witnessed. In an incredibly short time the trees in the neighbourhood were alive with clambering blacks each of whom had but one object in view, and that was to get out of reach in the quickest possible time. Gone were their dreams of impending riches. The old cook, who had not approved of the method of procedure, was watching proceedings from what he thought was a safe distance, and so intent was he on the race for the trees that he failed to realise that he was himself in the danger zone. Like Johan and me, he was enjoying the fun and shaking with laughter, but in the next instant the grin was wiped from his face. The bull suddenly changed direction and came straight for him. For a second the cook seemed unable to move, but as the bull came closer he took off in an undignified rush for a nearby ant-heap. He must have realised immediately after he took off that he would not be able to reach the ant-heap in time, but some fifteen yards away to the right there was a young sapling, and the cook now turned off his course sharply and made for the tree. During these few seconds, Johan swore he could see the whites of that nigger's eyes from a range of seventy-five yards! The albino was now gaining rapidly on the cook, but only about five more yards remained before he would reach the tree, and here, for the first time in my life, I saw the swallow dive performed in an upwards direction! That cook seemed to have an utter disregard for the law of gravitation and in a wild leap he landed midway up the tree as the buffalo rushed past him. The animal then turned around in a half-circle, some twenty yards away, and stood glaring at his intended victim. In his panic, the old man had climbed to the very top of the tree, and now it started to bend slowly towards the ground. This was the signal for renewed shouting and screaming for help. The situation was certainly dangerous, as the tree had already sagged low enough to bring the cook within range of the charge should the buffalo decide to renew hostilities. Johan and I were shaking so much with laughter that I doubt whether we should have been able to stop the buffalo in time had he resumed the charge, which, fortunately, he did not.

"We had now reached a deadlock; the buffalo was still full of fight and the natives had suddenly lost all interest in the cash prize. If we wanted the albino alive we would have to capture him ourselves. After some scheming we decided we would try to do so. Our plan was to use a long rope; each of us would hold on to an end and we would remain close together and walk boldly up to the buffalo. As soon as he took off to charge we would separate and pull the rope tight. In this manner we would trip the bull without much difficulty, as he had only the uninjured front leg on which to balance himself. Once we had got him down we would be able to tie him up before he could regain his feet; in this part of the undertaking Johan's eighteen stone would, at last, serve a good purpose. The plan seemed quite a good one; the only fault was that we made no allowance for the bull's view of it. We had not advanced more than five yards towards him when he came out at full speed, making straight for me. The time had come for me to run and I certainly lost no time! Johan's description of my headlong flight—zigzagging through the bush with the bull hot on my heels—made unpleasant listening later on in the day. He said, as in the case of the cook, that the whites of my eyeballs were showing up at 200 yards, whilst, with mouth wide open, I afforded him an excellent opportunity to count all my teeth at a similar distance! For a few yards I managed to hold my own, but now I could virtually feel the hot breath of the buffalo as he closed in to toss me. It was here that the zig-zag course I pursued proved so valuable. On two occasions the bull actually made contact. First, when he grazed my leg as he swept his horns in an upwards direction, and again when he hooked his horn into the extended palm of my left hand, inflicting a rather serious wound. Never was there a time that I was so thankful for the excellent Rugby training I had received at college! But I was beginning to come to the end of my physical resources; I could not maintain the speed at which I was running for more than a few seconds longer. The charge had got under way so quickly that it left me no choice of direction, and until now I had not noticed a tree a few yards ahead. At a pinch I might make it. Then, putting in the last ounce of energy left in me, I made straight for the tree. When only about three yards remained there came another vicious snort right at my heels, and the time had come for me to perform my own swallow dive in an upwards direction. Johan maintains that I improved considerably on the cook's performance! At last, I was safely seated in the branches of the tree, whilst away in the distance I could hear Johan roaring with laughter. I could not help wondering what would have happened had the bull elected to charge Johan instead of me. His eighteen stone might have contributed something in a stand-up fight, but in a flat all-out race, such as I had just completed, he would not have fared quite so well; and certainly he would not be laughing quite so loudly as he was doing now. The albino stood glaring at me for a few moments and then walked off slowly, apparently in utter disgust.

"After I had rested for a while and recovered from the effects of the exertion, I slowly descended the tree. The albino was at a safe distance and I was able to join up with Johan again. To him the whole episode was a great joke, and as he had not been through my experience, it was not difficult to understand his enthusiasm and determination to have another try at capturing the albino. For myself, I had lost a good deal of interest in the affair, and was beginning to think that a stuffed carcass in some museum might, after all, prove very interesting. Johan explained that there was no museum in Northern Rhodesia, whilst in his own back yard there was ample room to accommodate a live buffalo. The reason we had not succeeded the first time, he explained, was that I had not remained close enough to him before the buffalo charged. But now, if I would listen to him and follow his instructions, all would be well. The memory of that wild race for the tree had not entirely faded from my mind and it was with serious misgivings that I finally allowed myself to be persuaded to renew activities, hoping, as I did, that if there should be another charge it would be Johan who would figure at the end of it. All this time the natives were safely lodged in the tree tops in the immediate vicinity, our appeals to them to come forward and lend a hand having fallen on deaf ears.

"At last, all discussion came to an end and Johan and I set out again in the direction of the albino. This time I remained as close to Johan as possible. We were still thirty yards away when the albino started to lower his head and grunt again. Johan kept warning me not to run and open the gap between us until the bull had approached within five yards or so. I was about to remonstrate against the foolishness of such a procedure when Johan shouted, 'Here he comes!' There was no doubt, he was coming all right, and the scene looked to me dangerously familiar! It flashed through my mind that, were I to start running now I might again attract the notice of the buffalo and once more make myself the object of his charge. The best thing to do would be to remain stationary and take a chance.

When only about five yards separated us from the buffalo, Johan pushed me and shouted, 'Now!' We both made off in opposite directions, at the same time pulling the rope tight between us. In the next instant I was lying flat on my back, and as I scrambled to my feet I saw Johan rushing forward. His eighteen stone had resisted the shock as the buffalo rushed into the taut rope, and the albino was now lying on his side. Johan was first to him and threw a rope around one hind leg. As the buffalo struggled to regain his feet, I managed to get my end of the rope around the other leg, and we then started on what must surely be the strangest tug of war in history. Johan was shouting at the top of his voice for the natives to come down and help us, and in a few seconds two of them joined us, and not a moment too soon did they throw their weight into what was fast becoming a one-sided struggle, as the buffalo was now rapidly regaining an upright position. Soon more natives were on the scene, and after a hectic struggle we managed to tie the young bull securely and land him in the truck we had brought for the purpose. We had caught an albino buffalo alive, a feat no other man had done before; and this on my very first buffalo hunt!

"Johan soon reached heights of eloquence seldom attained by men of the hunting fraternity. Like the natives had done earlier in the day, he was now seeing visions of wealth and notoriety. What he did *not* see were the numerous pot holes and elephant tracks in the path we were following back home, and I frequently debated with myself as to which was the worst experience—to be chased by a buffalo, or be driven home over rough country by Johan with a buffalo on board.

"By the time we got back home the day was already well advanced. We managed to get the buffalo into an enclosure, where he kept up a vicious snorting all night; frequently he charged the sides of the enclosure, fortunately without success. Early next morning there was again an epic struggle to get the buffalo loaded into the truck, and when this was finally accomplished we set off for Old Fife where we called on Dr. Mills and asked him to try to re-set the fractured limb. After a careful examination the doctor informed us that there was no hope of this being done successfully, as the bone was badly splintered and would not yield to treatment. There was nothing for it but to destroy the animal to save him from unnecessary suffering, and all hopes and aspirations to immortal fame ended in thin smoke. Still, we managed to dissect the carcass carefully, and some day I hope this rare specimen will adorn one of our museums. That we failed to preserve this specimen alive is to be regretted, but I think we are entitled to some credit for the determined effort, not without danger, we made in this direction."

Mr. Combrinck is right; there is no need for me to comment on the daring and courage of these two men, complete strangers to the art of lassoing, who yet dared to capture a 500-pound specimen alive with the meagre equipment they had at their disposal.

It was some time after this that I made the personal acquaintance of Mr. Combrinck; our respective duties had brought us together at a point far from his first camp. Here he again recounted the story to me with additional passages of humor. We worked together for some weeks and shared the same camp. Late one afternoon he walked into my tent and by way of opening conversation he asked, "Have you ever seen an albino giraffe?" On my assuring him that I had never seen or heard of one, he casually remarked, "In that case you had better follow me, I'll take you out and show you one. I have left a native out there to look after the carcass."

A few minutes later we had mounted a truck and were on our way to examine this rare specimen. Half an hour later we reached the spot and, as Mr. Combrinck had assured me, there was the dead body of a perfect albino giraffe. The skin was snow white and the beauty of this wonderful specimen was enhanced by the pink lips, nostrils and eyes. Surely, one of the most beautiful animals it has ever been my good fortune to see. What had brought him to his untimely end—he was perhaps three years of age—is a complete mystery. The natives vowed that he had died as the result of a snake bite—a very logical explanation, in view of the large number of cobras and puff adders to be found in that area. I had myself lost a beautiful prize Great Dane a few days earlier as the result of a cobra bite.

Mr. Combrinck had gone out early that morning without seeing any signs of giraffe or other game. On his way back that afternoon his attention was attracted by vultures swooping down to the ground, and on proceeding to the spot he had made this remarkable discovery. For an amateur at the hunting game Mr. Combrinck has certainly enjoyed an astonishing run of luck. I doubt whether any hunter in Africa can claim to have been responsible for bringing to light two albino specimens so exceptionally rare.

9: STAMPEDE IN THE NIGHT

THE CONTINENT of Africa consists of some eleven million, five hundred thousand square miles, and of this vast area Tanganyika Territory occupies approximately three hundred and seventy-four thousand square miles. That, I think, should allow plenty of space for us all—man and beast—to move about freely without getting in each other's way. When I was camped on the Ipogolo River, a narrow stream about fifteen miles long, I built myself a rough shack of grass on its banks; I then occupied about one hundred square feet of the African continent. No one could rightly accuse me of being avaricious for allocating to myself such a small area. But, incredible as it may seem, with all these millions of square miles suitably adapted to their purpose, a great buffalo herd found it necessary one night, in trying to escape from a pride of lions, to overrun that one tiny spot.

In the simple shack I occupied I had placed all my personal belongings and camp equipment. There had been very little hunting for some time, and although buffalo was on the vermin list, I had encountered only one in several weeks—a decrepit specimen, blind in both eyes.

It had been a trying, hot day and shortly after dinner I had retired to bed. Some two hundred natives, of whom my safari consisted, were also tired out and by 9 p. m. the camp was quiet and in darkness. At 10 p. m. I was awakened by a rumbling sound which at first I took to be an earth tremour. But the sound came nearer, and I could distinctly hear the pounding of hoofs. I realised at once that this was a stampede by a great buffalo herd and they were coming straight towards my shack! The night was pitch black and it was impossible to tell just how close the herd had approached, but I was quite certain that within seconds they would reach my shack. In a flash I grabbed my rifle and a powerful torchlight, and made for the door. As I switched on the light I saw an array of fireballs rushing towards me in the dark. They were the eyes of hundreds of buffaloes reflected in the rays of my torch. The animals were then less than one hundred yards from me and coming in a direct line towards the shack. Frantically I fired a shot in their direction, hoping thereby to divert them from their path, but I might as well have tried to stem the flow of the Nile. By the greatest good fortune I had built my shelter close to a giant bao-bab tree, which I managed to reach with but a fraction of a second to spare. The tree's trunk measured fully twelve feet in diameter and it was quite impossible for me to climb to safety, but in my desperate position I clung to the trunk as though I were riveted to it. By now, the vanguard of the herd was rushing past the tree at top speed; those buffaloes were in a great hurry, and their immediate programme did not include wasting time on an insignificant being glued to a tree. I could hear the crashing of my pots and pans and other belongings as they were trampled by the herd. It was some time before the last members had passed—and finished the destruction of all I possessed.

Like myself, the natives had been awakened at almost the last moment, but they were camped well out of the path of the fleeing herd. They suffered nothing more than a great scare. They had scattered in all directions and those who could find suitable trees in the vicinity had lost no time in seeking safety in the topmost branches. (The speed at which an African native can scale a tree in time of danger is something incredible, and must be seen to be fully appreciated.)

With all danger past, the natives began to re-group around the remains of my shack. I was busy examining the debris when, in the distance, I could hear the bellowing of a buffalo, followed by the angry growls of a lion. This proved that the stampede had been caused by lions, and they had now run down their quarry. I was intensely annoyed at the senseless destruction of my belongings, and as I stood looking over the scene of devastation I heard one of the natives say, "It is all the fault of the lions; they chased the buffalo from the water." "It is true," agreed another, "but why could not the stupid buffaloes have run in some other direction?" Came the answer: "They never had time to think where they were running to; the lions took them unawares and they thought of nothing else but to get away from danger. The buffaloes are not to blame for this, it is all the fault of the lions."

Yes, it was all the fault of the lions, and now, with my belongings smashed I was faced with the prospect of sleeping out in the open without a bed, whereas they were about to settle down to a royal feast. No, I decided, they were not going to get away with it as easily as all that. With my heavy-bore rifle and a powerful spotlight I would drive them from their feast, and that meat, which I needed urgently, would go to my natives. If the lions objected to my programme—well, I knew just how to settle such a difference of opinion. In the beams of a spotlight the lion is a stupid beast—an easy target, and not likely to attack. I forthwith explained my intentions to the natives, but they would have none of my scheme. "Is it not enough to have lost all your property? Is it necessary now that you should go and look for trouble that might result in losing your life, as well?" queried the old headman. With this sentiment the rest of the gang was in perfect agreement; perhaps not so much on account of concern for my safety, as that it offered an excellent excuse for them not to follow me on such an expedition of vengeance. I finally persuaded one of them to accompany me. It was not very difficult to follow the trail of the herd with the aid of a spotlight, and I had a pretty good idea as to the location of the spot from which had come the bellowing and growling.

About three hundred yards from camp we would have to pass through a small creek on the banks of which there was considerable scrub. Up to this point the native had followed me without complaint. But now his courage failed him; he was not prepared to go through that creek in the dark—the kind of place where lions might be found at any moment of the day or night. He was perfectly right in his objection, as was proved by subsequent events. As we had already lost a lot of time, I did not enter into a further discussion with the native and decided to carry on by myself. I promptly went down the steep embankment and after I had mounted the far side of the creek I felt curious to know whether the native had returned to camp or would await my return, so I flashed the torch at the place where I had left him. Apparently he was too scared to go back to camp by himself, for he was still standing in the same place. For all I cared he could remain there all night. As I turned around to proceed on my way I thought my torch caught the flash of an eye a few yards to the left of where the native was standing, and not more than fifty yards from me. For a full minute I trained my light on the spot but I could see no sign of anything. I decided that I must have seen a firefly and was about to turn around again when two eyes moved into the beams of the torch. Only the head was visible, but the heavy mane identified this as a big male lion. He was in a crouching position and apparently stalking the native. The light from my torch had brought him to a stop, and there he was, with eyes glaring, a superb target at fifty yards! In a matter of seconds I aligned him in my sights and as I pressed the trigger I could hear the bullet strike. The eyes were still visible in the rays of the torch, but now the head was flat on the ground and I knew I had succeeded in placing a brain shot.

The native, quite unaware of his part in this tableau, now shouted, "Please, Bwana, don't kill me! I'll follow you; please, Bwana, I'm coming!" The fool was under the impression that I had opened fire on him because he had refused to follow me. In all truth that bullet had whizzed past him pretty close! He rushed to me, swearing fidelity and expressing willingness to follow me to the ends of the earth.

I was, of course, anxious to have a look at the trophy, but at the same time it struck me that I could have some fun at the expense of the foolish native. I promptly read him a lecture on the evils of abandoning a white man in the bush at night whilst out hunting, and assured him that the next time he attempted to do such a thing I would surely kill him. He admitted readily that the crime of which he was guilty deserved nothing less than death, and after giving him sufficient time to repent of the evil of his ways I informed him that I intended to return to camp. He was led to think that the shot I had presumably fired in anger had surely scared away any animal in the vicinity and we would come back to look for the lions the next day. I said we would go back the same way we had come and that he would take the lead. During this discussion I had occasionally turned the torch on the carcass; there was no doubt the lion was dead. The native needed no urging to get started back to camp in the quickest possible time. I kept about fifteen yards behind him and purposely kept the light of the torch well off the ground. But just as he reached the spot where I knew the lion was lying—still in a crouching position—I turned the light onto the carcass.

The native looked down to where I had focused the light, and for a moment appeared incapable of grasping the situation. Suddenly, he loosed a mighty yell, and the next moment he had vanished into space. All the way back to camp he screamed and called for help. The story he told in camp is best left to the imagination. In a few moments I could see a procession of flares and burning logs coming towards me; pans, pots and empty tins were being beaten with abandon in order to scare the lion away. The gang was coming out to collect what was left of me!

I had meanwhile extinguished the torch, after examining the trophy—a miserable old brute, in the final stages of senile decay. Nearer and nearer came the torchlight procession. It soon reached a spot quite close to where I sat. I could hear my recent companion calling on the others to stop and telling them that they had reached the exact spot where the lion had jumped at him. He rendered a graphic description of how the lion had stuck to his heels all the way back to camp, and he had no doubt that I, who could not run as fast as he could, had by now paid for my folly. I knew that they were all armed with spears, axes, and similar weapons and I did not think it advisable to allow them to approach too closely for fear I might find myself on the receiving end of a spear. I flashed the torch in their direction and called out that all was well, whereupon they came rushing up to find out what had happened. They found me seated comfortably on the carcass of the lion. As I had not fired again after the native had departed, they were at a loss to account for the dead lion and, knowing the credulity of the natives, I forthwith told them a hair-raising story of how the lion had attacked me and I had strangled him to death with my naked hands.

For some hours I enjoyed the reputation of being Africa's bravest and strongest man; but the telltale evidence of the bullet in the forehead ultimately dispelled my aspirations to immortal fame. The victim of my joke was subjected to a great deal of bantering, but could not be shaken from his statement that the lion had chased him all the way back to camp. If it was not the dead one, then certainly it was another!

The next morning early I was out on the trail again, and less than a mile from camp I caught up with the lions, a male and female. They had dragged their kill down a steep ravine and were lying next to the carcass. As soon as the male spotted us he started growling, and in a few seconds he came for us. It was easy to see from the manner in which he took off that the charge would not be sustained. (Lions often make bluff charges, when they are at the kill, in order to scare away intruders.) This one was now trying to scare us away; for about fifty yards he came out at a fast pace, but when only another fifty yards separated us he thought better of it and came to a sudden stop. I had kept him well covered all the time and as soon as he came to a stop he was met by a heavy slug between the eyes. Without another move he slumped down. The female had been watching proceedings closely and instead of being frightened away by the shot, she ran true to form and came out in full charge. It was apparent from the manner in which she took off that she was out for trouble. In my experience with lions I have found that, invariably, the female is much more aggressive than the male, and certainly much more impetuous.

Although I was well equipped, having at my disposal a double-barrel shotgun and a heavy-calibre .425 Express, I took no chances with her. She was coming at that peculiar gait that lions always adopt when running at full speed, and as the bullet struck her in the chest she was thrown right over on her back, where she remained until we came up to collect her. I had certainly avenged myself for the loss and inconvenience I had suffered as a result of the activities of those two lions. The old fellow who was accounted for the previous evening could not have been involved in the buffalo stampede. The most one could expect from him would be man-eating, and his determined stalk of the native indicated that he was out for such mischief.

My loss of the previous night included a splendid .318 Express rifle, the stock of which was broken into matchwood. As a precautionary measure I had allowed the headman to take my shotgun to the compound that night; but for that fortunate circumstance I should have lost that also.

Indeed, a buffalo herd stampeding in the still of night is a thing one does not like to encounter too often!

10: FIVE MAN-EATERS OF IDETE

Some years ago, shortly after I had migrated from the Congo, I landed in the Mahenga district in the southern part of Tanganyika Territory, where I was shooting elephants under special licence. As the elephants had become a nuisance and were causing a lot of damage to native plantations, the government decided to issue licences to a number of selected hunters. Each hunter was required to destroy twenty-five head and to operate in a district indicated by the Game Department. I was fortunate to be included in the Game Warden's selection, and was later instructed to complete additional licences, each authorizing the destruction of twenty-five head. Although a number of thrilling incidents occurred while shooting elephant on such a large scale, the present story is concerned mainly with lions.

Towards the end of March I was camped at a village called Idete. It had been raining in torrents all day but towards evening the sky cleared and the night was brilliantly moonlit. A huge campfire was burning outside my tent around which some thirty porters had turned in for the night. Although we had encountered no lions so far, there were persistent rumours about man-eaters and my natives took the precaution of remaining near camp and as much as possible in the immediate vicinity of the campfire.

About midnight I awoke, and looking through the open tent door I was astonished to see a lion standing between the porters and my tent. The porters were all asleep and in blissful ignorance of the presence of the intruder. As the sleeping natives were lying around in all directions, it was impossible to chance a shot at the lion without incurring the risk of shooting a native, so in order to awaken the camp I fired a shot in the air. In a few seconds every native in the camp was lustily exercising his vocal cords. The lion had by now departed and I decided to follow it with a shotgun. In spite of the bright moonlight and the open clearing, I could find no further trace of the lion, and on returning to camp I was busy arranging with my gun bearers to do guard for the rest of the night when there was a tremendous uproar in the village some three hundred yards away. Above the yells and screams of men and women we could hear the angry growls of a lion.

We immediately rushed over to the village and on arriving there found that the lion had broken down the door of a hut and carried off a man. The victim had apparently put up a desperate fight, as the broken shaft of his spear was found outside the hut, and later, when the lion had been accounted for, we found the blade of the spear embedded deeply in its rump. We tracked him as fast as was possible at night, but nevertheless lost all trace of the raider. However, we did come across a pool of blood and part of the intestines of the native at a spot where the beast had stopped to devour its prey—a feast that must have been interrupted by our approach. The villagers, needless to say, were not keen on following the lion any farther that night. The victim had been killed, beyond doubt, and apart from risking further accidents there was nothing to be gained by continuing the pursuit. It was decided to return to camp and track the lion early next day. The rest of that night was spent in a great beer-drink, and sleep was quite out of the question. The natives proceeded to fortify themselves with a liberal supply of "pombe" and eagerly awaited the break of day to track down their enemy.

At the crack of dawn all the villagers and porters assembled outside my tent, armed with throwing spears, bows and arrows, axes, wooden clubs and every semblance of weapon they could muster. My two gun bearers, both reliable men, paraded with my two heavy-calibre rifles, and I again took the shotgun, loaded with SSG ammunition (perhaps the safest weapon to use against soft-skinned animals at close range). Tracking the lion to a patch of "mateti" (long swamp grass, about twelve feet high), we found that he had not emerged from that cover. We felt sure that he was lying in the grass with the remains of his victim. The patch was about 400 yards long and 200 yards wide, tapering to a point at the farther end, and with an open area all around for a distance of more than a hundred yards. It seemed the ideal place for a "beat," if only the lion would do what was expected of him, i.e., remain in the long grass until he had got to the tapered point of the patch, from where he was expected to break cover. But I have known of so many cases of "beats" where lions did not do the expected thing, that I was rather doubtful as to the best spot to place the guns, for I felt sure the guns would play the leading part in the final scene. The natives refused to enter the grass without being covered by at least one gun, which left me only two guns for the outside positions. I selected the likeliest looking warriors with bows and arrows and posted them on the one flank. A gun bearer with a heavy-calibre rifle took up his position on the other flank, whilst I took up an open position near the point of the patch from where I could cover both flanks. The beaters formed in a crescent on the broad end of the patch, and all was in readiness for the "beat." As things turned out I could have saved myself the trouble of selecting strategic points, for no sooner had the order to advance been given than there was a mad rush, and in less than a minute the mob was on the lion. Apparently the beast was so bewildered by the sudden rush that he never attempted to move and in a few seconds hundreds of spears and arrows were driven into him. The carcass soon resembled a huge pin cushion with its protruding spears and arrows. Then pandemonium broke out, as the shouting and scream-ing was taken up by a crowd of women and children who had assembled at a safe distance from the scene of the killing. They forthwith staged an exhibition of the most grotesque acrobatics, with stately dames of grandmotherly age giving vent to their feelings by turning somersaults and cartwheels in the sand. Exit Man-eater No. 1.

FIVE MAN-EATERS OF IDETE

During the day news was brought in that a woman had been carried off during the preceding night from a village some five miles away. The report made it clear that more than one lion was operating in that vicinity and they had become a serious menace to the population. I immediately sent to the District Officer for any guns he might have available, and from a nearby mission I managed to borrow a rusty old spring trap. Then, the following night, a village two miles farther on was attacked by a lioness and a man was taken out of his hut. His wife had courageously followed the lioness outside and attacked her with a heavy wooden club, thereby distracting the brute's attention from her husband. The woman's screams awakened two men in a hut near by and they promptly attacked the lioness with their spears. They finally succeeded in driving her off, but during the struggle one of the men was so badly mauled that he died shortly after I arrived on the scene. Apart from injecting frequent doses of morphia there was little I could do for the poor fellow, as he was practically disemboweled and his scalp was in a dreadful condition. The man who had been taken in the first place escaped comparatively lightly by losing an arm, which was amputated by the fathers in the mission near by. After the wounded had been attended to we went in search of the marauder. We soon got onto a blood trail which we followed for about two miles, when one of the trackers stumbled onto the carcass. The lioness had been dead for some hours. The two plucky natives had driven no less than fourteen spears into the beast and one eyeball had been smashed to a pulp—apparently by the woman wielding the heavy club, which explained why the lioness did not turn on her immediately she commenced operations with the club. Exit Man-eater No. 2.

After this there was peace for a few days, until one day a native came in to report that a lion had taken a man from his hut the previous night. The village was three miles away and I set out immediately to see what could be done in the matter. On arriving there and after listening to the details of the occurrence I decided to organise a hunt. The entire male population of the village turned out with spears, bows and arrows, clubs, axes, etc. We followed the tracks of the lion which, after a few miles, led into a dense undergrowth. Here, I thought, the lion would have stopped to devour its prey, and after the feast would most probably go to sleep. I got the natives to surround the place and close in gradually whilst I took up a position at the end of the dense bush, where I felt certain the lion would break cover. No sooner had the natives started to close in on the centre than there was an outburst of wild shouting and a tremendous amount of action. When I got to the scene of the killing I found, as in the first case, a carcass resembling a pin cushion. It evidently was not necessary for me to have come to their assistance. But the knowledge that a European with rifles was at hand in case of an accident had given the natives the necessary courage, and without any difficulty they did what they could easily have done without my aid. The lion was a young one and in excellent condition, but, as in the case of the first, the skin was completely destroyed by the numerous spear cuts. Exit Man-eater No. 3—with myself still playing the role of spectator!

The following night there was again a commotion in the village and once more a man was carried off. In the dark it was impossible to follow the lion and it was decided to follow the tracks early the next morning. That day we scoured the countryside, but without success; we could find no trace of the lion or its victim. Tired and disappointed, we returned to camp as the sun was setting. Late that night the lion again visited the vicinity of the camp, but on this occasion the natives were mostly all awake and the campfires and noise kept the marauder at a safe distance. We went out again the following day, but again drew a blank. The following day I decided to use the spring trap I had previously borrowed from the mission. Owing to the prevalence of the tsetse fly, there were no domestic animals of any description to use for bait, but I decided to set the trap in the footpath which I felt sure the lion would follow in order to approach the village. I warned all the natives in the vicinity of this trap, and took the added precaution of placing two layers of grass on either side. An hour after the trap was set the village was startled by loud cries. We all thought that the lion had made another capture and promptly proceeded to the point of disturbance. On arriving at the trap we found that a native had foolishly walked into it, in spite of the warning. His leg was badly lacerated and much blood was lost, but fortunately no bones were fractured. After releasing him from the trap I had him carried to the village for medical attention, and then I re-set the trap. I was still busy dressing the wound of the unfortunate native when there was a loud roar in the direction of the trap. There was no mistake as to what had happened. The lion had been attracted by the smell of the native's blood and had walked into the trap. When we arrived on the scene he was struggling desperately to free himself and I had no difficulty in disposing of him. Like the others that had been killed previously, this lion was young and in excellent condition. Exit Man-eater No. 4, and this time not entirely without my assistance.

I remained in the vicinity of this village for several days, but as there was no further indication of lions in the neighbourhood I decided to return to my main camp and carry on with elephant hunting. The following morning everything was in readiness for an early start when a native came in to report more trouble. He had travelled ten miles from a village where a young lioness had accounted for no less than nine natives in as many days. She had become so bold that even the shelter of their huts was of no avail, and on one occasion she had actually broken down the grass roof and carried off her victim. As everything was ready for an immediate departure, I set off in the direction of the village of the latest disturbance. On my arrival there that afternoon, I found the inhabitants in a state of terror. That night six hundred natives abandoned their village and slept in my camp. Great campfires encircled the camp and were kept

Man-eating is not entirely the habit of old lions; the four man-eaters shown here were young and in good condition.

These male lions had killed several native hunters and created much havoc amongst the kraals.

burning all night. I sat up and waited for the raider but the fires and the noise had the effect of keeping her at bay, and she failed to put in an appearance. I went out on three consecutive days but could discover no trace of her. At night the campfires were kept burning and the lioness, although bold enough to approach the vicinity and give vent to her feelings with an occasional roar, never approached within shooting range.

On the fourth day I called on the natives to cut down the long grass and make a clearance of about thirty yards around the camp. There being bright moonlight, I decided to occupy the clearance at night with my gun bearer, who was a well-trained native and an excellent shot to boot. A few minutes after sunset we took up our position, back to back in the clearance. I was again using a shotgun, loaded with AAA ammunition, whilst the gun bearer had a .450-bore rifle. Quite early in the evening we became aware of the presence of the lioness. In the bright moonlight she could be seen peeping through the grass at intervals. I had decided not to shoot until she came into the open clearance and gave instructions to my gun bearer to that effect. For nearly three hours the lioness kept circling around us and then she decided to charge. I sat watching her every move. Carefully she was watching us, then suddenly she came towards us at a gallop. When she had approached to within ten yards she crouched and made her first spring. I waited for her to make her second spring from a distance of about five yards, and as soon as she left her crouching attitude to make the final spring I let her have the full benefit of both barrels. The force of the simultaneous shots knocked her over on her back, where she remained without a further move. My gun bearer, who had been out of the picture up to this stage, promptly served the carcass with two more bullets.

I have shot many lions and have had some exciting experiences with them but never have I been so fascinated as I was in the killing of this marauder. In the bright light of a full moon I had watched her every move for hours. Finally, when she had decided to charge, I watched that tell-tale wagging of her tail. Then, her determined expression when emerging into the open; the gallop before making her first spring; the deliberate crouch before making the final dash— it all seemed to be the rehearsal of a play, and for my special benefit. My nerves were in no way affected, for I felt certain that she could never pass the two barrels of my shotgun. As it was, I shot her at a range of less than five yards, and the impression the two shots made on her fully justified my confidence. What I had done was a flagrant transgression on all the laws of commonsense, but I felt no different than one would on a tennis court, playing a difficult shot of which he was confident. If the shooter is given the right conditions and possesses a steady nerve, it is physically impossible for a lion to penetrate the defence of a shotgun loaded with the right sort of ammunition. The rest of that night, and a few more nights, were spent in wild celebration in the village.

I was greatly puzzled to find five young lions in

such excellent physical condition resorting to man-eating. As a rule a man-eater is a decrepit, sickly old beast which is unable to catch its prey among other animals. The natives advanced the theory that at a certain time of the year the elephant grass in the vicinity is covered with a pollen which, if it enters the eyes of man or beast, sets up a severe inflammation and swelling. In view of this fact, they claimed that these lions had resorted to hunting man, for which purpose it was not necessary to enter the grass. Some years later I was interested to read a report by a Game Warden of Uganda, upholding this theory.

At all events, although I had done very little to deliver the natives from their prosecutors, I was looked upon as a great hero in their district, and they were only too pleased at all times to render me any assistance I needed.

11: CONGO COPPER

In the beginning of the year 1903 I landed at Elizabethville, in the Belgian Congo, to which place I had walked from Rhodesia. It was then seven years before the first train would run to the Congo. Shortly after my arrival I entered the service of the Tanganyika Concessions Ltd., of which George Grey was then the representative in the Katanga. I was instructed to proceed to Likasi, a hundred miles north of Elizabethville, and there join a small group of prospectors who had preceded me by a few days. At the head of this group was a Swede named Ericksen. Just about the time of my arrival Ericksen's group had discovered the Likasi Mine, where in later years a flourishing township sprang up and the great copper concentrating plant of the Union Miniere was installed. When I arrived on the scene there was still considerable excitement at the discovery of the new mine and the neighbourhood was being subjected to a thorough survey.

Conditions in those days were hard, as supplies were sent up only on rare occasions, and for the greater part we lived on the country. We exchanged game meat, of which we were never short, for native produce. One afternoon whilst out hunting with one of the natives of the locality Ericksen was using a rifle, the sight of which had been lost in a scrape with an elephant. To remedy the defect, Ericksen had modelled a makeshift sight out of candle grease, which he affixed in the presence of the native. Shortly afterwards they came across a herd of antelope and, in spite of the improvised sight, Ericksen did some good shooting, accounting for two roan in as many shots. The native, who had watched the proceedings from the beginning, immediately attributed the good shooting to the effects of the candle grease, which he believed to be "medicine." After the meat had been delivered at camp there was a long discussion between the natives, and finally one of them offered to show Ericksen a place where there were plenty of "green stones," in exchange for two pieces of "medicine." Ericksen promptly accepted the offer and set out to discover what later became the Star Mine, the first copper mine to be worked in the Belgian Congo. His guide was quite satisfied to walk a hundred miles to the place in exchange for two candles! If the candles played a prominent part in the development of the Congo, it is certain that similar satisfactory results were not obtained in the matter of hunting, as I heard afterwards that Ericksen had come to grief whilst using the rifle with the improvised sight against a buffalo.

In 1905 I was prospecting in the vicinity of Elizabethville when another prospector came in to report that a village chief named Katapemba had chased him out and threatened to kill him. George Grey immediately sent out word asking for a volunteer to go to Katapemba's village and prospect that area as far as the Lualaba River. (At that time the Lualaba district was inhabited by cannibal tribes. Another prospector named Hooke who had gone in that direction had not reported for several weeks and considerable uneasiness was felt on his account.) In reply to Grey's appeal for a volunteer, I offered to go on condition that I be provided with an armed bodyguard. In due course I was provided with twelve Matabele natives who were armed with Martini-Henry rifles, and who had had a fair amount of training in the use of firearms. After preparing my safari I duly set out in the direction of Katapemba's village, determined to prospect that area and, if possible, find out what had become of the prospector, Hooke.

When I arrived near Katapemba's village some weeks later, the chief sent me a message ordering me to quit the vicinity immediately, failing which he would have me brought in and my throat would be cut. Katapemba's village was a fairly large one, and there were certainly enough of his henchmen to carry out his throat under usual circumstances. But I knew that he depended entirely on native weapons and had no firearms in his possession. On receipt of his message I called up my Matabele bodyguard and explained the position to them. They all swore allegiance to me and said they would stand by me in the event of an attack. Following this consultation I sent a message to Katapemba, advising him that I intended to call on him that afternoon and that, if he really intended to carry out his threat, he would be solely responsible for any misfortune that might befall him.

After we had pitched camp in the afternoon I called up my bodyguard and proceeded to the village to interview the chief. The presence of the twelve armed men accompanying me had a soothing influence on the old chief's temper. He received me in a friendly spirit and forthwith offered me a goat as a present—the customary peace offering. The other inhabitants of the village were likewise very docile, and it was obvious that their earlier insolent attitude had undergone a change. No reference was made to the chief's earlier ultimatum, and before returning to my camp I informed him that I intended to move off at daybreak the next morning in search of the prospector Hooke, after which I intended to return to his village and prospect the district. As I did not know the Lualaba district, and in view of the early start I intended to make the next morning, I asked the chief to provide me with a guide who would sleep at my camp that night, and thus be at hand in the morning. The old chief readily agreed to my request and promised to send me a reliable guide before sunset.

Shortly before sunset the guide had not arrived and I decided to send my native capitao (captain) to remind the chief of his promise. The village was only a few hundred yards from my camp, and when half an hour later my capitao had not returned, I began to feel uneasy. I was just getting ready to proceed to the village to investigate when I heard shouting in the distance, and on looking towards the direction of the noise I saw the capitao making for camp as fast as his legs could carry him—with a mob of villagers in hot pursuit. The capitao had a good start on his pursuers and reached camp fully a hundred yards ahead of the leader. I allowed the mob to approach to within twenty yards of the camp and then called on them to halt. The twelve Matabeles had meanwhile taken up a position close to me and had the mob covered with their rifles. As the villagers appeared to ignore my order to halt, I ordered a volley to be fired over their heads. Those shots brought the desired result. The natives retired slowly, and a little farther away they settled down to an earnest discussion amongst themselves. After a while the leader came forward and said he wanted to speak to me. I allowed him to come to within five yards of me and then asked him for an explanation. He promptly explained that the whole episode was merely a little joke at the expense of my capitao. I was not very favourably impressed with this explanation, nor was my capitao, who informed me that he had actually been made a prisoner and that the villagers were making arrangements to kill him just before he managed to break away. What was more, he had overheard them arguing as to how his body was to be divided. The spokesman of the group, however, persisted that it was all a harmless joke. I told him that their kind of joke did not appeal to any of us and that I wanted the chief to come to my camp immediately and bring with him the guide he had promised to furnish. Should he not comply, I intended having a joke of my own by opening fire on the village. A few minutes later the chief arrived with the guide, and he also insisted that the whole affair was a joke. I let the matter drop there, but took the precaution to warn the chief that if any of the villagers should approach within a hundred yards of my camp during the night, in the same jocular mood, I would not hesitate to shoot. Katapemba forthwith instructed the guide to remain at my camp that night and escort the safari at daybreak, after which he left me with an avowal of eternal friendship. I had my own opinion as to the value of this newly discovered affection and promptly arranged to have sentries posted for the night, a precaution which probably explained why we were left in peace that night.

Early the next morning we set out for the Lualaba River, a distance of twelve miles from Katapemba's village. As we were going down the final hill in a narrow footpath which led into a dense forest, I noticed an interesting formation of reef running at right angles to the path. I decided to follow this formation and told the guide that as I would have no immediate need of his services he could return to his village. In following this formation I was led a considerable distance off the path. As it turned out subsequently, it was owing to this change of course that I am alive today. I spent several days in the vicinity and towards the end of that week I arrived at another village. I pitched camp about a hundred yards from that village and decided to go over and interview the chief. On arriving near the chief's hut I noticed a rope tied to two posts; over this rope several strips of meat were hung out to dry in the sun. On the suggestion of my capitao, I went to examine the meat and found that they were strips of human flesh. The victim had obviously been killed shortly before our arrival, as the flesh was still dripping blood. Although the village was considerably smaller than Katapemba's, I was thoroughly alarmed at this sight. Not suspecting any danger, I had foolishly left my rifle in camp, and apart from the capitao, only three of the Matabeles had followed me. Fortunately, they had brought their rifles along. I instructed them to remain close to me and proceeded to make my presence known to the chief. The chief belonged to the Mabunda tribe; he proved to be an insolent type of native and offered none of the usual courtesies. I decided to lose no time in imposing my authority and told him that I was accompanied by an armed force, and that I expected him to present himself at my camp as soon as possible. He did not appear keen to comply with my request, but after thinking things over for a while he promised to come over later in the day.

As soon as we returned to camp the news of what we had seen in the village spread quickly amongst the porters. The Matabeles did not appear very worried, but the porters were clearly alarmed. I warned them all to remain close to camp, and I had no reason to suspect that any of them would venture near the village. The aptitude of the African native for fishing out news has always intrigued me. In this case I felt certain that none of the porters had gone beyond the immediate neighbourhood of the camp, but for all that, in less than half an hour they brought me startling news. By means unknown to me, they had discovered that the chief was holding a European prisoner in his village. So convincing was their story that I determined to question the chief as soon as he arrived at my camp.

A few minutes later the chief arrived, accompanied by two other natives, and bringing the usual peace offering. I promptly asked him for an explanation of the presence of a white man in his village. The Matabeles had meanwhile gathered around us and were making a prominent display of their rifles. This, of course, was done to impress the chief. He informed me, in a rather sheepish manner, that the white man had been in the village for three weeks, and was being kept there for his own safety. I replied that I had come out especially to find my friend and that I would assume immediate responsibility for his safety. I ordered six of the Matabeles to accompany the chief to the village; they were to secure the white man and bring him back without interference. I had no doubt that the man was Hooke, and still less doubt as to the reason for his detention.

In due course Hooke arrived at my camp; he was the sole survivor of his expedition. Only that afternoon the last of his porters had been killed and the flesh we had seen in the village was that of the unfortunate native. Hooke related that when he was captured the chief told him he would be killed last, and in the meantime he would be fattened. That very morning the chief had informed him that he was now in a fit condition to provide a good feast and that he would be killed the next day. My unexpected arrival had upset all the arrangements, and on releasing Hooke the chief told him that it was all a little joke to frighten him. We decided to let the matter drop and not to stir up trouble. Sentries were posted in the usual way that night and we were not molested. Early the next day we proceeded on our way to Katapemba's village. We remained in that vicinity for twelve months and were then ordered to proceed to Lufupa, where we were joined by another prospector named Sharpe. (Sharpe had been engaged in London by George Grey, a brother of Sir Edward Grey, on the recommendation of Lady Grey, who at a family gathering had asked George to find a position for the young man. He was sent out in a very minor capacity, but many years later he discovered the world's richest uranium mine at Chinkolobwe, in the Belgian Congo.)

Shortly after Sharpe's arrival at Lufupa his caravan was attacked. One of his natives was killed and another wounded. The matter was immediately reported to headquarters and an armed column was sent out. We were all instructed to join this column and proceed to the scene of the outrage. Nightfall of the first day found us camped close to the village of the offending chief. Sentries were posted and instructed to keep a sharp lookout in the direction of the village. At dawn the next day we were subjected to a surprise attack from the side opposite the village. A volley of arrows was fired at our column, but luckily without causing any casualties. We immediately attacked the raiders and they ran back to the village. In the subsequent fighting twenty-six natives were killed, including the chief. The action was soon over and we took possession of the village.

On entering a hut where a wounded native was being attended, I found the wife of the dead chief. She told me that on no less than three occasions her husband had ordered his men to kill me whilst I was prospecting in the vicinity. The men had refused to carry out the chief's instructions because I had always supplied them with plenty of game meat and they could not see the sense of destroying their source of supplies. But this was not the only surprise I had, for farther down the village I recognised the guide who had accompanied me from Katapemba's village on my journey to the Lualaba the year before. He told me that on his return Katapemba had chased him out because he had failed to lead me into an ambush the chief had prepared for me near the spot where I had left the footpath to follow the reef formation. Instead of entering the dense forest, I had struck out into open country and turned away from certain death which awaited me a few yards ahead.

After this affair I remained in the district for two years, during which time we were left in peace to carry out our work. Our little group did much to open up the vast copper field of the Katanga and I have lived to see some of the death traps of those days converted into model townships; not very far from what was then Katapemba's village the enormous smelters of the Union Miniere are now turning out over a hundred thousand tons of copper each year.

12: THE CHINGANDA KILLER

Towards the end of October, 1945, I was hunting in the Rungwa area, near the Rift Valley. Some twelve miles from my camp was a little village named Chinganda. I had received many glowing reports about the large herds of game in the Chinganda area, but as I was doing quite well where I was I did not bother much about Chinganda—until late one afternoon, when a runner from there came rushing into my camp. He was in a very agitated state of mind, and it was obvious that he had something important to tell. After the usual greetings, I asked him what had brought him to my camp in such a hurry. The story I then heard was an alarming one indeed.

That morning a rogue buffalo bull had, for the third time, killed a member of Chinganda's small community. These killings, which were without provocation, had started only two weeks earlier. In that time the bull had accounted for three fishermen who were peacefully following their occupation near one of the pools in the river. This last killing was accomplished with particular vindictiveness. The unfortunate native, in trying to dodge into the grass, had received the full force of one of the horns in his temple and the horn was driven clear through the skull. The buffalo had carried the corpse for some distance suspended on his horn, and had then dashed it to the ground. Apparently unable to lift the dead man on his horns again, the bull had smashed the skull into a pulp with his heavy front hoofs. The friends of the victim were unarmed and unable to help him; they had found safety in a nearby tree, and here they were menaced for several hours by the infuriated beast.

A few months earlier a government official had escaped a mauling by what was suspected to be the same bull. The man was charged unexpectedly and had no time to shoot. Fortunately there was a tree near by and, discarding his rifle, he had just managed to get out of the bull's reach in the nick of time. At Rungwa village, only ten miles away, two natives had been killed the previous week by a lone bull. The natives were convinced that the same bull was responsible for all of these casualties.

The runner from Chinganda now brought me an urgent appeal from the local Sultan to come out and rid his village of this menace. In many years of assiduous buffalo hunting I have caught up with a good many killers, and I have listened to many stories about buffalo outlaws, but this monster at Chinganda had earned for himself the most evil reputation in my experience.

There are several experienced native hunters at Chinganda. They all use old muzzle-loading weapons, but even thus armed, native hunters generally manage to rid themselves of such an unwelcome animal. That they had failed in this case proved that this super-killer, apart from his vindictive nature, was possessed of unusual cunning. Upon my questioning the runner, he admitted that several shots had been fired at the brute, but none had laid him low. Thus, it was quite possible that he had been wounded on more than one occasion and this, of course would account for his bad temper. The muzzle-loading type of rifle used by natives in these parts can be quite effective at close range, and it frequently accounts for elephants. But this bull had apparently scared the hunting community at Chinganda so badly that none of them would approach him within shooting range of their muzzle-loaders, and such long-range shooting as they had indulged in had only aggravated matters.

This was a distinctly dangerous and unpleasant assignment, and one I was not at all keen to tackle. To clean up the dirty work of native hunters is, at the best of times, a bad business. In the case of buffalo it is deadly dangerous work. However, there it was; if this bull was left to his killing he could do a great deal more damage and, quite apart from human considerations, there was the question of my own prestige. I could not very well tell the natives that I was afraid of this brute! The matter was duly discussed with my hunting natives and finally it was agreed that we should go out to Chinganda and see what could be done. I sent the runner back to the Sultan with a message that I would come out within the next day or two.

The next morning I prepared kit and supplies for a seven days' outing and that afternoon we set out for Chinganda, where we arrived just before sunset. As could be expected, at Chinganda there was but one topic of conversation—the rogue buffalo. Natives are always prone to exaggerate an affair such as this and the present occasion was no exception. But even allowing for exaggeration, it was quite obvious that this killer was fighting with the gloves off; he was waging war with great cunning and ferocity. His "modus operandi" was to conceal himself in long grass, from where he could attack any unsuspecting passerby. In each case he had mauled the dead body of his victim, after which he showed no eagerness to depart from the scene. Invariably he would re-enter the thick grass where the natives would not dare to follow him. On several occasions they had seen him in the long grass, but always at a distance and well beyond the range of their antiquated weapons. There was no doubt about it, Chinganda's killer had reached the stage where man no longer inspired fear in him. On the contrary, he had inspired terror in every inhabitant of that village.

Throughout every discussion of the matter, the local natives repeatedly referred to the long and dense grass which, even at that time of the year, was still too green to burn. This was all in favour of the bull, and I realised that unless he was killed outright with the first shot the situation would be aggravated still further. Certainly there would be no possibility of following him should he take to cover after an unsuccessful shot. When finally I turned in for the night I had serious misgivings about the job in hand and I realised that Chinganda's killer was going to prove a very tough nut to crack.

Early next morning, accompanied by the trackers,

I went out to examine the locality where the score had to be settled with the bull. From what I had heard the previous evening I expected to find difficult country, but what I saw on the spot filled me with dismay. The kind of country the bull had selected for his nefarious work was unapproachable and quite impenetrable. A small footpath had been hacked out from the village to enable the inhabitants to reach the river and the fishing pools, and it was in the immediate vicinity of this path that all three accidents had occurred.

Chinganda village is built on a high sandbank and overlooks a basin-like depression which stretches out to the present Rungwa River, nearly a mile away to the east. The entire basin is overgrown with long reeds and elephant grass—country so dense that visibility is reduced to only a few feet. From the village itself there is a splendid view of the valley below, but in that dense vegetation a large buffalo herd could easily hide and escape detection. In this valley I would have to settle the score with the killer. Unless something altogether unexpected and unhoped-for happened, I could not see how this was to be done. Certainly I had no intention of abandoning the hunt without making some effort to get the bull under fire. Whilst I was busy examining the position, the Sultan and a crowd of hangers-on had gathered around me, all anxious to see what I would do. Just what they expected me to do I do not know, but I forthwith explained to the Sultan that I was willing to do all I could to rid them of their enemy, but I was not going to risk my life by looking for him in the long grass. I suggested that observers be posted all along the embankment and that I be notified as soon as the buffalo put in an appearance. To this they all agreed, and as there was nothing further for me to do I returned to my camp. All that day I waited for a call, but by nightfall nothing had happened.

Next morning, early, I had to see about meat for the camp followers and I was taken to a spot not far from the village where bushbuck were plentiful. I had not been out long when the natives put up one of those antelopes, which I had no difficulty in shooting. That shot not only provided the necessary meat for the camp, but it also awakened the bull in the long grass near by. In a few minutes a runner came up to report that the buffalo had been sighted. The animal had left his hiding place, walked a short distance, and then had lain down again near the embankment, from where they could see him easily. This was good news; the unhoped-for had happened!

I immediately made for the spot where a crowd of natives had now gathered and from where they were pointing at a place in the grass below. I could see no sign of the buffalo, but the natives were all emphatic that they could see him clearly and that he was not far away. After I had wasted some time in unsuccessful efforts to see the animal, I finally got one of their hunters to train my rifle on the target and in this manner I eventually detected the bull, or at least what was visible of him. He was fully two hundred yards away, and the entire target did not amount to more than twelve inches of black hide. It was quite impossible to tell which part of the body was exposed to view. To shoot at such a target would be merely guesswork and might easily aggravate matters.

The entire village had now turned out and I immediately got them to beat drums and tins and make all other noise they could to make the bull move. But all the noise those villagers could create in half an hour failed to move that black devil. I could understand now why the native hunters with their muzzleloaders had failed to get within reach of the cunning brute. Tired of beating drums and screaming, the natives now insisted that I should fire at the black spot. Unsatisfactory as such a procedure undoubtedly was, I realised that it was the only way of moving the bull, and after I had lined the black object up well in my sights I pressed the trigger. I was using a heavy-calibre .404, and could clearly hear the soft-nose bullet strike home. In the next instant the black spot came to life; the bull was making frantic efforts to rise. He was clearly in difficulties, and as he finally got to a standing position I gave him another shot. Again I could hear my bullet strike home, but instead of going down as I had expected him to do, the bull now rushed deeper into the long grass. At 400 yards he once more came into view; I fired, and again I could hear the thud of my bullet finding its mark. But the buffalo showed no signs of distress and stuck to his course, towards a bend in the river some 800 to 1,000 yards away. From where we were, on the high embankment, we could see the grass being pushed down as the bull moved forward. Occasionally his black figure came into view, but he was now beyond my range and soon we would lose sight of him entirely. But at this stage of the proceedings a flock of white tick birds came to our assistance; they circled around the running buffalo, and as he went down into the river bed we could see the birds swooping down at the same spot.

The situation now was just about as bad as it could be. I felt certain I had registered a hit on each occasion, but just where the three shots were placed it was impossible to tell. There was only one course open to us now and that was to follow him down the river. I was convinced that the punishment he had taken from the heavy-calibre rifle had driven him to shelter and that he would not willingly expose himself to further danger—unless we approached him within charging distance, which, of course, I had no intention of doing. My plan was to proceed within 100 yards from the river and from that point onward to burn the grass down all along the bank of the river. This scheme found favour with the villagers and in a short time they had all turned out with burning logs. Green as the grass was I was determined to clear the decks for action. If fires failed we would resort to hoes. It took us an hour to burn down the grass near the river bank, and by the time the fires had died out for the hundredth time I had an open space 500 yards long and 100 yards wide. Here, at least, I could meet the bull on something like even terms.

The problem now was to coax the killer from the river bed, where he was shielded by heavy reeds and grass which would not burn and, for obvious reasons, could not be cleared. This was the danger zone, and inside the long reeds I knew the bull was lying and awaiting our approach. The most important thing was to determine his exact whereabouts, and in this I decided the tick birds could help us. The natives were now called upon to throw burning logs in the direction where we presumed the bull to be hiding, and this, in addition to the beating of drums, soon had the desired result. As one of the logs fell near his hideout there was a violent snort and the birds took off. We knew the bull had jumped to his feet and very little more provocation would send him out in full charge. The villagers had now made up their minds that it was time to quit the scene and on all sides they were making for the embankment at the village. Only my hunting natives remained with me and between us we would have to carry on from where the villagers had left off. We now had gained the advantage of knowing the exact whereabouts of the bull, but to get him to come out into the open was the next difficulty. We all knew that the next time he came into view it would be in full charge and the only way to coax him into a charge would be for someone to go near enough to provoke him. Obviously I could not do this myself as, in order to handle such a situation, I would require the necessary time and space. But once again luck seemed to favour us, for at this stage a native hunter with a pack of mongrel dogs appeared on the scene. I firmly believed that the dogs would save the situation, and as they went down the river bank slowly I prepared for the charge which I expected would follow. But before the dogs had gone far there was another violent snort and in a fraction of the time it took them to descend, that mongrel pack rushed from the river bed. Buffalo baiting definitely was not their strong forte!

We had now reached a stalemate; I could think of nothing else to provoke a charge. Certainly, I did not think it worth while to suggest to any of my own natives that they offer themselves as bait. But now, to my amazement, they came forward and offered to go nearer and tempt the bull. They assured me that all I had to do was to arrange the respective positions we were to take up and they would do the rest. Those natives certainly had more faith in my ability to deal with the situation than I had myself. In quick time we were all posted in line, and then six natives closed in on the river and started to throw burning logs. At first there was no response, but when the third fusillade of logs went toward the river there came another violent snort and this was quickly followed by a huge black body. Chinganda's killer was making his last determined charge. But his speed was very much reduced by the punishment he had taken, and as he came into full view on the river bank he was met by a slug between the eyes. Once again I could hear my bullet strike, but this time there was no mistake and the big bull slumped to the ground. The triple killer of Chinganda had come to the end of his trail of violence and destruction.

It was exactly three hours after I had fired my first shot that proceedings finally came to a halt. The

Horned Death

Sultan and his people had enjoyed a grandstand view from beginning to end. This pleased them immensely, as they could watch the destruction of their enemy from absolute safety and see and appreciate every movement of the three-hour struggle. It was certainly one of the trickiest jobs I had ever handled and I heaved a sigh of relief when it was all over.

When I came to examine the carcass it was not difficult to see why that bull had become such a terrible menace, for apart from the three stomach wounds and the brain shot he had taken from me, I removed no less than nine slugs from his body.

In view of the terrible vengeance this bull had exacted, one would have thought the villagers would have taken heed. But no; only a few days later another native hunter paid toll to a wounded buffalo at Chinganda. When the news reached me I was almost tempted to say, "It served him right."

13: PYGMIES OF THE ITURI FOREST

I WAS sitting comfortably in the hotel lounge in Nairobi one night, where I had landed after a protracted hunting safari, when a stranger approached me and stated that he was acting for a wealthy American patron who was in need of the services of a professional hunter to take him out on a big safari. He explained that the arrangement he had made with another hunter had been cancelled at the last moment, and he had then been advised to approach me with a view to overcoming the difficulty. I was not keen to undertake such a safari at that particular time as I had for some days been concentrating on my own preparations for a holiday down South. My newly-made acquaintance was persistent; the terms he offered were generous, and when he mentioned that the safari would include a couple of months in the Ituri Forest, where I had not hunted previously, the project began to appeal to me.

I had often contemplated a trip to the Ituri. Stories of the forest and its Pygmy inhabitants had always stirred my imagination. Here, at last, was an opportunity to satisfy my curiosity; I would see the Pygmies in their natural haunts. The okapi also, at that time, was filling the headlines. Like the Pygmy, this strange animal was to be found only in the great

Ituri Forest. Thus, the germ of a new adventure entered my system once again, and it did not require much added persuasion to divert my interest from the proposed holiday.

The next day found me in a whirl of activity, preparing foodstuffs, rifles, and ammunition, recruiting the necessary staff, engaging motor lorries, and doing the thousand and one things that go to make up a successful safari. It was apparent from the outset that the patron had come out to enjoy the best sport obtainable, regardless of cost. Everything had to be prepared in grand style. In addition to a male secretary, whose job was to record the history of the safari, the patron was accompanied by his wife.

We were on the road only a few days when it became very apparent that the presence of the lady would severely mar whatever good sport the trip might offer. Just what she expected from a hunting trip I was not able to understand. She protested vehemently against the "senseless slaughter" of every good trophy we bagged. In addition, she had fixed views on most other subjects—views that did not always coincide with our own, and which were sure to rob the trip of all interest. Her husband, like many good husbands, suffered all this interference in silence whilst in her presence. But the moment we were alone he was loud in his denunciation of her attitudes. As I felt more or less responsible for the success of the trip, I hit upon a plan which I submitted to the patron and which met with his full approval.

We left the main road that afternoon and made

The patron displays his trophies from the Ituri safari.

A motorcar halts at the edge of the vast, impenetrable
Ituri Forest.

for a big swamp near a river. The place swarmed with mosquitoes, gnats and every other kind of flying and crawling insect. At the edge of this swamp we made camp for the night. When the time came to prepare our beds not a mosquito net could be found. Always, when things disappear in this part of Africa, the natives are immediately blamed, so, forthwith, their baggage was searched thoroughly for the missing nets. I held out small hope of ever recovering the nets as I maintained that natives are never caught red handed with the proceeds of any theft—their procedure being to "plant" the loot in a safe place for future recovery. It was fortunate that the victim of our plot did not understand Ki-swahili, for whilst the search was in progress the natives protested violently that they had seen me hiding the nets in one of my suitcases earlier in the day! That night we were left to the mercy of every insect in the vicinity of the swamp. It was a nightmare experience, and the husband, although party to the scheme, was much louder in his imprecations than the wife, who suffered in silence.

The following morning we awoke with swollen faces and hands, and in this respect the lady was by far the greatest sufferer. As soon as breakfast was over she insisted that we should depart from the vicinity. But misfortunes, like sorrows, seem not to come singly, and there was yet another piece of ill luck awaiting us. Now, the mechanic had suddenly discovered that the truck with our foodstuffs aboard was damaged beyond repair. A spare part would have to be obtained in Nairobi before we could proceed on our journey. I had meanwhile emphasized the fact that our experience at the swamp was only a mild taste of what awaited us farther ahead. When, a short time later, the car left for Nairobi in search of an unnecessary spare, the lady was a willing passenger. She felt sorry for her husband who had to face the hardships of such a safari, but that was "his own foolishness," as he had refused to abandon the trip and return to Nairobi with her. In a few days the safari was on its way again—minus the lady.

In the beginning I found it somewhat difficult to cater to the requirements of the patron. His obsession was to collect record specimens of horns and tusks, and these, he insisted, should fall to his own rifle. He was only a moderate shot under favourable conditions, and the risk involved in leaving him to shoot up dangerous game was apparent to everyone but himself, especially since he took violent exception to being "covered."

During one afternoon the patron and I came across a lone buffalo bull, whereupon he insisted that I stay in the background and permit him to carry on. I had the most serious misgivings on the subject. Any solitary bull is a doubtful customer, as there is no immediate way of telling whether he has a grievance to settle. An animal of such uncertain status is not a fit subject for the amusement of an amateur hunter, but the patron turned a deaf ear to my arguments, and when he finally settled down to reduce the distance between himself and the bull I decided to disobey instructions and "stick around." Up to then the bull had not seen either of us, but when the patron had approached within seventy-five yards the buffalo picked up his scent. In the next instant the bull's head was lifted high as he stood sniffing the air. It was at that moment that the patron went into action. The resulting shot was badly placed and drew an immediate charge. I had kept the bull covered and as soon as he took off I fired for the shoulder with a heavy .425 Express. The shot was luckily placed well in the heart, although the effect was not immediate. My second shot missed the target completely, and I was about to fire a third time when the bull sprawled headlong just two yards in front of the terrified patron, who, at that stage of the action, way lying on his back. From the moment the charge had got under way the patron made no attempt to shoot again, or to get out of the way, but simply went into a "freeze" and fell backwards—apparently from shock! By the time I reached him he had regained a sitting position, from which he refused to move. There he sat, mumbling to himself, and that part of the monologue which was intelligible to me is not exactly fit for repetition! Suddenly he turned to me and demanded, "Say, how much do I owe you for this?" I had not thought of translating my timely interference into terms of cash, and replied, "Your life, for one thing, and whatever a good lesson is worth, for another."

The amount of the cheque with which I was presented on our return to camp gave me the impression that he valued his life fairly high! I had become quite a hero in his estimation. As he pointed out, I had, in the course of a few days, saved him from an interfering wife and from a charging buffalo. He maintained that he did not know which was the greater of the two services I had rendered him, but since no second cheque was proffered, I presume that it was the latter service he appreciated most! After this incident I found it much easier to reason with him and we remained in that camp for some time. There we obtained a good specimen of elephant and also lions. A little later we had another unfortunate session with a buffalo.

We had caught up with a herd, and a big bull was the first to go down. As the herd was running away from us the patron kept up a rapid fire on the disappearing animals, and on following the trail we soon came across a wounded cow which we dispatched. A native runner was sent back to call porters to carry in the meat. After the runner had departed we decided to follow the trail farther, in case there might be other wounded animals to account for. When we returned about an hour later we could hear cries in the distance, and on following up the sound we were astonished to find our runner sitting in a very small tree, whilst below a buffalo bull menaced him. We disposed of the buffalo, and on examining the native, who had been crying and groaning during the proceeding, we found his right leg badly lacerated and bleeding profusely; much of the flesh had been scraped to the bone. The native explained that he had not been able to get entirely out of the reach of the buffalo, as the tree would not support his weight higher up and, whereas he had got beyond the reach of the horns, the buffalo had promptly started to *lick* his leg! It was a bad wound, extending over a considerable part of the leg, and quite consistent with the native's explanation. Another explanation is that in his prolonged efforts to keep out of reach of the buffalo's horns the damage could have been done by the rough trunk of the tree. The native, however, was quite emphatic that such was not the case. For my own part I am willing to accept either possibility. I have had ample evidence of the vindictiveness of a wounded buffalo, and the native's account is quite in keeping with the animal's true character. This bull had been wounded in the wild shooting and had dropped out of the herd. On his return to our camp the runner had approached within charging distance, and he was then very lucky to have had even so small a tree at hand. The leg yielded to treatment but the victim did not recover fully from the effects of the injury, for he was still limping badly eight months later. This incident raises an interesting issue, as I know of no other case on record where a buffalo has resorted to such a novel method of retaliation.

After this unfortunate incident we continued our journey for some weeks until we reached Budiaba, on Lake Albert, and from there on to Irumu, thence into the Ituri Forest. The Ituri is perhaps the largest and densest forest in Africa. So dense is it in parts that frequently we all but walked into sleeping elephants before we were aware of their presence. It was somewhat disconcerting to walk behind the Pygmy guides and see them stop suddenly and point toward the front or one side, and invariably there would be an elephant, or a herd, a few feet from us! Without these amazing little guides it is quite impossible to travel in the heart of the forest. The trees are literally infested with weighted spears, the Pygmy trap for elephants and other game. The spear is weighted with a heavy block of timber and suspended from the overhanging branches of a large tree, and is released by touching a cord which is stretched along the ground across the game path. A comparatively light touch will spring the trap. Such devices present a positive danger to any stranger who may venture into the forest without the guides, who know precisely where the traps are set. In addition, there are numerous pits, skillfully covered by grass and brush, and in the bottom of these pits are planted sharp stakes and spears. The main industry in the forest, so far as the Pygmies are concerned, is the capture or killing of game. They are a peaceful and harmless tribe and ever willing to accompany any traveller who can ensure a liberal supply of meat. Reliable guides can easily be obtained from their chiefs and interpreters are not difficult to obtain. The Pygmy language, if such it can be called, is incomprehensible to any but those who live in the immediate vicinity and are in frequent contact with them.

The Pygmy guides caused us endless trouble and delays. At the slightest movement in the forest they would disappear in pursuit. Snakes, lizards, rats or birds, everything that moved, was legitimate prey and would be eaten raw. Whilst they were absent in pursuit of their quarry we would have to stand and wait until they had effected a kill or lost all sight and trace of it. The killing of an elephant by our party would mean an enforced delay of many days. Although we had only eight guides with our safari, there were hundreds of hangers-on dogging our footsteps. No sooner would an elephant be accounted for than there would be a mad rush for the carcass from every side, and then would follow a free-for-all fight for possession of the meat. Spears, knives and axes would fly in all directions, and frequently we had to deal with severe injuries amongst the small people. When fighting was in progress amongst one faction, others would open the stomach and as soon as the entrails were dragged from the carcass another wild scramble would be started in order to gain entrance to the carcass. Those who were able to effect an entrance would remain inside and commence operations from within! Frequently they would gorge themselves until they were unable to move. The meat, of course, is eaten raw. The amount of meat those diminutive creatures can account for is something incredible. We soon realised that it would be necessary to curtail our operations in so far as elephant or big game was concerned, for every killing resulted in a wild orgy and a serious delay. Just how much meat the Pygmies are able to obtain by their own efforts it is difficult to say. The ones we saw appeared to be well fed. Assuming that they are always able to supply their wants in meat, they must be considered one of the happiest tribes on earth. They pay no taxes; the forest is home to them; they are not aggressive, and live on terms of friendship with other natives in their vicinity. They do no work in the sense that other natives do, for they are not concerned with plantations or gardens. They appreciate maize, meal and other native foodstuffs, but such food is not essential to them. Occasionally they will exchange meat for bananas or such other foodstuff as may be obtainable. It is a strange form of barter in which the participants rarely see each other. The wares for barter are deposited at the edge of the forest during the night and are removed by both parties without personal contact. Since there is no contact there is no bickering or quarreling as to the respective values of the goods exchanged.

But above all, the Pygmy is a hunter of the very first order. He is the most amazing craftsman in the forest and appears to be guided by an unerring instinct. His powers of observation are uncanny. In spite of his diminutive proportions he is absolutely fearless. In exchange for a cigarette or a plug of tobacco we frequently induced them to crawl underneath the stomach of a sleeping elephant and emerge on the other side in order to collect our contribution to the bargain. Before commencing such operations they would divest themselves of any rags or skins they might have on their bodies. The entire body is then covered with fresh elephant dung so as to destroy the human scent, and after that they are not very particular as to how they proceed. The recklessness with which they will enter such an escapade is something astonishing. The

A group of Ituri Pygmies in their kraal. A safari's rifles
bring the promise of more meat for everyone.

Working from without and within, Pygmies make short
work of removing an elephant's flesh and entrails.

same methods are employed in order to hamstring the elephant.

If the Pygmy is a craftsman of the first order, the tiny little dogs they keep are no less so; they are expert hunters and extremely intelligent. In order to follow the dogs' movement in the dense forest the Pygmies tie wooden bells around their necks. They seldom, if ever, bark; when danger threatens a low grunt will warn their master. These little dogs have enjoyed great popularity in England in later years. Not only is the Pygmy a craftsman in the hunting business, he is also an expert in fashioning his own weapons. Nails and all scraps of iron are keenly sought after and turned into knives of razor-edge keenness.

We remained in the forest for two months and saw almost all there was to see of interest—with one notable exception, and that was the okapi. In spite of every effort to catch up with this rare animal we never got within a reasonable distance of one. The nearest we ever got to seeing anything of an okapi was on the rare occasions when pieces of its skin adorned a Pygmy hunter's body.

On our way back we managed to buy a young chimpanzee from one of the native chiefs. The intelligence of these animals is said to rank next to that of the human being—with no great distinction if taken by and large—and like human beings, they are prone to all sorts of vices. Before three months had elapsed our chimp had developed a distinct weakness for alcoholic refreshment. Whisky, beer, or wine were all alike to him, and we had to exercise the greatest care in order to keep alcoholic drinks out of his reach. This reminds me of an incident that occurred some years later, when I wrote to an agent in Coquilhatville, up in the Belgian Congo, regarding the purchase of two chimps he had for sale. I received a telegram stating the price and details about age and character; one chimp was given an excellent character, but the telegram concluded ominously, "the other a confirmed drunkard, has other vices which may be curbed." Apparently the drink-vice was incurable! Our Jacko, for that was his name, was fast developing similar tendencies, and at sundowner time he was always very much in evidence. A couple of good tots of whisky would set him well on the road, and then his antics were screamingly funny. Although he provided us with lots of laughter, he resented any merriment at his expense. The preparation of his bed at night was a job to which he attended with meticulous care; frequently it would take all of half an hour before he would be satisfied that it was comfortable and in accordance with his requirements.

On our journey back from the Ituri we came to a large native village whose Jumbe asked us to destroy a vagabond elephant that was causing trouble and damage. We accepted this assignment and were promptly followed on the excursion by nearly all the meat-hungry inhabitants of the village. It did not take very long to find the old fellow and he was brought down with a shot in the head. As soon as the elephant had fallen to the ground the Jumbe mounted the carcass and began to shout instructions as to how the meat would be divided. He had just announced—with considerable patting of his chest—that the fat behind the eye, a great delicacy amongst natives, would be allocated to himself, when the elephant surprisingly revived and started to struggle to his feet. For a moment the old Jumbe appeared incapable of making any movement at all, and then he made an undignified leap to the solid earth and ran for his life. The elephant had been badly stunned by the shot that brought him down and fortunately we were able to dispose of him before he could do any damage. Whilst this was happening some four hundred natives had vanished as if by magic. It was some time before they were all back on the scene again, and the Jumbe resumed his interrupted speech—this time from a safe distance and with a wary eye fixed on the big carcass.

When eventually the safari came to a close we had been on the road for more than eight months. We brought back many fine specimens of horns, tusks and hides. The largest elephant to fall to our rifles produced a pair of tusks that weighed close to a hundred and fifteen pounds each. We secured no record animals, but in every other way the trip was a success—in spite of the unpromising start.

14: ELASTIC JUSTICE

W<small>HEN</small> the Union Miniere, the great Belgian mining company in the Katanga, commenced the exploitation of its vast copper field some thirty years ago, it was only natural that many of us wanderers in Central Africa were attracted to this new field of adventure.

At that time there were more Britishers and other foreigners employed in the Congo than Belgians. And in those days the administration of law and the public services, such as they were, was of a very haphazard nature. I well remember in the early days of the railway service how the train was often stopped in the bush whilst the driver or guard would go out in search of game or partake of the hospitality of any European who might happen to be camped in the vicinity of the railroad.

Life in Elisabethville was free and easy and the dignity of the law was not what it is today. The town then was little more than a glorified "boma" in the heart of the forest. For all that, there was no shortage of cafes or institutions where one could forget the troubles and trials of the day under the soothing influence of a bottle of Scotch.

Public holidays were unfailingly, if not wisely, observed, and when the occasion happened to be Empire Day, the British community did full justice to their sense of loyalty and patriotism. On one particular occasion this day had been well celebrated at the leading cafe of the town and the British community were ably assisted by their Belgian friends, who were not opposed to a liberal indulgence of Scotch on such a festive occasion. When the fun had become fast and furious a Belgian, in a moment of indiscretion, gave vent to his feelings in a manner that was strongly resented by the British community. This difference of opinion ended up in a come-as-you-like fight for all. Bottles, chairs, and table legs were freely resorted to in order to emphasize the different points of view. No serious damage was done, but one of King Albert's subjects was dished up a particularly raw deal when he was caressed on the head with a table leg. That little attention necessitated fifteen stitches in order to restore the Belgian's scalp to its correct shape. Such affectionate treatment could not be left to pass unnoticed and the matter duly reached the stage where the Crown Prosecutor took a hand.

A day or two later the British culprit received a friendly invitation to present himself at the police station for the purpose of interrogation. The offender promptly replied, expressing great surprise at the fact that he was expected to leave his work, of which he had plenty, in order to attend such an enquiry. Back came a reply apologising for any inconvenience that may have been caused, but emphasizing the point that the enquiry would be postponed for ten days and that in the event of absence of the accused, judgment might even be pronounced during his absence. Judgment was to the effect that the accused would have to pay 1,000 francs in order to soothe the pain and compensate his victim for the inconvenience he had suffered. At that time 1,000 francs amounted to £40 and represented the better part of a month's salary. The penalized man would not suffer such an outrage in silence. He complained, "An appeal must be made to reason and common sense." And, forthwith, he sent a letter to the Judge explaining that, apart from the fact that 1,000 francs exceeded by far the value of any skull in the Congo, the appellant had no visible means by which he could raise that amount of money. Besides, he now considered himself a martyr in the cause of patriotism, for had he not wielded a strong and energetic arm in defence of King and Country, whose honour and dignity had been assailed in a public bar?

This appeal was partly successful. The matter was "carefully considered"—it was not stated whether on the grounds of logic or patriotism!—and it was decided to reduce the fine by half. It had, however, to be clearly understood that this amount must be paid by the end of the month, failing which, an order for imprisonment would be made.

The five hundred francs were not paid on the stipulated date. The offender was invited to attend the court and stand ready to receive a sentence of imprisonment. This was done in due course. After much discussion and many voluble explanations, it was decided that ten days "hard" would meet the majesty of the law. It was agreed, however, that this term of imprisonment would be served on the installment system. In order to enable the accused to earn his living whilst meeting the demands of justice, he would be required to do penance in the Elisabethville gaol every Saturday and Sunday for a period of five weeks.

This arrangement, being acceptable to both sides, was duly put into execution and on the following Saturday the accused presented himself at the gaol and faithfully carried out his agreement for the day. On Sunday everything proceeded normally for some hours, when it occurred to the convict that he had promised to be present at the celebration of a friend's birthday. The position was forthwith explained to the gaoler who agreed that, as the occasion demanded the man's presence elsewhere, the demands of the law would be satisfied if he was back in his cell by 9 p.m. Should the prisoner fail to return at that time, the doors would be locked against him.

I met this man on the Tanganyika goldfields fifteen years later and reminded him about this escapade. "Ah yes," he replied, "I still owe them three days on the deal."

The foregoing was by no means an isolated case of lackadaisical justice. I remember the matter concerning a young accountant who was found guilty of having defrauded his employers of a large sum of money. After his guilt had been conclusively established there was a long discussion as to what would be the best method of procedure. Finally it was decided to find the accused another billet, which would enable him to redeem his character as well as indemnify his previous employers for the loss they had suffered.

In due course a responsible billet was found for the erring accountant. For six months all went well. Then one morning he failed to put in an appearance, nor was the reason difficult to explain. He had relieved his benefactors of a sum of money far in excess of the amount involved in the first case!

But the old order passes and makes way for the new. The days of move-as-you-like trains, of dilatory justice and free fights, have long since passed. The hovels of twenty-five years ago have given way to imposing double-story structures. Elīsabethville with its theatres, its social clubs, its Grand Palais de Justice, its sports grounds and athletic fields and the enormous installations of the Union Miniére, takes second place to no town north of the Zambesi. Before the great slump—during the years of prosperity, 1926-30—the Belgian Congo was the outstanding and most delightful of all Central African colonies.

15: THE ONE-HORNED DEVIL OF CHERIDA

AGAIN Ndege, my head tracker, was speaking on a somewhat worn theme. Said he, "Ati Bwana, that big bull down Cherida way is up to mischief again. We should go out and get him tomorrow. Unless someone puts a stop to his mischief he will finish up by killing somebody. This morning he treed a party of men coming from the Ufipa country and kept them in the trees for hours. I have just spoken to these men and they all say he is a bad character. Why can't we go out again and try to get him?"

On three occasions previously I had allowed myself to be persuaded to go after a buffalo bull that was said to be causing trouble for the natives who used the footpath which runs past the water hole at Cherida, some ten miles from our camp. On each occasion the hunt had ended in failure. Now I had almost begun to doubt the truth of the reports. My skepticism was supported by the belief that even if this bull had been in bad evidence that very morning, there was no assurance he would be in that vicinity again the next day. Also, a twenty-mile walk in October is not exactly a pleasure!

But Ndege is an incurable optimist in such matters and he explained at some length the better features attending another try. According to him, the bull was with a herd in which there were many calves and this fact alone would ensure a return to the water hole during the night. Also, owing to the presence of the calves, the herd would not go far afield, and if we made an early start we would certainly catch up with the animals before the day's intense heat had set in. The troublesome bull could be identified easily because he had but half a horn on one side. The missing half had apparently been shot away by native hunters, or it might have been lost in a fight with other bulls, but in any case the broken horn could have been the cause of his bad temper.

I was inclined to share Ndege's enthusiasm in the matter, but first I thought it best to talk to victims of the latest attack. Some of them were then in my camp and upon being summoned they soon convinced me that this bull at Cherida needed curbing. They said that with no provocation at all he had emerged from the herd and scattered the terrified natives, and only the presence of climable trees had allowed them to escape uninjured. My informants expressed every willingness to take me to the spot where the trouble had occurred.

With such evidence at hand I had no particular reason to turn down the hunt. After all, buffaloes were what I was after, and meat supplies were running low. The meat of an aggressive buffalo is no different from that of a docile one and, securing him, I would at the same time render a service to the entire community. I made known my decision to start early next morning on the trail, and in view of my previous failures to track the bull down, we would take equip-

ment and food for a three-day outing. Personnel for
the trip was to include some twenty porters in addition
to myself and the trackers.

Cherida village itself is a desolate place, in spite
of beautiful surroundings at the foot of a mountain.
At one time the village was the centre of a large native
population, but in later years the entire area was
vacated owing to the prevalence of sleeping sickness.
All that now remains of the village are many hundreds
of charred huts. The pools of crystal-clear mountain
water that once supplied the wants of the village are
now the main attraction for herds of buffaloes and
other large game. At the time of our visit seasonal
conditions had reduced the water supply to one perma-
nent pool which was fed by a mountain brook. This
pool was easily accessible to all animals and, once
there, they could be observed from convenient hideouts.
These vantage points could be had in the belt of forest
which extended along the mountainside above the pool;
the valley below the pool was unsuited to that purpose,
as it was filled with dense reed beds and elephant grass.

We arrived at Cherida by ten o'clock in the morning and proceeded to pitch camp about a mile from the
water hole. At four o'clock in the afternoon I was
comfortably installed in the branches of a big tree, a
short distance from the pool. Every detail had been
attended to and I waited patiently for the appearance
of the herd—and the troublesome bull. I fully expected the animals to turn up at the pool before dark,
as buffaloes will frequently drink twice daily during
the dry season if water is close at hand. But sunset

came and no animal of any kind had appeared at the pool. Our plan for that day had failed, and as darkness fell we returned to camp.

At the campfire council that night we decided to return to the observation post before daybreak. We reasoned that the herd would visit the pool during the night and then graze in its vicinity until daybreak. If we lacked sufficient light to see the bull, it would be a simple matter to follow the herd. At bedtime I had no doubt that the score with Cherida's bad bull would be settled before breakfast next morning. The day had been a scorcher and the herd was certain to come to water during the night.

Ndege roused me from a deep sleep; the time was one-thirty in the morning. The herd was coming to water. Louder and louder from the blackness came the grunting and bellowing; as the animals approached water they broke into a wild rush. Although we were camped well away from the herd's path, the porters lost no time in getting into trees. Nor could I blame them greatly, as I had no difficulty in remembering the night when a herd had actually stampeded through camp and I had barely saved my life.

This sudden appearance of the Cherida herd had taken us unawares and now it was decidedly unsafe to make our way through the darkness to the observation post at the water hole. For three long hours we listened to the trampling of hooves, the grunts of bulls and the lusty bellowing of calves. Then, quite abruptly, the herd moved off to the forest country near by. It was still too dark to follow the trail and I called for early morning coffee. An hour later we were on the trail.

Two hours of trailing brought us up with the herd, in long grass. The animals were scattered and grazing peacefully, quite unaware of our presence. Under such conditions there was no hope of identifying the bad bull, and I knew it would be another two hours before the herd would regroup and seek shelter from the sun. To approach closer now would be risky, as there was always the possibility that a stray member might spot us or pick up our scent and spread alarm. I decided to call in the trackers by signal and await the herd's natural movement, for then only would we have a fair opportunity to single out our quarry.

In response to my signal, the tracker on the far end of the line had moved hardly two yards when there sounded a wild snort. He had come unexpectedly upon a cow grazing in the long grass. Her panic was transmitted to the herd and immediately all were off in a great cloud of dust. Then followed two hours of tiresome trailing. At the end of that time a tracker approached me dejectedly and said the hunt was at an end. He had found the tracks of native hunters between us and the herd; the other hunters were certain to catch up with the herd before we could hope to do so. At two o'clock that afternoon we straggled back to camp, hungry, thirsty, footsore and disappointed. The bad bull of Cherida was still very much at large.

In the early hours of the following morning our camp was awakened by the roaring of a pride of lions in the vicinity of the pool, whilst on the plain beyond we could hear the sounds of a restive buffalo herd.

At daylight we examined the ground at the water hole
and immediately found the tracks of lions and a small
herd of roan antelope. We then struck out in the
direction from whence the sounds of buffalo had come
and in a short time were back on the trail of the big
herd. The presence of lions at the pool had evidently
kept the herd away from water during the night.
(Lions will not, as a rule, attack an adult buffalo, but
this herd was fearful for the safety of its calves, which
are even subject to attack by wild dogs.) The herd had
stampeded in a northerly direction and away from the
area it usually frequented. A half-hour of trailing
brought us to the half-eaten carcass of a young bull.
We had disturbed the lions at their kill, for bad-
humoured growls came from thick grass near by. The
country was rough and I did not consider it advisable
to look for trouble with a peevish lion. I was there
to settle the score with a bull and now, on the third
day, I had nothing but blistered feet to show for my
efforts.

All that morning we stuck to the trail and ordi-
narily would have come up with the herd by midday,
but the alarm of the previous night had kept the animals moving. At noon the trail led into a great swamp
with grass so dense that visibility was reduced to nearly
zero. An encounter in such surroundings would be
distinctly dangerous and was not to be considered.
Once again the hunt had ended in failure and we were
obliged to return to camp empty-handed. The cir-
cuitous walk that had brought us to the swamp had
involved at least twelve miles and a return by that

[172]

route in the day's heat held no appeal. A short-cut would reduce the trip back by at least two miles, and deciding upon this we struck out.

Soon we were in strange country, and in two hours of walking we saw no game tracks. Eventually we struck a worn footpath that had many game tracks leading into it. The tracks came from wooded country which lay beyond the freshly burned-over area adjacent to the footpath. It was obvious that so many animals must be using the path for a very good reason, and the course was now leading directly towards our camp at Cherida, some six miles away. Another hour's walk brought us to a point not far from our camp and at the base of the same mountain. Here we found a stream-fed pool similar to the one at Cherida, but much smaller. The country about this pool was exceptionally open and the tracks around the water hole itself indicated that it served hundreds of animals daily. The pool did not exceed fifteen feet in diameter and the most unusual feature of all was the great tree which grew in its centre. This tree afforded a perfect hideout and from its lowest branches one might all but touch any animal that came to drink. The whole arrangement was perfect and even our fatigue could not dampen our enthusiasm for it. There and then we decided to shift camp from Cherida. I instructed some of the natives to erect a scaffold in the branches of the tree, whilst the rest of us proceeded to Cherida to effect the removal of our camp to its new location. I was certain that the move invited a night of real adventure.

At this point I must digress from the subject of our quest for the bad bull of Cherida. Just prior to this safari a friend had informed me of having had much trouble with lions at his camp, which in itself is not an unusual nocturnal occurrence in these parts. But there was more to it than that. He had assured me that, without the aid of lamp or spotlight, the lions' eyes could be seen at night "like balls of fire." I had serious doubts that such a thing was possible. In fact, I suspected that he was suffering from hallucinations brought about by exposure to the sun. Never in all the years I had knocked about in the African bush had I heard of such a phenomenon. I was filled with disbelief, even though my friend's reports had always been marked by reliability. But now, on my arrival in the Cherida area, I heard from the natives a story identical to that told by my friend. They said they had often seen a lion's eyes at night without the aid of an artificial light. I was surprised to hear of this thing again, and from new sources, but I was fairly content to rely upon the contradictory evidence furnished by my own experiences, some of which had been quite recent. Only a short time before I had shot a lion at night and he had had every opportunity to display naturally luminous eyes, but he had not done so. On three different occasions he had approached within a few yards and it was not until I flashed a torchlight on him that there were any signs of eyes at all. On another night I had an eight-hour session with a lion; I was without a spotlight, and during the entire time I saw no eyes. That lion finally got away. These experiences and all that had gone before could do naught but make me extremely dubious of the existence of lions' eyes that shown of their own accord. I certainly was not expecting to see anything of that kind as we prepared for my night's vigil at the smaller pool of Cherida.

Shortly after sunset I was comfortably installed in my observation post a few feet above the surface of the pool. In the branches above me were Ndege and Abeli. By nine o'clock no animal had come to the pool and shortly thereafter both natives commenced to snore. I, too, was tired from our exertions in the hot sun, but the prospect of obtaining an unusually fine flashlight photograph kept me on the alert. Camera, rifles and spotlights were all close at hand. At ten o'clock my attention was drawn to two moving balls of fire; they were advancing slowly towards the pool. They could hardly be anything but the eyes of an animal. What others had seen I also was seeing! I watched the eyes for fully five minutes; there could be no doubt, an animal was lurking beyond the pool.

The trackers were sound asleep and in my efforts to awaken them I raised my voice. At this sound the balls of fire disappeared. Both trackers were now wide awake and I told them what I had seen. Like myself, they had previously ridiculed the "balls of fire" stories. Now we all watched and for some minutes nothing happened; then, the balls of fire reappeared at a place close to where I had seen them last. We each were certain the eyes belonged to a lion. The distance was too great to attempt a night shot, and for fully half an hour we watched those luminous orbs moving about in the area beyond the pool. At long last I shouted out, and again the balls of fire disappeared.

Now we could hear the buffalo herd in the distance; they were coming to the pool. My nerves became taut, for in a few moments the great animals would be shouldering each other for places around the pool and at a little more than arm's length from me. I was well hidden in the leaves, the night was moonless, and the wind sat in our favour—there seemed no chance whatever of our being discovered. We could hear the herd break into the last fast trot that would bring them to water—and then they came to a dead stop. Sharp snorts sounded throughout the herd, such snorts as the buffalo hunter knows as the warning of a charge or of alarm. This herd was thoroughly alarmed, and in a few moments we could hear the hoofs pounding a rapid retreat.

I was disgusted, and felt certain that lions were the cause of the herd's flight. As I mulled over our latest disappointment my attention was drawn again to a pair of glowing eyes, far to our right. As they moved in our direction they could easily have been mistaken for the headlamps of a distant car or lorry. But such a thing was not possible, as there was no road and much of the area was so rough as to offer difficulties for foot travel. The eyes were again approaching the pool; at times they would flicker and vanish momentarily, no doubt when the animal turned its head. I was satisfied that the owner of the eyes was some distance away, possibly two hundred yards; I tried to catch an animal shape in the beam of my spotlight but failed to do so. The trackers and I watched those unearthly eyes for half an hour, and there in the deathly still night I experienced the most eerie feeling of all my years in the bush. Eleven o'clock passed and no animals other than the buffaloes had attempted to approach the pool. At half past eleven the eyes vanished and did not reappear.

I consulted with Ndege and Abeli on the matter of our next move. My suggestion was that we descend from our perch and investigate with the aid of the spotlight. This they flatly refused to do, and it was not because they were frightened by what we had seen; they were simply convinced that the eyes belonged to a lion who was bent on mischief. Their only recommendation was to remain in the tree and await further developments. This we did. At one o'clock Ndege heard the faint sounds of an approaching buffalo herd and we all hunched forward with renewed anticipation. But our interest was of short duration. The herd approached within a few hundred yards of the pool— and then there were sounds of the wildest disorder. Once again those supernatural eyes glowed far over to our right! The herd thundered away, and the eyes shortly disappeared. We continued our watch. At four o'clock a herd approached the pool again and, for the third time, the entire disappointing performance was repeated. After that, we agreed that there was nothing to be gained by sitting in the hideout any longer, and sleepily we retraced our steps to camp.

It was too late now for sleep; in little more than an

hour day would break. I was anxious to investigate the scene of the night's events as soon as possible, and had breakfast prepared hurriedly. Just before sunrise we were out again on the trail.

In addition to those peerless trackers, Ndege and Abeli, I was accompanied by several other experienced hunters. We went directly to the place where we had seen the eyes and Ndege soon found the tracks of two lions, male and female. Thenceforward it was a simple matter to reconstruct the happenings of the night before. There was no doubt that the lions were responsible for the buffalo stampedes and the failure of other animals to come close to the pool. Also, the lions had in each instance pursued the herds for a considerable distance. The final chase had proved successful for, about two miles from the pool, we came upon the two lions, and they were still at the kill—a young calf. Our appearance on the scene did not frighten them; on the contrary, the male snarled viciously at us. Before his resentment could assume dangerous proportions I terminated his part in the affair with a heavy-calibre slug in the brain. I fully expected the female to attack, as they frequently do when harm befalls the male, but in this instance she lost no time in getting away.

After the encounter with the lions there seemed to be no point in remaining afield in that area. The sun was becoming unpleasantly hot and there was small hope of locating the buffaloes. The frequent attacks by the lions were too fresh in the consciousness of the herd to permit it to remain in the close vicinity. Things had not gone at all well on this excursion, which was to have lasted only three days; we were now in the fourth day and had not so much as glimpsed the one-horned bull. The porters were hungry, tired and disgruntled; they had no more interest in the business, especially in view of their not having had meat for several days. And for myself, I was now much too tired to go out and look for meat supplies. I would simply have to admit failure and return to the main camp empty-handed. It was hunter's luck—and largely bad.

After our return to the camp near the large pool at Cherida I immediately got the safari under way on the fourteen-mile trip back to my main camp. By four in the afternoon walking had become almost a mechanical function; I was completely tired out from the work and sun of the previous days and from the sleepless nights. I had handed my rifle to Ndege, and as I plodded wearily along the thoughts of a one-horned buffalo and lions with balls-of-fire eyes were far, far from my mind. I was thinking that only a few miles remained before we would reach camp, food, and above all, rest. I would eat; I would sleep . . . ugh! My surroundings came into focus with a rush as I became aware of natives scurrying in all directions, each making for the nearest tree. At my side was Ndege, pushing the rifle into my hands. His words carried the impact of an explosive—"Bwana! Bwana! There he is! The hornless one! Quick, Bwana, he is going to charge!"

The "hornless one" did *not* charge. A heavy-calibre slug in the neck, fired at fifty yards, took care of that.

So there the hunt ended, three miles from my camp. In summing up, I could not ignore the painful fact that during the previous three days I had walked nearly a hundred miles in my efforts to trail that bull down. Well, hunting buffaloes is just like that!

Now, along with my memory of the one-horned devil of Cherida Village, persists even more vividly the impression of moving, luminous eyes in the black of night. There is definite evidence to show that the eyes of some animals do glow in the darkness and that the strange ability does not depend upon refraction from an outside source of light. But do the eyes of lions, at least on occasion, possess that property? I am quite convinced that their eyes can glow, although distance prevented my seeing a lion that night. Henceforward I must listen with genuine interest and respect to any hunter who can recount an experience with a lion whose eyes shone like balls of fire in the night.

16: AND ESPECIALLY, ERNEST!

THE BUFFALO trail has led me to remote and strange places, and whilst on that trail I have met some remarkable characters, but surely none are more memorable than those I met on one eventful trip of long ago. I had just completed an engagement to shoot meat for the military forces on the northern border of Rhodesia and I was forced to proceed to a more healthful climate in order to restore my fast dwindling physical resources. I was to have medical treatment and a spell of recuperative leave in Southern Rhodesia.

I had left the New Langenberg area, now Tukuyu, some days earlier in a mashila (hammock), as persistent recurrences of malaria had reduced me to a point where walking was no longer possible. This particular day was sultry and hot, and by 3 p. m. the porters had carried me a distance of eighteen miles since our early morning start. They were tired, and only about a mile remained before we would reach a water hole near the edge of what was known then as the Valley of Death. This valley was isolated and forbidden country, owing to the prevalence of sleeping sickness. Few Europeans frequented the territory, and on my way through it I did not expect to encounter any signs of civilisation for a hundred miles or more.

So it was with great surprise that, on looking down the valley from a vantage point, I spotted a tent in the distance. Further scrutiny with the aid of binoculars revealed signs of life around the tent. No African native in those parts ever lived in a tent and I was puzzled at this unexpected sign of white habitation in the valley of ill repute. The porters were instructed to make for that point so that I might satisfy my curiosity. On the way down to the tent I tried to think of an explanation for its presence in that desolate place and finally decided that some misguided hunter, perhaps a stranger to these parts, had ventured too far afield and was even at that moment paying for his indiscretion. My surprise can well be imagined when, on stepping out of my mashila, I was met by a young woman, smartly dressed, and apparently the tent's sole occupant.

The story the young woman told me was even less conventional than was our meeting in this strange place. Fifteen months earlier she had been a chorus girl on the English stage, and during one of her tours in the counties she had met a well-known hunter whose stories of adventure in the African bush had fascinated her. So much did his description of the life in the bush appeal to her imagination that she forthwith severed relations with the stage, married her hero, and came out to share his life of adventure. From the heart of the city of London she was transported to the heart of the African forest, and if appearance was a criterion, she was quite happy and content with her choice. At the time of my arrival her husband had been absent for several days on the trail of elephant. Apart from her native servants she was living absolutely alone and with no personal protection other than a light sporting rifle. The roar of the lion and the cry of the hyena, terrifying and eerie in the still of night—a test for the nerves of the average man—made no impression upon this lone young woman. She seemed to accept the situation as being perfectly normal and regular. On my pointing out the obvious dangers of her position, she reminded me that even in the streets of London one was not exempt from danger to life and limb. At home, crimes of violence are frequently committed against women, but here in the forest no native would dream of harming her; on the contrary, if needs be, they would protect her at the cost of their own lives. As for the danger to her husband, it was negligible. He knew the habits and ways of animals and he would not risk danger unnecessarily.

It all seemed incredible to me, but I was also impressed with the logic in her arguments. Her husband returned the following day. His trip had not been very successful, but he was cheerful and happy and, like his wife, seemed perfectly satisfied with this extraordinary scheme.

The logic of this lady's argument was sadly confirmed a few years later. Her husband had gone to America to arrange for a cinematograph expedition to East Africa and was accidentally killed in a motor accident in the streets of New York. The lady had spoken truly: in the heart of the forest they had found greater safety than in the streets of a great city. But theirs was an exceptional case, for in the African forest of those days death lurked ever near by. Sometimes it came swiftly and without warning, at other times slowly but surely after long spells of delirium and wasting fever. Death also followed the ravages of sleeping sickness, which even today exacts its toll from the unwary wanderer who ventures too far afield.

Since the time of my passage, this part of Africa has assumed a totally different aspect. Slowly but surely the advance of civilisation has become apparent in all directions. The Valley of Death remains but a name, remembered only by the wanderers of those distant days. That vast country has since been carefully surveyed and photographed, but in such work the mashila and the native porters have played an insignificant part. They have been superseded by the automobile and the aeroplane. The safari of earlier days is obsolete, and if one such is encountered now on the vast Copper Belt it becomes an object of wonder and surprise, in much the same way an aeroplane was once viewed. The type of adventure that appealed so much to my hostess at the Valley of Death must now be looked for much farther afield, and it is doubtful if the setting of the adventure of that man and wife could be duplicated.

It was with feelings of regret when, a week later, I bade farewell to those two delightful adventurers. I proceeded to Kasama, where the East African campaign was finally to come to an end with the surrender of von Lettow. At Kasama I was met by one of the most notorious Central African characters of the

time and upon whom, for the present purpose, I
bestow the name "Ernest Hakon." I had not met him
previously, but his reputation was well known to me.
Hakon had come out to South Africa some years previously as leading violinist to a famous prima donna.
In Johannesburg he had got mixed up in bad company
and, together with two others, became involved in a
bank robbery. His companions were eventually captured, but Ernest escaped to East Africa where for
years he lived amongst the natives, very much as one
of them. Subsequently he migrated to the Belgian
Congo where he held up and robbed a mail train,
some eight miles from Elisabethville. His loot from
the train included, amongst other things, a complete set
of dental forceps. Ernest did not trouble to leave the
scene of the robbery, and a few days later a posse of
armed askaris called on him to surrender. Ernest had
no intention of surrendering and told them so. When
the askaris became too persistent Ernest fell back on
a simple and effective expedient—which proved fatal
to several of the representatives of the law. He then
decamped, and amongst other activities he included
that of travelling dentist for the special benefit of the
natives in those parts. On the northern border of
Rhodesia he became involved in a dispute with a
native chief, an affair which ended fatally for the
latter.

When war broke out Hakon, under an assumed
name, managed to secure a contract to shoot meat for
the porters who were bringing up supplies to the troops
on the northern border. (I was also at that time shoot-

ing meat for the front-line troops, but at a place farther north.) When I met Hakon at Kasama he was convalescing from the after-effects of an encounter with a buffalo. As he related it, he had fallen into the foolish habit of leaving his rifles to be reloaded by his gunbearers. On this occasion he had wounded a buffalo bull, which immediately charged him. He was a deadly shot and it never occurred to him to look for safety in a nearby tree. When he attempted to stop the charge with a second shot he discovered that the magazine was empty; in the next instant the infuriated beast was on top of him. At the moment of impact Hakon's rifle was thrown some distance to the side and in some inexplicable manner he managed to get in between the front legs of the buffalo, and to one of these legs he clung for life. Whilst the buffalo was trying to disentangle himself the gunbearer had reloaded and shot the animal. Hakon was unable to escape the falling beast and sustained two broken ribs, a fractured leg and arm. His was an astonishing escape and he owed his life to the courage of his gunbearer. It is rare for a native to remain on terra firma when there is trouble brewing with a buffalo, and this is one of the few cases I can remember.

Whilst Hakon was receiving treatment for the injuries he had sustained with the buffalo he contracted blackwater fever, one of the most deadly diseases in the tropics. When I met him he was well on the road to recovery, but, to all intents and purposes, a physical wreck. For all that, he was of a jovial disposition and I was treated with the greatest hospitality. On the

AND ESPECIALLY, ERNEST!

second day after my arrival Hakon informed me that he was due to perform "a little social function" that evening and I was invited to attend. The affair was to be held in the camp of a friend not far from his own quarters. When I arrived at the camp in question I found Ernest sitting beside a table. Hand in hand before him stood a bearded European and a native woman, whilst squatting on the floor in a circle were a dozen native women and a like number of chocolate-coloured pickaninnies. Ernest was holding an illustrated journal in his hands, and from this, with the aid of an enormous pair of spectacles suspended well down his nose, he was busy reading out the marriage service —*á la* Hakon. He was conducting the service with all the decorum and earnestness that the situation demanded. His added advice and suggestions as to how perfect matrimonial bliss could be achieved were instructive indeed. The audience consisted of the twelve dames who had gone through a similar ceremony with the bearded one. They, and the children, were present in order to see father tie one more nuptial knot—to be joined in "holy blasphemy," as Ernest termed it.

Shortly after this strange ceremony Hakon informed me that he had decided to return to the old country and would accompany me on the journey south. Here was I, in Central Africa and in a delicate state of health, destined to become the travelling companion of a murderer and robber! The prospect was not a very alluring one, but I could think of no excuse to escape from it, and in due course we set off on our journey. The trip south was uneventful and Hakon's behaviour never gave me the least cause for uneasiness. In spite of his unenviable reputation his conduct showed unmistakable signs of culture and refinement. In discussing his past life he explained that he was merely "a victim of circumstances." I listened for many hours to tales of those contributory circumstances.

Ernest continued to carry the dental equipment with him. These tools, he maintained, were a boon and a blessing to the poor heathens. Needless to say he knew nothing about dentistry, but he diagnosed every complaint as being due to faulty dentition. Headaches, stomach disorders, boils and ulcers, and the thousand and one ailments from which the African native suffers —these were all due to this great source of evil, and Ernest had the proper means to deal effectively with the scourge. I cannot remember ever having seen so many toothless natives in so small a body of porters.

After Hakon and I had travelled for a week the strain of the journey proved too much for him, and he decided to halt for a few days. I was unable to stay over and it was decided that I would proceed to Kashitu from where I would send him some provisions. This I did on my arrival there, and from that point onward my journey was completed by train. A fortnight later I received a telegram in Bulawayo; it was from Hakon, asking me to meet him on his arrival by the next train. I duly presented myself at the proper time. Hakon stepped from the train as I approached his carriage, but before I could speak to him he was accosted by two men. They were C.I.D. officials and they forthwith took him into custody. That was the last I ever saw or heard of Hakon, and I do not know on which of the many charges against him he was arrested. I left for Salisbury a short time thereafter.

I have been back in Central Africa now for some years. In this part one never knows who or what is awaiting around the next bend. It would not surprise me if, during my wanderings on the trail of adventure, I should again come across that amiable rascal, Ernest Hakon.

17: ACTION ON THE GROUND

WHEN A BOXER enters the arena to face an adversary, he knows just what to expect from that adversary. The rules of the game are carefully codified, and inside that framework the methods of attack and defence are clearly defined. But if the boxer should discover that, during the process of a contest, his adversary had suddenly developed an extra pair of arms, he would find the situation somewhat disconcerting and difficult to deal with. It is true, there were many occasions in my misguided youth (when I firmly, but mistakenly, believed I was cut out for a career in the roped square), when I would have sworn that the other fellow had suddenly turned octopus! But these were merely illusions—mental aberrations, brought about by the stress and strain of the moment.

When a hunter goes out to take the arena against the buffalo, he has no prescribed rules to follow. The framework of codified rules is replaced by his fund of experience. In an emergency he draws on this fund; if it is adequate he manages to pull out a plum from the bag of experience, and he survives. If the bag is empty the situation can become alarming indeed, and generally he does *not* survive. In my numerous encounters with the Bovine Monarch, I frequently have had to dip deep into the bag in order to find the right solution and, fortunately, I have always managed to succeed somehow or other.

But there was one fateful day when I found the bag of experience completely empty. The "octopus" element had entered the contest, and its presence could not be laid to an illusion or mental aberration on my part. The situation was truly desperate.

During the second great war I often had opportunities to take out young soldiers on short trips, and invariably they would ask to be shown elephant, buffalo, and lion. Elephant and lion are not always easily encountered, but I generally managed to stir up the odd buffalo, and frequently I had much fun at the expense of some of these lads. Many of them were excellent shots on the target range, but on game they fell far short of expectations, and I often witnessed a dissipation of ammunition—hard to procure during the war years—that almost moved me to tears. But there was one morning when the dissipation of a thousand rounds per second would have been music to my ears. On this occasion I had taken out two young officers of the R. A. F. and, as usual, they wanted "big stuff." One of these fellows had seen buffalo from a plane, whilst the other had seen them only in picture books. When I assured them that I would take them to a place where large herds could be seen and hunted daily, they were overjoyed with the prospect—but that was at the beginning of the hunt. When we returned that night they both expressed a fervent hope that they would never encounter another buffalo for the rest of their lives—unless it should be from an aeroplane! I have good reason to believe they meant every word they said.

Shortly after sunrise that morning we spotted an

immense herd in the distance. It took us an hour to close up with this herd, which numbered about five hundred head. When we had approached within 500 yards, the animals became restive and soon were moving off at a fast gallop. A strong wind was sweeping the plain at the time and, unfortunately for us, we were on the receiving end of that wind. In a few seconds we were enveloped in dense clouds of dust which made it impossible for us to see more than a few yards ahead. As the herd ran across our line of approach the dust suddenly lifted and a hundred yards or so away I could see the dim outline of a buffalo, the rearmost member of the herd. I took a quick shot at that fast-moving target, hoping that it would be a good specimen and that the bullet, which I had clearly heard striking the target, would have the desired result. We waited for a minute or two for the dust to clear and then went up to ascertain the result of my shot. The hit proved to be well placed, high on the shoulder, and the buffalo had dropped in his tracks at the moment the bullet made contact. But I was disappointed to find that I had shot what must have been the poorest specimen in the herd. In weight he did not amount to much and the horns were not worth collecting. There appeared to be nothing else to do but collect the meat and scout out for something better. The column of dust was then moving rapidly in a westerly direction, as the great herd made for forest country some miles away. I felt certain they would not come to a stop until they had entered wooded country, where I did not feel disposed to follow them with two inexperienced hunters on my hands.

Buffalo hunting is full of disappointments and surprises and I was certainly having my share of the former. Out of this enormous herd it was my luck to shoot a specimen that I felt ashamed to pass off as a buffalo, and now the others were making for safety. I was not at all certain that we would come across more buffaloes in the limited time at our disposal. But as I stood looking disgustedly at the moving herd, they suddenly stopped and turned around, about two miles away.

I quickly decided to follow up, but that we would move around in a semi-circle, so as to keep out of sight until we could work to a point between the herd and the dense forest. This time I decided to remain above wind—a bad policy under normal conditions, as the buffalo is a keen-scented animal; but I felt that it would be better to take the risk of their picking up our scent than to be blacked out again in a column of dust, should the herd take off before I could select a worthwhile specimen. Everything worked according to plan for some minutes, but as we were about to pass the herd some 500 yards to their right, a cow with a young calf must have picked up our scent, and quickly she communicated her alarm to the rest of the herd. In a second they were on the move again, but instead of making for the wooded country they now moved towards the point from where the chase had started. The herd was now between us and the column of dust, as I had intended, and as they moved slowly in extended line I had a good opportunity to select a worth-while specimen. They were coming in closer to us and this was all to the good, as it reduced the range considerably, and the bull I had selected showed no inclination to become mixed up with the rest of the herd. Things were going extremely well up to this point. But now, suddenly, the head of the column started to wheel around in our direction, describing a half-circle around us. I was distinctly puzzled at these tactics and decided to wait for a moment longer to see what they would do next. They came to a dead stop, and the entire column turned and faced us. The herd was now about 300 yards from us and the obvious thing to do, in the light of subsequent events, would have been to open fire. But I have always disliked head-on shots on buffalo, and the range was rather long for the lighter rifles of my companions, so I pur-posely delayed shooting in the hope that the big bull I had selected would turn and present a broadside to me. My companions were anxious to start the ball rolling, but I stressed the range, and advised them to hang on for a little longer whilst we tried to reduce the distance between us and the animals.

I had hardly finished talking when, as though in response to a command, five hundred buffaloes lowered their heads and charged straight for us! This was one of the most terrifying moments I had ever experienced on the buffalo trail. We were almost entirely encircled, and every one of those buffaloes seemed to have but one object in view—to reduce the distance between them and us in the quickest possible time.

[194]

I know all about the buffaloes' "curiosity close-up," with the subsequent wild dash for safety as soon as they have satisfied their curiosity. Also do I know the wild stampede when a herd is aware of danger, but unable to determine its source or direction. In such cases they run, often with their heads well up, until the object of their curiosity or alarm is identified, and then they will suddenly turn off at a sharp angle. But this herd was not actuated by either curiosity or alarm. They had watched us intently for some time before they took off in our direction. This was a deliberate and determined charge; they were coming straight for us, heads well down! We were watching a mass demonstration of the fear-inspiring spectacle I had witnessed on so many other occasions when I had had to deal with individual charges.

To turn a stampeding herd is not very difficult, and well within the repertoire of every experienced hunter. A brisk movement, the waving of a hat, a random shot at the leader—any of these artifices, if resorted to in time, will serve to turn a herd, irrespective of whether their approach is prompted by fear or curiosity. But this was different; we were face to face with a situation completely foreign to me. The bag of experience was empty! There was no trick I could pull from it that would help us in our dire predicament. There was no leader whose course could be diverted; every single member of that herd was acting independently, and seemed to have made up his mind to get at us regardless of what the others might do. To run away from this avalanche would be madness and, at best, would only delay the inevitable for a few seconds. The herd had thundered to a little more than 100 yards from us, and still there was no sign that one of them would take the lead and change their direction. The natives, petrified by fear until now, suddenly found the right use for their legs, and as they started their wild dash for safety a heaven-sent inspiration came to my rescue. "Stand by, stand by," I shouted at my companions, "and shoot for the end of the column." I fired immediately on the bull at the extreme end of the line. I was using a heavy calibre .404 rifle, with soft-nose ammunition, and as the bullet hit the bull's shoulder he was thrown from his course and, unexpectedly, he followed the direction the impact of the bullet had prescribed for him. At that moment two more shots rang out, and then the line started to straighten out, as though a giant magnet were drawing the herd in the direction the wounded bull had taken. We kept up a rapid fire until our magazines were empty, and by the time we had again reloaded, the tail-end of the column was dashing past us—less than fifty yards away!

It was fortunate that I had loaded with soft-nose ammunition as, on making contact, the bullet had mushroomed and this helped to impart the full force of the load. That end bull was thrown off his course so suddenly that the rest of the herd must have thought he had turned off deliberately. Blindly they had followed him! A hard-nose bullet probably would not have given a similar result, as it would most likely have penetrated without imparting the full shock, or, it

This young bull had just killed a native hunter; the festering sore near his eye explains his bad temper.

Previously wounded by native hunters, this bull charged the lorry seen in the background.

might have dropped the bull in his tracks. In neither case would my shot have contributed much towards turning him off his course. In complete and abject despair I had pulled a ripe plum from the empty bag of experience.

As we stood watching the great herd moving away from us, a vast cloud of dust was again in evidence, but now the wind was blowing away from us and we could keep them under observation all the time. It was a wonderful sight, and a very welcome one for all three of us. A minute or so later we could see the big bull falling out of line. He was heading for a patch of dry grass close to him. As he reached the grass he turned around deliberately to face us, and then he sagged to the ground slowly. I knew exactly what that meant. The cunning brute had taken up a position from where he could watch, and was waiting there for us to approach him. His cover was only a small patch of grass of medium height, so I decided at once to move in a circle and force him to turn around in order to keep us under observation. When we had approached within 100 yards we could see the tell-tale evidence of the grass being pushed down as he turned slowly in our direction. My companions were watching proceedings closely and I now asked one of them to fire a shot at the moving grass. No sooner had the report of the shot died down than the bull was up on all fours. There was no mistaking his intention, and as he swung his head preparatory to the charge he was met by a .404 slug in the chest. He went down, and I assumed that it was all over, but as we walked in his direction he once again struggled to his feet and started swinging his head viciously. This time he was hit by two .303 slugs and he sank down slowly. A few seconds later we could hear two long-drawn-out grunts. The show was over.

On collecting the trophy we found him to be an exceptional specimen, with an enormous horn spread of magnificent curve, and bosses fully fifteen inches deep. Less than a mile away the herd again came to a stop, and I was quite satisfied to leave them there without further molestation. None of our party appeared to be anxious to resume hostilities, and after we had dissected the carcass we got the porters on the way to carry the meat to where a truck was waiting for us on the open plain, some four miles away.

Just what it was that had prompted this herd to stage such a determined charge is a mystery to me. None of the cows or calves had been killed or wounded. Had such been the case it would have offered a possible explanation, as I have heard of cases where a small herd had resented injury to one of its members and a charge had resulted. But for a large herd's adoption of such tactics I can offer no explanation.

It was quite late in the afternoon before the meat of the two buffaloes had been carried across the rough plain and loaded on the truck. When finally we moved off only a few minutes of sunlight remained. At a point about a mile farther on I stopped the truck and gave the plain a thorough going-over with a pair of powerful binoculars. All over the open plain there were innumerable patches of short dry grass, dotted at intervals of a few hundred yards. I saw no sign of game of any description. With that, we packed up our rifles and handed them over to the gun bearers, keeping back only a light 6.5 mm. rifle which I handed to one of my companions, who remained seated on the hood of the open truck.

I was sitting looking at the horns of the big bull in the interior of the moving truck when suddenly there was a shouting and screaming all around me. As I got to my feet I was just in time to see the black mass of a buffalo bull charging down on the truck. He was not more than five yards from us, and at that moment a shot rang out. As the bull "took it" there was a spasmodic jerk of the great frame, then a sickening crash as a headlamp was smashed. The impact of the infuriated bull, rushing head-on at full speed, had also brought the truck to an abrupt stop. Now there was another report of a rifle, and again a violent bump as a mudguard was staved in, and all this time I was shouting frantically at the gun-bearer to hand me my heavy-calibre rifle. As I reached for it there was another violent bump; this time it was the radiator that received the full benefit of the vicious lunge. At that moment two more shots sounded and the bull rolled over, dead.

Examination of the carcass showed that this bull had been wounded previously by native hunters, and was suffering from a large festering wound in his side. He had apparently been to the water pool that afternoon, and on his return had gone to sleep in one of the patches of grass. He was awakened by our truck, which had approached within ten yards before he got to his feet. The resulting charge was inevitable, and is an excellent demonstration of the indomitable courage of the buffalo. With his ire aroused, no odds on earth are too great for him.

My flier-companions had witnessed two extremely rare occurrences in buffalo hunting, and those on their first, and only, outing. The experience made a deep impression on them. A week later I received news that one of them had been killed in an aeroplane crash. I often wondered whether, during those last moments when he was crashing to his doom, his emotions had been stirred to the same extent as they were when he stood watching the great herd charging down on us.

Those two lads of the R.A.F. made an excellent impression on me during the stirring moments of that great charge. There was no sign of panic or fear, and when the natives decided it was time to quit I fully expected that they would do likewise, following the example of more experienced men than themselves. But they stood their ground and saw it through. When I asked them later whether it had not occurred to them to shoot at the herd earlier during the charge, they replied that buffalo hunting was not their business; they did not know what one was supposed to do under such circumstances, and they would not do anything that might aggravate the situation. Had I told them to shoot earlier they would have done so. If only they had known at the time that I, also, "did not know what one was supposed to do under such circumstances" they might not have been quite so content to leave it to me!

[200]

18: KIVU - HOME OF THE GORILLA

THE HUNTING season was close at hand, and a safari for which I had made extensive arrangements had suddenly fallen through. It was then necessary to make preparations for something else, but the difficulty was to decide just what would offer a suitable alternative. It was at this time that an old friend came to me and suggested a safari through the Kivu. I had heard much about that country, its dense forests and snow-clad mountains, its scenic beauty and, last but not least, the gorilla which, as was then believed, could be found only in the Kivu forests. I was easily induced to fall in with this scheme, and in due course we were on our way with guns and cameras to the home of the great anthropoid apes.

The Kivu forest is not as large as its famous neighbour, the Ituri, but for scenic beauty it surpasses by far anything I ever saw in the Ituri. To the botanist and the lover of plant life the Kivu is a veritable Garden of Eden, for plants and ferns of all descriptions abound there in endless variety. At the time of our passage the Kivu was still very much uncharted territory; few Europeans had ever ventured so far afield.

Part of our journey was completed by means of native canoes on the Irumu River, and that voyage was also through a land of breath-taking beauty. The natives in those parts, although not hostile to us, were still extremely backward, and many of them had never seen a European before. It was only with the greatest difficulty that we could persuade them to approach us, and even with the lure of unlimited meat supplies we found it difficult to recruit guides for our safari. Our column was continually flanked by small groups who looked on in wonder at everything we did. The shooting of an animal created a profound impression on them and was attributed immediately to the supernatural properties of our rifles. I firmly believe that it was the natives' awesome respect for our weapons that helped us to make the trip through the forest without any unpleasant incidents. The farther west we proceeded the more primitive we found the natives to be. They were of an extremely superstitious nature, and here, more than in any other part I had previously visited, the witch doctor held complete sway and dispensed "medicine" in its most primitive form.

We frequently came to places near the native villages where high poles were planted in the ground on both sides of the paths, whilst from a crossbeam there were suspended numerous gruesome relics, such as human skulls and other bones of the human frame. These bones, we were told, were particularly efficacious in warding off evil spirits. There must have been a great many evil spirits in these parts, for almost every village we came to was thus protected by ghastly human remains.

The bush telegraph, as usual, kept the inhabitants

of the neighbouring kraals well informed of our movements. Often we came to large villages and found them almost completely deserted, the aged and the ailing being left behind to face the terror from which the more robust inhabitants had fled. As we neared one large village a group of natives approached our column; they were armed with long spears and the usual bows and arrows. They appeared to be very perturbed by our presence and kept up a rapid discourse, at the same time pointing towards an array of bones and skulls hanging across the path. It was obvious that they were not in favour of our entering the village, and the skeletal relics marked the limits of our approach. In order to convince them that we dispensed magic of a more potent nature than their own, I leaned against a tree and, with much ceremony and display, lifted my rifle and shot down two of the skulls. The distance was about one hundred yards. The natives were immediately convinced of the potency of our "medicine." In a few seconds they had all disappeared into the bush and we passed on into their village. The place was deserted.

Our explorations in this village brought us to a large hut, surrounded by a fence some eight yards square. The floors of both hut and backyard were constructed of clay, into which was cemented a vast collection of bones of all shapes and sizes. There was hardly an inch of the entire surface that was not covered by these gruesome relics, the human representation again predominating. This must have been the headquarters of the village "doctor," and if evil spirits are affected adversely by bones it is quite certain none ever entered that stronghold.

My friend was strongly in favour of spending the night in this chamber of horrors "for the fun of the thing." I am devoid of all sense of humour in such matters, and that night we camped a mile or so from the outskirts of the village. Because the ground was damp and this part of the country was infested with white ants, I instructed the tent boy to cut some timber on which to mount our trunks and provision cases. I took no further interest in the execution of this duty, but whilst we were sitting at dinner that evening my friend smilingly inquired whether it was the quality, or the quantity, of the bones that had prevented me from occupying the "doctor's" quarters in the village, at the same time pointing in the direction of our trunks. The joke was decidedly against me, for instead of mounting the trunks on timber as I had instructed him to do, the tent boy had collected four skulls, and on these our trunks were firmly mounted. Although this native had come with us from Northern Rhodesia and did not belong to the local tribe, the bug of superstition had eaten deep into his mind and he was merely taking precautions! I have often wondered at what stage of his mental development the African native could discard his fear of the supernatural and his faith in the witch doctor. No matter how well he may be instructed, he always retains a lingering fear of both.

In the way of hunting, our trip up to this stage had proved distinctly disappointing. Elephants were scarce, and such specimens as we came across were not interesting. We had seen no buffalo or lion and, worst of all, no traces of gorilla. At this point we decided to change our course. We now struck out for the volcanic region of the Mount Virungu range. Soon we were crossing the immense lava beds; so dense was the forest here that frequently we had to hack our way through the undergrowth in order to make any progress at all. Away up in the distance were the fiery peaks of giant Mt. Mikeno. The awe-inspiring spectacle of this volcanic region, where high up in the glowing peaks thunderstorms rage incessantly, is a sight that beggars all description. The going was extremely difficult, for down the mountain sides deep rents had been torn in the earth by ancient lava streams. Along the higher slopes of the mountain are the dense rain forests, vast primordial regions, evil smelling, eternally dripping—the home of the great anthropoid apes. Even to see the creatures depends more on luck than design, for visibility is extremely limited, and the gorilla is perhaps the world's most difficult animal to track down.

We spent ten days in this utterly primeval wilderness before we caught up with a gorilla family. It was late one afternoon and another of the country's incessant thunderstorms was threatening to break. As the dark clouds came scudding overhead we decided to make for camp at the foot of the mountain. We had not gone far down the rugged slope when our guide touched my shoulder. He pointed towards the right at a high cliff that jutted from the mountainside forest. At the brink of the precipice, and perhaps fifty yards from us, stood a great male gorilla. Unaware of us, he was completely absorbed in watching the gathering storm. His proximity in the eerie half-light and our own great surprise conspired to render us incapable of immediate action. We could only gape. Lightning crackled in the rolling jet clouds and a blast of thunder shook the very mountain, but that hulking anthropoid figure stood calmly, interestedly—watching. Indeed, it was as if he were taking a lesson in the technique of unbridled fury. He turned quickly and saw us. At that instant a blinding flash of lightning enveloped the scene—and then the cliff was vacant. The great black ape had vanished as neatly as any Satan of the variety stage. Near by we glimpsed two more dusky forms, but they too slipped away in the forest. The storm then broke over us and we continued the descent to our camp.

As we plodded along in the pouring rain I could not help thinking of the many strange stories I had heard about the gorilla mingling with natives in their villages, and carrying off their women folks. Such stories may excite the imagination, but they have no foundation in fact. The natives here knew nothing about such incidents. They were afraid of the gorilla, as they are afraid of all dangerous animals. But the gorilla was even more afraid of them, and it was only on rare occasions that these natives, living in close proximity to the great apes, were ever privileged to see them in their natural haunts.

Our expedition in search of the gorilla had so far proved distinctly disappointing. During the time

Thunderstorms rage incessantly amongst the glowering
peaks of the Kivu.

we had spent in this vicinity we had fleetingly encountered only one family, and the conditions were so altogether unfavourable that photography was out of the question. When information reached us that natives near Mt. Sabinio had captured a baby gorilla, we immediately left for that point. Weather conditions on this part of our journey were appalling, alternating between violent thunderstorms and freezing cold. The natives gave a graphic description of the capture of the baby gorilla, but during the process of the hunt he had sustained serious injuries from which he died the next day. The skin had been put out to dry and a prowling hyena had taken it. (I have often wondered how much truth there was in that story.) As usual when white hunters are about, the natives assured us that gorillas were plentiful in that area, but when, after two more days of fruitless wandering, we had failed to locate the great apes, we decided to call it a day. The weather conditions, the difficult terrain, and the bad luck that seemed to dog our footsteps all convinced us that there were easier and more profitable activities in the hunting field than gorilla baiting, and we decided to strike out in the direction of Lake Albert. Our journey as far as the Uganda border was without incident, but the next stage was adventurous in the extreme, and productive of two major tragedies. It marked also the beginning of my adventures on the buffalo trail.

Our arrival on the Uganda border coincided with the release of the Government notice withdrawing the buffalo from the hunting licence and placing him on the vermin list. This was due to the spread of the tsetse fly, of which the buffalo is a carrier. At that time buffalo hides were valuable, and prices of five pounds and upwards could be had for the hide of a bull, whilst that of a cow brought only slightly less. Apart from sleeping sickness which was rampant in this area, the prospects appeared to be good and I decided to stay and collect any surplus cash there might be floating about. My friend of the Kivu expedition had lost interest in the venture, and decided to return south, whilst I decided to make for Lake George. There I would pitch camp and prepare to commence hostilities against the buffalo. Around Lake George buffaloes were plentiful, and it was said that they frequently grazed amongst the native cattle. Lions were equally plentiful and destructive, and the natives rarely enjoyed a full night's sleep, being kept awake by these marauders in their attempts to raid the cattle kraals.

My first night in camp at Lake George was a hectic affair. I had covered the door leading to the sleeping quarters of my tent with a raw buffalo hide— a precaution against lions. During the night I was awakened from a deep sleep by what I thought was a swarm of bees in my bed clothes. On turning on my light I found that the tent was being raided by a community of soldier ants. I quickly threw the buffalo hide out, for it was obviously this that had attracted the unwelcome visitors. For the rest of that night I sat outside in a drizzling rain whilst the ants made merry in my tent! When these intruders take possession there is no room for anyone else. (In later years

I often enlisted their support to clean the skulls of trophies for me, an unpleasant job which natives will seldom do well in the field. These ants would clean a skull thoroughly in an incredibly short time, free of cost and without effort!)

As I sat out in the open that night I saw the natives hurling burning logs at intruding lions on several occasions. Just beyond the campfires the hyenas kept up an unearthly din, which was varied occasionally by the angry grunts of a lion. Slightly before dawn there was a tremendous uproar in the camp, and logs of fire were thrown in all directions. I felt relieved when, on investigating the cause of the disturbance, I found that there had been no casualties. A lion had grabbed a native who was rolled up in a blanket and in the ensuing struggle the lion had departed with the blanket, leaving behind a badly frightened native. My camp appeared to be in an unhealthy spot and early next morning I moved to a point about five miles away where, later in the day, I welcomed the arrival of the two well-known German hunters, von Roelen and Mischaert, who had just returned from a safari in Abyssinia. We all settled down at this place and opened a campaign against the buffalo which ended in the previously mentioned tragedies.

The following morning we each went out in a different direction, and both Mischaert and I did a useful morning's work. Von Roelen was less fortunate. He wounded a bull and was charged in long grass. Fortunately there was a tree near by, but before he could avail himself of its protection the buffalo had grazed his side and hooked its horn through his ammunition belt. The toss landed him against the trunk of the tree, which he lost no time in climbing. From this position he dispatched the bull with a heavy-calibre revolver. "Coming events cast their shadows," and this was decidedly an early warning!

The following day we again hunted in separate directions, and von Roelen was the first to put up a herd. Again he wounded a bull and, profiting by the experience of the previous day, he was more careful about following it in long grass. Quite close to the spot where he had wounded the bull was an old tree stump, about five feet high. Von Roelen mounted this stump and tried to balance himself on it so as to get a better view of the surroundings. On finding his perch unsuitable for the purpose he called on his gun bearer to approach and, resting one foot on the shoulder of the native and the other on the stump, he started to look ahead for traces of the buffalo. At that moment the bull charged from behind and the native was in the direct line of charge. Von Roelen recovered from his fall just in time to see the native being carried off into the long grass, suspended on the horns of the bull. It was some hours later before we found the corpse lying next to the carcass of the dead buffalo. To a newcomer to the buffalo-hunting game, such as I was at that time, this was not a very cheerful start, and the five pounds did not look quite as good as it had a few days earlier.

The next day von Roelen decided to stay in camp, as the incidents of the two preceding days had unnerved him. He also thought that it would be better if we all desisted from hunting for a day or two. He had a strong premonition that there was further trouble in the offing. In this he was proved correct, and, had we followed his advice, a second tragedy might have been averted. Mischaert and I left shortly before sunrise, striking out in opposite directions. My nerves were distinctly on edge and I exercised the greatest possible care in all I did that day. This extreme caution made me pass up several easy opportunities and I returned to camp with only two trophies by four o'clock that afternoon. Mischaert had not returned. It was with difficulty that von Roelen and I hid our uneasiness on his account. A short time after my return von Roelen went to the tent door and looked out in the direction Mischaert had gone that morning. Turning around to me he said, "There is a native running in our direction from the bottom of the rise; I have a feeling that he is bringing bad news." I asked von Roelen not to worry, but the next moment he was on his way to meet the runner. A few minutes later the two reached the tent and then I learned that von Roelen's presentiment had proved only too true. The native had come in to report that his master had been killed by a buffalo. He gave an incoherent account of a struggle between Mischaert and a wounded bull, during which Mischaert was killed and the bull finally disposed of by one of the native porters.

We left immediately with an improvised stretcher to bring in the dead man, and after an hour's walk we came to the scene of the tragedy. We found Mischaert lying with his legs entwined around the neck of the dead buffalo and his clothes gone from his body. He was not dead, but he was not far from it. One of the buffalo's horns had penetrated his side and left a ghastly wound; several ribs appeared to be fractured, but fortunately the lung was not punctured. In addition a leg was broken and there were several other injuries. We carried him back to camp and attended to his wounds as best we could, after which we hurriedly constructed a mashila and set out for the mission station at Torro where medical attention was obtainable. We gave Mischaert frequent injections of morphia during the long journey to the mission and he was unconscious most of the time. There did not appear to be much hope of saving him, and when we finally reached the mission he was indeed at the end of his tether. Two days later he showed some signs of improvement, and it was more than three months before he finally left the mission. At the time of Mischaert's departure I was no longer in the vicinity, but during the fortnight we remained with him, prior to returning to Lake George, I got a full account from him as to what had happened on that fateful hunt:

On leaving camp that morning he had walked for about an hour before he came across any buffaloes. Then he had put up a bull and a cow. The cow offered an easy target, and he dropped her with his first shot. Before he could get a shot at the bull the animal had disappeared into the bush. Mischaert decided to have the hide removed from the dead cow before setting out on the trail of the bull, and whilst the natives were busy skinning he had taken a seat on a stump under a nearby tree. A few seconds later his attention was drawn to a rustling in the grass, and as he looked up he saw the bull charging down on him. There was still some distance between them and he managed to get in two shots, both of which took effect, but the bull did not go down, and before he could get in a third shot the enraged beast was on top of him. After he had been tossed for the second time he managed to get hold of the buffalo's horns and hang on grimly for life. The bull was then too weak to toss him again and was slowly making for the tree where, undoubtedly, he would have brought proceedings to an end quickly, when the gun bearer came up from behind and put an end to the buffalo.

Mischaert's was a miraculous escape, and he is one of the few hunters who have lived to tell the tale after coming to grips with an enraged buffalo. But that escape proved of no great benefit to him, for he died a short time later from heart trouble which must have been aggravated by his terrifying experience. I was puzzled for a long time by the unexpected and largely unprovoked attack on Mischaert. But in discussing the incident with an old hunter some years later, he suggested that it must have occurred in the mating season, which accounted, in all probability, for the aggressive behaviour of that bull.

When von Roelen and I returned to Lake George we hunted for a short while longer with varying success, but when, some time later, he had another narrow escape in which he evaded a charging bull by a margin of inches only, we decided that Lake George was unhealthy in too many ways. Five pounds is good money for a buffalo hide, but it is of no earthly use to a dead man!

This experience at Lake George was my introduction to the business of buffalo hunting, and it was somewhat discouraging, if not alarming. But these early practical demonstrations of the Black Devil's ferociousness and cunning were valuable lessons which stood me in good stead in after years. I was taught right at the outset that one dare not stand on ceremony when the time comes to settle an argument with these dangerous customers. The humane consideration that prompts every hunter to trail down a wounded animal and put it out of misery as soon as possible is a highly commendable attitude, but it is this same spirit that has led to the death of many a hunter of buffaloes.

In later years I frequently had no choice in the matter of trailing down wounded buffaloes; generally when the wounding had occurred in thickly populated areas and the animal could not be left to endanger the inhabitants. In such a situation the sense of fair play will prompt every hunter to "see the business through" at all costs. But in cases where these conditions did not apply I was always content to follow the advice of the best hunters of all—the native "fundis," and that is: "When you have wounded a buffalo and do not hear him grunt when he goes down, there is no need to hurry to find out what has happened to him. If he is dead vultures will soon be on the spot; they have better eyes and better means of making sure what has happened.

If a vulture, with wings to help him out of trouble, is afraid to go near—all the more reason for a man on his flat feet to keep well out of the way." This is sound logic. The reference to the grunting as a safety signal is virtually infallible. The well-hit buffalo will emit a half-bellow, and usually it is repeated three to five times. On the hundreds of occasions when I have stood and waited for that signal, and followed up after hearing it, I have not been involved in one untoward incident. With that sound the big fellow is giving up the ghost. It is just as well that the buffalo, with his inherent cunning, has not yet discovered how much significance we hunters attach to that death-grunt!

19: THE FINICKY PROFESSOR

Nᴏᴛ ꜱᴜʀᴘʀɪꜱɪɴɢʟʏ, my learned client had come to regard the animals of the plain with a personal and definitely selfish interest. The man was very hungry! He enquired, "Do you think you could shoot another of those little antelopes like the one you got day before yesterday?" Then, with more than a hint of desperation in his voice, he added, "Something will have to be done to get us out of this unfortunate predicament."

I replied, "There would be no difficulty in shooting as many such antelopes as we might require, but surely, professor, you are not asking me to do that?"

"Well, you see," the professor said, with an air of defeat, "the circumstances would seem to demand it. I've been without food for two days, and this cannot go on indefinitely."

"Quite, quite," I agreed, "But is this not rather a *volte face* on your part? You seem to have thrown all your scruples overboard quite easily. In fact, you are now asking me to do something which only a short time ago you condemned very strongly."

My companion was a famous scientist who had come out from London on a special research job. Arriving at my camp the day before we set out on this trip, he had persuaded me to accompany him to a place where large herds of buffaloes and other big game could easily be filmed, and he was particularly anxious to obtain the buffalo shots. My knowledge of the area was calculated to be of some assistance to him, and I had agreed to accompany him. But right at the outset a difficulty arose which led me to tell the professor that, if he persisted in his attitude, I should be forced to call the trip off. He was totally averse to hunting in all forms, a fact he explained to me when making arrangements for the trip. Now, as my rifles were being brought to the car, he objected to our taking them. His view was that since there was to be no hunting there was no necessity for bringing the rifles along. I explained that, hunting or no hunting, I was not prepared to travel about the bush, especially where buffalo would be encountered, without firearms. If he did not agree on that point, he could carry on without me. I would go armed, or I would not go at all. I had already given instructions to have my kit removed from the car when the old man reluctantly agreed to let me have my own way. During the greater part of the four-hour journey I was treated to a tirade against hunting and hunters, and the professor was so dogmatic in his views that I felt there was nothing to gain by entering into a discussion with him. My only comment was to the effect that a week earlier there had been a fatal accident in the very area we were setting out for and that I was not particularly anxious just yet to hear the angels sing. On our arrival at the spot that afternoon, there was very little game to be seen, and no buffalo at all. I explained that the morning, rather than the afternoon, was the time for buffaloes to come to water and graze in the vicinity. I felt certain he would have all the pictures he needed before noon the next day, and that we would be back in camp before 5 p.m.

By 10 o'clock the next morning the professor had taken all the films he wanted, and we prepared to return to camp. Bedding, cameras, rifles and the rest of the kit were packed into the car, and we were ready to start. But during our brief stay some imp of mischief had entered that bus and, in spite of our combined efforts, it refused to move. By midday we were completely exhausted with pushing, pulling, cranking and trying the numerous devices that might help to set the wheels in motion. My mechanical knowledge amounted to exactly zero, and from what I could see of it, the professor's was slightly less. The two natives we had brought with us were unable to offer any assistance. There was no ignition spark, which indicated a discharged battery, and all that remained for us to do was to send a runner back on foot to get help from the nearest garage, a hundred miles away. That would mean an enforced delay of four days or more. We had brought provisions to last us until that night, and things looked anything but cheerful. To me it made no serious difference, as I can live on meat exclusively for weeks on end so long as water is obtainable. But the old man would find it somewhat awkward, having told me previously that he would not eat venison. That afternoon, whilst the professor had gone to sleep, utterly fatigued from the strenuous efforts earlier in the day, I went a mile or so from camp and shot a duiker. The food problem, for me at least, was solved. I had the duiker carried to camp and left it in the improvised shack the natives had previously erected.

Early the next morning we were out again for more pictures, and when we returned at 9 a.m. we both felt hungry, but all that was left in the larder was a bottle of beer. The professor was soon immersed in an illustrated volume on game which I had loaned him, and whilst the old man was thus occupied I set about to prepare a grill over the fire. When the steak was finally brought to the table the professor refused to have any of it, and I was once again treated to a lecture on the beauty and grace of these antelopes and the reason why they should not be hunted. To this I could only reply that there were times when we all liked to see them roaming about, or on the pages of an illustrated volume. There were times, however, when I preferred to see them on a plate, and the present was such a time. We were both in a position to give expression to our likes and desires, and there was nothing to stop either of us from enjoying the idea of putting our views into practice. I was quite certain that no man had ever appeased his hunger by *looking* at food, or a photograph thereof!

The rest of the story is of no interest except that, before we got back to camp, the professor's views had undergone a remarkable change, and he had done full justice to the fare I provided from antelope meat. I also heard later that he suspected me of wilfully sabotaging the car in order to have a joke at his expense—which is so much foolishness.

The above incident is but one more illustration of the extremist views of the anti-hunt community. Their uncompromising attitude is difficult to understand and indicates a lack of serious reflection. There are few, if any, cases of excessive and indiscriminate killing in the hunting field today. Those who hunt for sport do so on rare occasions only, and their activities are controlled by game laws. In cases where game is hunted in order to supply food for human consumption, it is obviously foolish to condemn such a procedure. There are large tracts of country in Central and East Africa where game meat has for a long time filled an urgent need. In many cases it has been the sole source of supplying the needs of hungry and, in some cases, starving people. Frequently this starvation is brought about by game, as it is due entirely to their depredations. Damage done by game animals to native plantations is far more serious than is generally believed. Surely no thinking person will have the temerity to suggest that the pleasure of seeing game animals in their natural state is sufficient reason to allow them to increase, unrestrained and uncontrolled, to the detriment of the highest form of animal life—*Homo sapiens*.

Throughout Africa today there are hundreds of thousands of square miles set apart for the protection of game animals of all species. In these sanctuaries, parks and reserves, no hunter ever molests them, and I have no doubt that, if there is any justification for increasing these areas, this could easily be done. But if the "anti-hunts" have it their way, we will arrive at a position where the game inside the sanctuaries is protected by law, whilst outside the sanctuaries the game will be protected by sympathy. This is a misguided sympathy that takes no account of the human animal, nor does it function where he is concerned. And if it is really a question of sentiment and aversion to seeing animals killed, one is prompted to ask: "Why all this discrimination in favour of game as compared to domestic animals, since, to a very large extent, the killing is done for the same purpose and helps to meet the same demands?" Death must be as repulsive to the one animal as it is to the other, and between the killing of domestic animals and the killing of game there is a vast difference. The former we tame, and by virtue of their close association with human beings for centuries, the instinct of self-protection has been lulled to sleep. They place their confidence in us and in return they are treacherously murdered, without one chance in a million to escape. Even the most fanatical protectionist will agree that, in the normal course of events, the chances of escape favour game by a million to one when compared to domestic animals. It is unfortunately true that the law of murder is also the law of growth, and no animal can rise to excellence without being fatal to the lives of others. Since this law provides that we shall kill in order to survive, I cannot see why there should be so much discrimination in favour of game animals who, in many cases, are harmful to man, yet serve the same purpose after they are killed as do the domestic animals. The claim that we can breed the latter in accordance with our demands, whereas we cannot do so in the case of game, does not appear to be a very sound argument. If it were, one might well be prompted to ask, "What then is the object of setting aside such vast stretches of country in the form of national parks, reserves and game sanctuaries, where all species of game are protected and allowed to breed and propagate their kind without hindrance or molestation?"

In this modest plea for a more compromising and tolerant attitude, I at once dissociate myself from the other type of extremists who have been responsible for bringing about legislation that has led to the senseless destruction of hundreds of thousands of animals, the carcasses of which were left to putrefy the veld. This is a monstrous crime which has led to an aggravation of the evil it sought to destroy. Here is a rich field to which the anti-hunt community may devote their energies with profit.

20: A PACKET OF SHOCKS

I HAVE WRITTEN much about narrow escapes and awkward situations during encounters with buffaloes, but when I come to review my adventures on the buffalo trail I must confess that the greatest shocks have not been experienced whilst actually shooting it out with the "bad boys." My genuine spinetinglers have always sprung from unforeseen circumstances. When one goes in to shoot it out with a wounded buffalo, or prepares to face an expected charge, he faces a known situation. One keeps cool, calm and collected; one adjusts himself to a recognised situation, for to do otherwise will almost certainly lead to disaster. It is when the completely unexpected happens that the nerves are liable to "play up."

During one October, away down on the Kafuvu River, we got on the trail of a big buffalo herd, and the size of certain tracks indicated the presence of at least two outstanding bulls. Also, by studying the tracks closely, we determined that the herd was not running but was grazing towards a destination. These animals had come from a water hole near by and were grazing out in the direction of the forest country. Thus, if not disturbed, they would reach that shelter not later than 10 a.m. Before arriving at the forest they would have to cross a large plain, from six to ten miles wide. Throughout the plain were extensive patches of dry grass, each a square mile or more in area, and much of that growth was so long and dense that visibility was reduced to a few feet.

The trail of this herd had already led through two or more of those dense grass patches, and now only one large patch lay between us and the forest. We had not yet seen an animal, even though a herd will sometimes lie up in a grass patch and sleep during the heat of the day. (When the trail leads into such thick clusters of grass the procedure generally is not to follow that trail, but to send trackers to circle the cluster and find out if, and where, the herd emerged.) Our trail now led us into the largest patch of grass we had so far encountered. It stretched for fully two miles across the plain, and was a mile or more wide at its narrowest point. Quite close to the grass was a big tree, and here I decided to remain in the shade whilst the trackers went out to ascertain whether or not the herd had left the grass. An hour or so later they returned and reported that the herd had passed through and had made for the forest beyond.

It was now close to 10 a.m. and in view of the assurance that the herd had traversed the grass I felt that there was no point in walking around the big patch. The quickest route would be to stick to the trail, as the grass would be trampled down to a large extent and easy to negotiate. As I did not expect to use any of my rifles before we entered forest country, I handed them over to the gunbearers and set out at the head of the trackers and porters. Following the trail through the long grass was an easy matter and did not require the services of an expert tracker. I was walking ten yards ahead of the nearest gunbearer, head down and deep in thought—just walking and following the trail automatically. In one instant I all but strode onto the back of a buffalo, fast asleep in the long grass! The wind was blowing in our direction and the first intimation a troup of sleeping buffaloes had of our presence was when I was about to stumble over the one in my path. I do not know who had the greatest shock—the buffalo, the porters, or I. I do know that the old saying of "jumping out of one's skin" could have applied to me literally at that moment. The buffaloes bolted off and for several moments I could hear the grass crumpling as they ran. The porters also left that spot in a great hurry. A grandfatherly old fellow who had complained all morning that the going was too hard for him was at the head of the flight and busy setting up a new record for the 100 yards.

A shock such as this is only temporary and one gets over it quickly. In a few minutes we were all back on the trail, the usual bantering and leg-pulling bringing comic relief to a tiring job.

Now we were approaching dense trees and everyone was on the alert. The main herd had made straight for the forest and in a few minutes we would find them under shelter. I soon heard a tracker's warning whistle. (Good trackers always imitate the whistle of some bird or other, and this they do so well that I have never known an occasion when animals have been alarmed by the signal.) The herd was found, but as yet they were still circling around, looking for suitable shade in which to lie down during the heat of the day. Finally they settled down under a big tree some 300 yards from us. I have always considered any shooting distance over 250 yards to be risky so far as buffaloes are concerned, no matter what rifle I used. I now tried to reduce the distance, but some slight movement in stalking attracted the notice of one of the cows, and at once she communicated her alarm to the rest of the herd. They were restless and ready to move off. I did not fancy a trailing job at that time of day, and in picking out one of the big bulls before he could move off, I did not allow sufficient time and care in aiming. As the shot rang out the herd took off at top speed. I did not hear the bullet strike and felt certain that I had missed. The trackers, however, were equally certain that the bull had "taken it." There was nothing to do but follow the tracks and look out for a blood trail. For nearly a mile we stuck to the trail without finding any signs of blood. Then one of the trackers picked up a dry leaf on which there was a mere speck of fresh blood. This indicated a flesh wound and one not likely to have much effect. The echo of my shot in the dense trees on the far side of the forest had sent the herd back in a circle; they were now making for the extreme left side of the patch of grass in which we had had the alarming experience earlier in the day.

Much has been written about buffaloes inevitably charging when they are wounded, but experience has taught me that a lightly wounded animal will rarely charge, and it will even go to a lot of trouble to escape added injury. Only when a buffalo is mortally or seriously wounded will it try to settle its grievances. I felt comparatively safe in following this herd; the wounded bull would do his best to keep out of the way. Back into the grass we again followed the trail; once again visibility was reduced to a minimum. But in such cases, with a herd on the move, one does not depend entirely on seeing the quarry in order to determine its whereabouts; in dry grass a big herd on the move can be heard a long way off. In following this trail we stopped on two occasions and listened intently, but there was no sound of any movement. After an hour of tracking we came to a halt. The trail had led us within a few hundred yards of the extreme edge of the long grass and in that intervening space the herd was in hiding, as they had not shown up in the open plain beyond. We had hardly come to a stop when I heard the grass ahead of me being trampled down; the herd was moving less than twenty yards in front of me. I watched attentively in an effort to discover the wounded bull, and as I did so the herd came to a stop. They were quite unaware of my presence. Suddenly, a strange feeling came over me that all was not well. It is difficult to explain this sort of thing—the nearest I can get to it is that I felt I was being watched. I then realised I had gone too far forward without making sure that all was clear on the flanks. "Get back, get back," a voice seemed to call out to me. Quickly I made up my mind to retreat. As I turned around I looked straight into the scowling face of a bull at not more than three yards on my right. He was looking at me intently, his eyes glaring beneath the heavy bosses and, withal, such a complete picture of menace and truculence that a tingling feeling swept down my spine. In the next instant, before I could raise my rifle to my shoulder, that bull whirled around on his hind legs and set off at top speed in the opposite direction. I resumed the business of breathing!

The trackers and porters were several yards behind me, but for all that, they had again scattered in all directions. When I suggested later that we track the herd down, for the third time, they there and then pronounced me completely mad. Wild horses could not drag that mob out again on the trail of the herd. Later on I heard myself described as a "very brave man to stand and face a wounded buffalo at arm's length." Little did those fellows know that at the time I was petrified with shock and quite incapable of movement for some seconds!

* * * * *

One—or was it two?—of the outstanding shocks I have had on the buffalo trail was on a day when buffalo was not the quarry, yet proved the means of supplying the fireworks.

On this occasion a friend and I set out early in the morning for a swamp, some three miles from home, in search of impala. The larder was empty and impala were plentiful in the swamp. As no buffaloes had been encountered in the area for fully twelve months, there was no reason to suppose that they had suddenly returned. We expected nothing bigger than impala and carried only light rifles. We arrived at the swamp shortly after sunrise and soon came across a small herd

[228]

of impala. Unfortunately the wind sat in the wrong direction and before we could get a shot at them they had picked up our scent and had run into the long grass. I started to follow the trail, well ahead of my friend who was still walking slowly down the embankment leading into the swamp, when suddenly there was a violent commotion in the grass, right at my side. As I looked in that direction I was horrified to see a pair of buffalo horns coming straight for me; at that moment they were not more than five yards away. The shock was great, and I had not even started to raise my rifle when a shot rang out some distance behind me. Instantly, the black mass of a buffalo cow sprawled right at my feet.

The whole business had started and finished so suddenly that I had no time to realise what had happened. But, most certainly, a dead buffalo lay in front of me! I immediately wished to examine the carcass, to discover where that timely shot had been placed. As I bent forward to do this there sounded a loud "BAAH" right behind me and in the same instant I received a violent bump in the buttocks which sent me headlong across the carcass of the cow. This unexpected attack bewildered me completely, and as I scrambled to my feet I had the mental picture of an enraged bull waiting to complete his work of destruction. In this my surmise proved correct, for as I turned around to face the inevitable I looked straight into the face of a buffalo bull—barely one month old!

My encounter with the cow and her calf was easily understood when, a little farther ahead, my friend and

I found the tracks of a buffalo herd. The cow had dropped out of the herd in order to rest the calf in the long grass and, unknowingly, I had walked into the hornet's nest.

My friend explained later that he had remained behind on the embankment intentionally, as he expected me to put up the impala in long grass, in which case he would be in a better position to shoot. He had kept a close watch on my movements and had fortunately spotted the cow at the very moment the charge got under way. Excellent shot that he is, he brought proceedings to an end with a bullet in the cow's neck.

That calf was an astonishing little fellow, for with the death of his mother he promptly transferred his affections to us and followed us all the way back to camp, baah-ing lustily all the way. The new surroundings in camp did not appear to upset him at all. His love for us grew until finally it became impossible for either of us to move about without having him at our heels. We kept the calf on a diet of cow's milk, but after a few weeks he developed stomach trouble, from which he died.

It is strange how trifles can affect serious issues. Just before this outing I had acquired a splendid .275 Express. I had sung the rifle's praises to my friend, and on this occasion he asked me to allow him to test it, a request I willingly granted. In exchange for the .275 I had taken his .22 Hornet—an excellent little weapon for small game, but one totally inadequate where a buffalo is concerned. But for this fortuitous exchange—and the excellent marksmanship of my friend—I would not be writing this.

* * * * *

Up on the Katuma River, north of Lake Katavi, I ran into a solitary old bull one morning. He had been sleeping under a tree, but had picked up our scent, and before I could get a shot at him he was making for the river bed at top speed. As he turned to descend the embankment he offered a broadside target; there was but little time to aim, but I could hear the thud of the bullet striking home. It was impossible to tell just where the bullet had landed. The bull stuck to his course and in the next instant he had disappeared into the river bed, where I was not anxious to follow him. Solitary bulls are always doubtful customers and usually persistent in the matter of settling grievances; the guilty and the innocent look alike to them. It was quite likely that this old fellow was not at peace with the world, and the fresh injury he had suffered would not improve his temper.

The country at this place was absolutely flat and I figured that it would be easy to observe any movement from the top of a nearby large tree, should the bull leave the river bed. Soon the trackers and I were up in the tree. On both sides of the river bed, where the bull had disappeared, grew long green grass, and beyond this grass on the far bank was a burned area. A mile beyond this barren patch was an old water course, covered by dense bush and reeds. At the spot where the bull had disappeared the river itself was waist-deep. We watched the spot for several minutes without seeing any sign of life; the animal had either died from the bullet wound or he was in hiding. In order to make quite sure I fired a shot at random at the spot in the river bed where I suspected him to be. A few seconds later he emerged on the far bank and started for the old water course in the distance. Before he again offered a suitable target he was fully 400 yards away, and as I pressed the trigger I saw a cloud of dust arise in front of him. My shot was slightly high and the bullet must have thrown sand in the old fellow's face. The next moment he turned around and came straight back towards us. Slowly he trotted until he regained the far bank, and there he came to a stand-still. Only his horns and the ridge of his back showed up, but it was quite a good target, as I could easily judge the location of his shoulders. I fired, and the bull went down in his tracks. For several minutes we watched for a movement, but all remained quiet. I felt certain that the bull was dead, but there was always the possibility that he was only stunned and would lie in wait for us to approach him. A wounded buffalo, in long grass, holds all the aces, and he knows exactly when to play them. However, there it was; something had to be done to make sure he was dead before trying to collect him. Another random shot brought no response. The trackers were not at all impressed with my suggestion that we go down and see what had happened. Their view was that if the bull was dead the vultures would soon be on the scene, and only then would they make a move towards collecting the spoils. Sometimes one can persuade a native to do something against his wish; at other times he shows no comprehension whatever. My trackers now were—just dumb. I decided that I would go down there myself; the two trackers were to remain in the tree whilst I crossed over. They would keep a close watch on the spot where the bull had gone down and, as there was no landmark to guide me, they would keep me informed when I entered the danger zone.

After crossing the river I soon got on to a heavy trail of blood; the bull was evidently bleeding from the lungs. I was getting rapidly into what I considered dangerous territory; the trackers were shouting out instructions to me. It was still "mbali" (far). Even without their assistance I could determine my safety for at least ten yards, the distance ahead of me where the blood was visible on the long grass. Another twenty yards, and now there was no more blood to be seen, but the grass appeared to be trodden down. I stopped for a moment for further guidance from the trackers; it was still "mbali kidogo," that subtle native expression which means "a little bit far" in their language but which, in fact, means nothing where distances are concerned. Once again I had a good look ahead of me; definitely there was no more blood, but the trodden-down grass trail was quite obvious. Now, with rifle at the ready and eyes fixed intently ten yards ahead, I continued on the grass trail. The next moment I stumbled and fell flat on my face, rifle falling to one side. I had fallen over the dead body of the bull! The leap that took me off that carcass will remain a classic example of the perfect high jump! If any reminder were necessary, this incident helped me once again to realise how effectively a buffalo can take cover in long and dense grass.

*   *   *   *   *

On the Rungwa River, late in October, we once got on to the trail of a tremendous buffalo bull. Like all other hunters, I am continually on the lookout for a record trophy. It is true, record horns are not always found on the largest animals, for a moderate-sized animal will sometimes carry an excellent pair of horns. But it is generally amongst the big "beef trusts" that one looks for the best trophies. If footprints were a guide, then this bull which we had followed since early morning was something quite out of the ordinary. Now, after many such failures, we had again lost the trail. (At that time of year, in the Rift Valley, the black cotton soil is so hard that tracking at times becomes extremely difficult, if not impossible.) The sun was beating down with the intensity of a blast furnace, and for fully ten minutes we had been walking in circles in our efforts to pick up the trail again, but it had vanished. The only thing to do in such a case is to return to the spot where there was the last positive evidence of a trail. I had sent the trackers back to that spot, some 500 yards away. About a hundred yards ahead of me was one of the clusters of dense bush with which the Valley is dotted. They are frequently twenty yards in diameter and extremely dense. (I believe that the Good Lord placed these clusters in the Valley as an afterthought, to help poor

[234]

hunters who find themselves on the trail in the heat of the day.)

This particular cluster was so dense that I had to crawl on hands and knees in order to gain the interior, where I intended to have an overdue and hurried breakfast whilst the trackers went back on the trail. However, long after I had eaten, the trackers were still far off and following the trail with great difficulty. The going was so slow that I determined to abandon the trail and I was about to call to the distant trackers when one of them shouted to me. In the next instant my immediate shelter seemed to spring to life. Branches crashed down, and a violent snort right at my side caused me to scramble to my feet. There was a sickening crash of bottles, as my haversack was sent sprawling to one side. Then, in an instant I realised that the big bull had taken refuge from the sun in the same cluster I had chosen, and there he had fallen asleep. The shout of the tracker had awakened him. On making his exit he passed within a few feet of me but luckily he was concerned only with his own safety and paid scant notice to me. Those few moments were packed with shock—for me and the bull. It was very fortunate that I was not in the direct path of his escape. I had my heavy-calibre rifle at my side and before the bull had gone a hundred yards I had added to his shock-score with a slug in the heart. He proved to be an excellent specimen in the matter of size but had far from a record in horn-spread.

The tracker who called to me and thereby precipitated the trouble had again found the bull's trail and

was convinced that the animal was in the same cluster
of bush as I was. That bull and I had got away from
the sun—and then from each other!

*　　*　　*　　*　　*

When the gold rush was at its height on the Lupa
River I was doing fairly well on some claims I had
pegged near the confluence of the Chunya and Ipogolo
Rivers. The Chunya, near the location of my camp,
swept through sandy country and in several places
its banks were nearly twenty feet high, although at
that time its water was little more than a trickle. For
several weeks we had seen no game of the usual
description, but guinea fowls were plentiful. Late one
afternoon I was out on the trail of birds with a shotgun.
Away on the Chunya's opposite bank we could hear
the birds. Guinea fowls, as is generally known, are the
most cunning of birds, and as I got nearer to them
their calls ceased. No sound or movement could I
detect from where I stood. A few yards ahead was a
big sand bank and from there I hoped to get a better
view of the other side of the river. I climbed the
bank and was watching the far side intently for a movement, when suddenly the bank collapsed and I went
down into the water. My descent was so rapid that I
had no time to look around, but now I stood in the
river, covered with slime and mud. Before I could
fully take stock of the position I was aware of a movement at my side. A big buffalo bull had just scrambled
to his feet and stood sniffing the air. Luckily for me,
I had loaded with buckshot and during my descent
I had stuck to the gun. Now, face to face with im-

A PACKET OF SHOCKS

pending death, I acted by instinct. At point blank range I aimed behind the bull's ear and pulled both triggers. The great brute made no move other than to sink to the ground, stone dead.

For a time I was completely puzzled at what had happened. The bull, normally, should have made some effort to escape or attack me. Instead of that he gave me sufficient time to recover from my shock and shoot him at point blank range. Never before had I heard of such an occurrence, and I daresay this is the only instance of a buffalo's being killed instantly by charges from a shotgun. But when I came to examine the old fellow closely the mystery was dissipated. The beast was completely blind in both eyes. In standing up as he did before I shot him, he was apparently trying to pick up my scent before trying to effect an escape. I felt mean to have taken advantage of the afflicted creature, but of course at the time I did not know that he was blind and—perhaps it was better so.

* * * * *

Of all the shocks I have had on the buffalo trail, there is one that always produces a queasy feeling in my stomach when I think of it. This incident happened some years ago on the Ruhaha River. For more than a year I had struck a blank so far as buffaloes were concerned. During that time I had walked and motored more than a thousand miles in search of the elusive bovine, but always the trail ended in failure. Then one day natives reported buffaloes in an area where I had not previously looked for them.

HORNED DEATH

I left home on a Saturday afternoon and motored some fifty miles on the main road. That night we had the first heavy rain of the season, and it rained continuously for several hours. Early the next morning we were out and soon on the tracks of a solitary bull. Tracking was easy on the wet ground. For six hours we stuck to the trail, but nowhere was there a sign of the buffalo. At long last I decided we had gone far enough, and as a final effort we would mount a small hill to obtain a better view of the surrounding country. If there were still no signs of the buffalo we would call it a day and return to camp. Once on top of the hill, we reached a small open clearing from which I intended to view the countryside. With Ndege close behind me, I had come to a stop and was busy adjusting my field glasses, when I was jerked sharply by the shoulder. "Nyoka, Bwana," (snake, sir) cried Ndege. I looked down as the head of a big puff adder whipped past my knee. He had missed me by the fraction of an inch and I actually looked down his wide-open mouth as he struck. In coming to a stop I had not looked on the ground in front of me, and of all places in the vast territory of Tanganyika, I had put my foot on the tail of a puff adder.

Such a close call was something to think about. I had no serum or other antidote with me, and I was at least eighteen miles from camp. Only the two trackers were present and they were by then pretty well played out. If that snake had struck me, the two natives, tired as they were, could never have carried me back to camp. Even had they succeeded in doing

A 25¼-foot python which had swallowed the antelope seen
on the ground.

The disgorged antelope, more clearly seen in relation to
the size of a man.

so I would have had to travel at least seventy-five miles to the nearest doctor, by which time I would have been beyond all human aid. Even now, when I think of the adder incident, I can see that wide-open mouth striking at me, and the thought of the miserable and painful death that would have followed makes me shudder. ·To be killed by a buffalo, lion or any other dangerous animal is always a possibility in the hunting game. But in such cases one generally has a fighting chance, and if it comes to the worst, the killing, one way or another, is generally done in quick time. But to die from a puff adder bite, a lingering and painful death, without help, is quite another matter.

The buffalo trail can be strewn with things other than roses!

As I write of the adder, I am reminded of another snake affair, but this time the shock was one of a more pleasant variety. Some years ago a friend in America wrote and asked me for a skin each of the mamba and puff adder. Puff adders were extremely plentiful near my camp, but in over twenty years I had not encountered a mamba. I had even begun to believe that mambas were nonexistent in our part of Tanganyika. Frequently snakes had been pointed out to me and the claim made that they were black mambas when, in fact, they were not mambas at all. To some people any black snake of considerable length is a mamba. The mamba, Africa's deadliest snake, is easily identified by its small head, the slender neck, the position of its fangs—under the nose—and the distance between the fangs.

I had received this letter shortly before Christmas, and had mentioned to my hunting natives that I would like a good specimen of adder and, if possible, a black mamba—emphasizing the fact that I did not want a cobra (kipili) or boomslang. During the next few days I was busy on other work and did not think again about the snakes. On Christmas morning the entire crew of hunting boys assembled outside my house and announced that they had brought me a Christmas gift. The head tracker handed me a basket, which they had covered with green leaves. Frequently natives will bring gifts of eggs, fruit or other edibles, and I naturally assumed that they had brought me something of that nature. Thinking thus, I pulled off the leaves. The first things to meet my eyes were two freshly killed puff adders—still wiggling. The basket also contained a dead black mamba, twelve feet long; several more adders and, for good measure, two large cobras. To say that I got a shock would be to put it mildly.

The mamba proved to be an interesting specimen and the skin was duly sent to my friend in America who subsequently sent it on to Professor Ditmars, the world-famous authority on snakes. The professor considered it one of the best specimens he had ever seen. He mentions it in the last work he wrote on the subject, just before he died in New York.

21: THE CANNIBALS OF UBANGI

Not long ago a friend sent me a journal in which was published the views of a representative of a famous film company which specialises in travelogue films. The writer had come out to South Africa to make a travelogue and at the same time to consider the possibilities of making an important film based on the history of South Africa. His views were illuminating, if for no other reason than that it is always interesting to see ourselves as others see us. But when the author took it upon himself to say that most of what has been written on the seamy side of the Dark Continent is gross exaggeration and merely figments of imaginative minds, one felt that he was not quite conversant with his subject. It was not difficult to see that his knowledge of Africa was acquired during a trip by air from Durban to Johannesburg, where the article was written shortly after his arrival. It is not in this manner that one can judge Africa. I should like to have had that author with me on a trip which I once made through the Ubangi many years ago! He would have found there all material proofs to convince him that imagination does not always play a prominent part in the stories about Africa. The Africa of gold mines, of hustle and bustle, of theatres and skyscrapers, is but an insignificant part of the great continent. There is another aspect of this vast land mass with which sightseers and visitors to the populous parts of South Africa never come in contact. It is with that side of Africa that my story deals.

During the winter of 1908 I had drifted to the region of Kilo, the now famous gold mining district of the Belgian Congo, which lies to the northwest of Lake Victoria Nyanza. Kilo was then the private property of Leopold II of Belgium, and I found conditions there so unfavourable, in so far as a foreigner was concerned, that I decided to quit the vicinity and make my way to the French Congo, through the Ubangi. Having had a good fill of "Africa in the raw," it was my intention to make for the Congo River and from there go by boat as far as Matadi, from which place I intended to proceed to England on a well-earned holiday.

Having spent several weeks in the vicinity of Kilo, I had a fairly good idea as to what a trip through Ubangi might mean. But Ubangi was one of the "dark spots" of Africa which I had not previously visited, and in spite of the repeated warnings to abandon the project, I determined to carry out my intentions. Like the aforesaid writer, I was convinced that most of the lurid reports were greatly exaggerated, and in due course I set out on this safari with guns, ammunition, provisions and an army of porters. It was my intention to collect as much ivory as possible before I reached Matadi on the West Coast.

Several days after leaving Kilo we reached the summit of a hill from which we could see great plains stretching far into the distance. The natives on these plains were very suspicious of any European. By means of their bush telegraphy, which, by the way, no European ever understands, our movements were known days ahead. From the high ground we could see the natives driving their cattle out of the line of our approach and abandoning their villages. But soon the news spread that our mission was a peaceful one and ere long we were on friendly terms with the inhabitants of the villages on our route. At most places they approached us to barter produce for salt and meat, which we carried in ample supply. (Wherever I have travelled in Africa, in savage or civilized parts, I have always found that in exchange for meat it is possible to barter almost anything with the native—one's personal safety not excluded.)

As the plains gave way to lowlands we came to a remarkable subterranean passage. On first examination it appeared to be an excavation made by the natives, but it was actually an ancient water course. It extended for more than two miles in the granite formation, and on passing through it I found bones scattered everywhere—many of human origin. At one time this passage must have served as a refuge from wild beasts or raiding tribes. The natives in the vicinity were quite tractable. Theirs was a beautiful country and fertile, and many of them did considerable cultivation. This part of Ubangi had much the appearance of a great park. Vegetation of every description grew in wild profusion and the numerous streams of crystal-clear water were lined with towering palms.

HORNED DEATH

Up to this point our journey had proved to be a normal and pleasant one, but shortly thereafter I began to experience considerable trouble through the daily desertions of porters. Both the country and its people were assuming a more savage appearance. The desertions were due to fear of what the porters called the "Leopard People." Although I have never seen any of these marauders, I have no doubt whatever as to their existence. I have heard accounts of them in widely separated parts; the details never vary, and in several other ways I have satisfied myself as to the truth of these accounts.

The Leopard People are a marauding tribe of savages whose dress consists of leopard skins, and out of wood and iron they manufacture claws similar to but larger than those of the leopard. These claws are fitted over the fingers and secured around the wrists and, like the leopard's, are used with deadly effect. In addition to the claws these people are armed with bows and arrows and spears. They make human sacrifices and practise cannibalism. They do not settle down for long in any place but, also like the leopard, they wander from one place to another in search of prey.

We were then in Ubangi East and before long came to a stream of water near a native village. On going to the village I found it deserted with the exception of two old women who were too feeble to walk and had been abandoned by the rest of the villagers. They told me that the rest of the natives had cleared out for fear of the white man. I decided to camp near the

THE CANNIBALS OF UBANGI

stream for the night. After pitching the tent, my native cook went to the stream for water. A few minutes later he ran back into camp in a state of obvious terror. So unnerved was he that it was impossible to obtain an intelligent account from him. He insisted that I return to the stream with him and bring my rifle with me. Arming myself, I lost no time in accompanying him. On the way to the stream he kept repeating that none of us would live to see the sun rise the next day; his aged mother was going to be rendered childless, and the fault was mine for having brought him here to be eaten like an animal. Previously he had laughed at what he called the stupidity of the porters, and seeing him in such a terrified state I realised that something serious had happened to upset him.

Shortly I was viewing that which had inspired terror in the cook. I was similarly affected, but unlike him, I dared not show it. In the stream and partly submerged were three native men, tied together. Their arms and legs had been fractured, but they were still alive. I stood petrified before this horrible spectacle and shuddered to think what might have been the methods used to fracture the limbs. (I learned afterwards that the arms and legs had been broken with heavy clubs so as to prevent the victims from escaping; leaving them in water until they died was held to be an effective method of rendering the flesh tender. Previously I had come across cases in which natives had fractured the wings and legs of birds and the legs of animals to prevent their escape, but I never dreamt that the lowest savages would apply such brutal

[245]

measure to human beings.) These unfortunate men were in terrible agony and beyond all help, they had been in the water for three days, and all we could do was to remove them to our camp.

No sooner had we brought the poor creatures in than all the porters came up to my tent; they were terrified and looked to me to get them away safely. It was obvious that unless I could do something to pacify them they would all desert during the night. As I was well armed I felt certain that as long as we remained in a large body there was not much likelihood of being attacked, but to persuade the terrified porters to take the same view was an altogether different matter. Finally I resorted to threats and warned them that the first one who attempted to escape would be shot down without compunction; I also pointed out that there was much greater danger in being caught in the bush away from the column than in remaining together. This seemed to pacify them and I felt comparatively safe for the night.

That night we kept the camp well illuminated by means of big fires, and I had sentries posted at all points. Although I was tired, I did not dare to sleep. Outside my tent were the three wounded men. For hours they moaned, whilst from a tree near by an owl sent forth its cheerless calls.

It is strange how one can be affected by unimportant things in such circumstances. Up to now the real danger we were in had not affected my nerves in any noticeable manner, but the hooting of that owl served to completely unnerve me. It would have been easy enough to drive it away by firing at it, but I feared that a shot in the dark might be taken for an alarm by my porters and be the signal for a wholesale desertion under cover of darkness, the thing I wished most to avoid. Finally my nerves were worked up to such a pitch that I began to regard the hooting of the stupid bird as a foreboding of impending evil. I went out in the dark and fired two shots in the direction from which the sounds had come. After that all was quiet except for the groaning of the three natives outside my tent. My cook-boy pleaded with me to put the men out of their misery, and for several minutes I sat turning the idea over in my mind. Theirs was a hopeless situation; it was impossible to save them or alleviate their suffering. I could not take them with me nor could I prolong my stay, for my natives were terrified and only by threats had I persuaded them to stay for the night. There was no likelihood of my being able to keep them for another night in this vicinity, and I was certain that if I did not move off with the coming of daylight they would desert me at the first opportunity. It was now past midnight and at daybreak I would have to be on the move. I felt that the best thing to do would be to put an end to the suffering of the three men. There was no doubt as to the soundness of the argument, but whatever the justification, the idea of killing a man in cold blood is revolting, and reason as I would I could not bring myself to do it.

I went out and appealed to my sleepless porters to rearrange their loads so as to leave six men free to carry the wounded men. This, however, they would not do; they feared that such an act of sympathy would incite the cannibals to attack them.

At daybreak, when we were ready to move off, the three men were dead. I had taken the final desperate step and put an end to their suffering. My porters all insisted on returning the same way we had come, but this I refused to do, for I knew that the cannibalistic savages would regard any indication of fear on our part as a sign of weakness. For three weeks we had seen little or nothing of natives in the forest and during that time I had not had the slightest suspicion that we were actually amongst cannibals. That we had not been attacked before was due to the fact that we were in a large body and I had used firearms on many occasions along the way. Should we now return the same way we had come, immediately after seeing the cannibals' gruesome handiwork, they would rightly infer that we were afraid, and that would be fatal. I realised also that taking the porters back over a road with which they were acquainted would be further inducement for them to desert. I finally compromised with them and we agreed to strike out in the direction of the nearest police post, which was about two hundred miles away.

At best, my position was desperate, although I had no great fear of the cannibals whilst I could keep the column up to its present strength. The serious problem lay in preventing desertions. Up to now I had reasoned successfully with the porters and they appreciated the soundness of my arguments, but I knew that should anything happen to frighten them again, their reasoning powers would be paralysed by fear and then no arguments would hold them back. Once our number was reduced to a point where it could no longer command respect, I had no doubt as to what our fate would be. I never allowed an opportunity to pass without enlarging upon the obvious dangers of desertion. In this manner I managed to keep the column together, and for four days all went well.

We frequently came across honey-filled earthenware pots hanging on trees, a sure sign of human habitation, but we saw no natives. The villages we came to were newly deserted and as a rule we camped as far away from them as possible. On the fifth day we arrived at a large village and were surprised to find it inhabited. I was met by a native who appeared to be the chief; I explained that I was on my way to the police station and offered to exchange meat for such foodstuffs as he could supply. I was treated with the usual respect and taken to a hut where I was told I could do all my bartering with the villagers. I intended to remain at the hut only until I had exchanged sufficient foodstuffs for my natives and then to move off as far as possible from the village before camping for the night. Whilst waiting for the natives to bring their wares, in exchange for meat, I looked into the hut. Beaten tree bark was stacked around the walls to a height of about three feet. I was aware of an unpleasant odour in the place but as I could not detect the cause of it I took no further notice. In a short while I traded out all the meat I had and decided to move on. Whilst waiting for the porters to rearrange their loads, the cook came to me and asked if I had seen what was inside the hut. On my replying that there was only bark in the hut he said he could show me something more sinister. My curiosity aroused, I went and had a look. As he pulled aside some of the bark I could see the cause of the unpleasant smell I had noticed previously. It was part of the putrefying remains of a human body. I warned the cook to say nothing about it to the porters, and I immediately got the column on the move. We met several natives on the way who were not afraid to approach us and seemed more civilised, but for all that, I had had ample proof that cannibalism was an active practise in the district.

Two days later I came across a prospector near Kanga. He had a large gang of natives with him and all were returning to Kilo. He had been in the vicinity for two weeks and told me he had found a hundred and forty ounces of gold. He had also experienced trouble with his natives and, as they would not remain in the district, he was compelled to return to Kilo. At this point most of my natives decided to accompany the safari of the prospector; they had had enough of the district we were in and looked upon the advent of the prospector as a piece of fortune especially designed for their escape. I could not induce them to stay with me. The prospector, however, informed me that about three kilometres farther on I would find a large village where it would be possible to recruit all the porters I needed. I eventually persuaded the porters to see me through as far as the village, where I could replace

[250]

those who wanted to return. The prospector obligingly consented to accompany me to the village and there camp the night with me. He was better acquainted with the region than I was and seemed surprised that I had come so far on my journey without accidents. He told me that the district we were then in was ruled over by another chief, and although cannibalism was practically extinct the tribal customs did not differ much from those of the place I had just left. He said that there was no danger in so far as a European was concerned, and assured me that from there on to the police camp there was no risk of being molested provided I paid tribute to the chiefs according to custom.

We arrived at the village late in the afternoon and immediately set out to find the chief; on making inquiries we were told that he was at the other end of the village. We were puzzled at the vague manner in which the natives described the whereabouts of their chief, and could make little headway in locating him. Finally we got a native to guide us to his presence.

I have seen some of the worst aspects of cruelty in African native life, but I never saw anything so horrible as the scene which awaited us here. About 500 yards beyond the confines of the village some scaffolding had been erected to a height of about ten feet, and from a distance we could see nothing abnormal about it. But as we approached the meaning of it was brought home to us in no uncertain manner. This chief had died four days previously and we were now at the scene of the funeral rites. The corpse rested at the top of the scaffold, on flooring composed of thin poles. On the ground beneath the platform lay the five wives of the deceased man. They were bound together and, like the natives I had seen before, their arms and legs had been fractured. Here the women were to remain until the liquid which exuded from the corpse had dropped and anointed their heads. If by that time they themselves had not succumbed to their injuries, they would be killed and interred with the remains of their husband.

The horror of this nauseating scene left me speechless. The rite's unspeakable cruelty and the suffering of the victims meant nothing to those savages. It was of no use to argue with them. It was the custom; it had been done by their fathers before them, and they would continue to do likewise. Even now the attendants were gathering around and soon the final scene would be enacted. We did not wait, but hurriedly retraced our steps.

That night I thought matters over. I did not want to waste any more time in this accursed country, nor was there anything to induce me to return to Kilo; Kilo was much farther away than the Boma, and the latter place was only a few miles from the Uganda border. My prospector friend advised me that the best thing to do would be to recruit sufficient porters on the morrow and proceed to Langley's village. (I have never been able to discover how a native chief in this part came to be the possessor of an English name.) The march to Langley's village would require five days' time. My friend assured me that the natives in that section were much more civilised, and that I would be absolutely safe as long as I paid tribute. He had no doubt that the natives to be recruited the following day would see me through, especially if I were to supply them with an abundance of meat. This would be easy enough to do, as there was plenty of game about.

The following morning I was not surprised to learn that my own porters had become thoroughly aware of the gruesome funeral rite of the previous day. That was the last straw, and with the exception of my cook, a personal boy, and two gunbearers, they all demanded to be paid off; nothing could persuade any of them to continue with me. I then recruited an ample staff of one hundred porters from amongst the villagers. I had serious doubts as to the advisability of carrying on the trip with porters secured in a village where such barbarous rites were observed, but my friend eased my mind on that score. By nine o'clock we parted company and I set out for Langley's village.

On the third day thereafter we arrived at another village. So far everything had gone well, but no sooner did we arrive at the chief's hut and my porters deposited their loads, which consisted mainly of salt and ivory, than they departed en masse, leaving only a few to ensure that I removed nothing before I had seen the chief and paid the tribute. My new porters' bad behaviour and the excited manner in which various groups were talking convinced me that something had happened to upset the tranquillity. The harrowing experiences of the past weeks led me to believe that they were plotting against me, and I heartily cursed my foolishness for allowing myself to be persuaded that there was no danger in carrying on with the trip. I quickly examined my firearms—I carried two of each, shotgun, rifle, and revolver—and after filling the magazines I sat down and waited, determined to sell my life as dearly as possible. But the precaution was unnecessary. A while later the chief, Gulu by name, arrived. After explaining that I was on my way to Langley's village and was going from there to the Boma, I asked him to collect his customary tribute. He promptly took nine loads of salt, after which he instructed my porters, who had now all returned, to take my belongings to a suitable spot where I could camp for the night.

Shortly after I had pitched my tent and settled down I was favoured with a visit from Gulu. He was greatly agitated. Earlier in the day, and before my arrival, a neighbouring tribe had successfully raided his village and taken a number of women and goats. Amongst the captured women were Gulu's wives. He had now come to ask my assistance in recovering the wives and other property. He was quite certain that this would not be difficult, with the aid of firearms. Then, if the expedition was successful, my remuneration for the part I had to play was to be one goat. This was a totally unexpected development and one fraught with danger. I had no intention of getting mixed up in a tribal dispute, for my recent experiences thereabouts had convinced me that the least I had to do with these people the better it would be for me. On the other hand, to refuse the assistance Gulu expected might also involve me in unpleasantness and danger. I was painfully aware that my entire gang of natives was newly recruited and might at any moment decide to desert and leave me at the mercy of the chief, and without his assistance I knew I would not be able to recruit one porter. Here, if ever, was a situation which needed diplomacy.

After assuring the chief that even if the outrage had been committed against me personally I could not be more concerned than I was at that moment, I pointed out that we were ill-equipped for an expedition of revenge. Did he not know that my gang had been recruited at the previous village, and were ignorant in the use of firearms? To this he replied that I had four natives who had not been recruited at the previous village and that each of them would be able to handle a rifle. I assured him that although these natives had been with me for some time, I had never instructed them in the art of shooting—a statement my natives stoutly supported. In order to convince him that to fire a rifle needed special training, I slipped my rifle's safety-catch to "safe" and invited him to fire a shot. After he had failed to do so, I took the rifle and fired at a stone some distance away, the force of the bullet smashing it to bits. So far the bluff had worked well, and he was quite convinced that the firing of a gun needed special training. I then suggested that as I was due to meet a friend at Langley's village, which was little more than a day's march from there, I would hasten to that point and return with my friend. This was, of course, untrue. I had not the slightest idea that there was any European within a hundred miles of the chief's village. But, in scheming out my own salvation, I was unknowingly signing the death warrant of a fellow wanderer.

The chief accepted my suggestion, and then to make sure that I would return with the necessary assistance he asked me as a guarantee of good faith to leave another nine loads of salt, a request I was only too willing to meet. Shortly after he left me a group of natives from the village came and installed themselves near my camp. On being asked what they wanted they said they were staying for the night. I suspected that they had been sent by the chief to prevent my escape under cover of darkness; but, on the other hand, my porters were all in league with the chief and it was therefore not necessary for him to take this precaution. Could it be that they had come to wait for a favourable opportunity to dispose of me during the night, so as to secure my rifles? It was a delicate position and caused me much uneasiness. The craving for tribal revenge could incite this savage chief to commit an outrage which, under normal conditions, he would not think of doing. I discussed the matter with my cook and we decided that the best plan would be to keep guard all night and not allow my three other natives to go to sleep. He was quite convinced that we were to be murdered that night, and again started to reproach me with the old saw about his mother being left childless. On no other occasion did he mention her, but in times like these he was a most dutiful son.

As soon as darkness set in I handed each of my

Members of a Ubangi cannibal tribe.

The Ubangi killers of Dickson. Photographed some days
later in their village, by the author.

four natives a gun and warned them that if they permitted themselves to drop off to sleep their sleep would be a lasting one. The natives from the village kept up a continual conversation and, like us, they kept awake all night. I was happy when dawn arrived. To this day I have not been able to decide whether those natives were sent there to prevent me from escaping, or whether they were simply biding their time for a favourable opportunity to dispose of us.

That morning, as soon as possible, we set out for Langley's village. There, I knew, I would be beyond the reach of Chief Gulu. Langley was a powerful chief, a comparatively civilised native, and in no way hostile to Europeans. From there to the Boma was only a short distance, and I felt certain that if I could reach his village my safety would be assured.

Under pretext of being in a hurry to return, so as to carry out my agreement with Gulu, I persuaded the porters to do a double march that day. In accomplishing this I forged one more link in the chain of circumstances that was to lead to the death of another. For, travelling along a road that intersected the one on which I was travelling, and making for the same village from which I had escaped that morning, was a European named Dickson. From the information available after the tragedy it was apparent that Dickson arrived at the place where the two roads intersected only a few minutes after I had passed that point. Had I met this stranger on his way to Gulu's village I should naturally have warned him of the danger in proceeding there.

Late that night I arrived at Langley's village. I explained to him all that had happened to me at Gulu's village. He told me that I had acted very wisely in absenting myself from the vicinity, and said that nine bags of salt was a small price to pay in exchange for one's life. He knew Gulu, and was quite certain that blood alone would wipe out his grievance against the raiding chief. He surprised me further by saying that another European was camped near by, and offered to take me there.

Some hundreds of yards from Langley's village a young man named Bancock was camped. He had advanced to that place and was now awaiting the remainder of his expedition. He was on his way to the Sudan border for a six months' elephant hunt. I related to him my experiences of the past month and my failure to reach Matadi on my way to England via the West Coast. My plans having failed, I was more or less at a dead end, and had nothing definite in view. We discussed matters for a while, and as I was well equipped and able to come in on equal terms, we decided to hunt in partnership. I accepted this as the best possible consolation for my failure to carry out my original plan. Bancock gave promise of being an excellent companion and I considered myself lucky, on the whole, to have met him at this point. I was completely exhausted after my adventurous journey and decided to rest for a few days.

The following morning I paid off all the porters and told them to go back and tell Gulu that my "friend" did not wish to take part in the expedition to recover his wives and property, and that it was of no use for me to return on my own. With this I expected to have done with Gulu and his troubles, and considered the nine loads of salt and the goat I was to have received a small sacrifice to make in exchange for my safety. But the matter did not end with that, for on the fifth day after my arrival at Langley's village a runner passed through on his way to report at the Boma that a European had been murdered at Gulu's village.

It happened that Dickson had arrived at Gulu's village on the day after my departure from that place. His arrival could not have been more inopportune, for the chief naturally took him to be the mythical friend whom I had mentioned. The return of the porters, who carried my negative message to the chief, effectively closed all avenues of escape to the unfortunate Dickson. Gulu did not intend to let a second opportunity for revenge slip through his fingers. Armed Europeans rarely visited those parts and he must have regarded the arrival of Dickson and his firearms as timely aid to his cause. Dickson was landed on the horns of a dilemma and evidently choosing what must have appeared to him the lesser of two evils, he accompanied the chief on his expedition of vengeance. The expedition was successful and Gulu recovered his wives and property, plus interest. Up to this point everything had worked according to plan, but for some inexplicable reason Dickson had elected to camp two miles from Gulu's village and in the direction of the village they had raided. Dickson remained in this camp whilst Gulu and his men returned to their village to celebrate the victory.

Later in the day some of the victims of the raid turned up at Dickson's camp and demanded that he restore their losses or otherwise lend his assistance in evening matters with Gulu. They were all armed with bows and arrows and other implements of native warfare. Their attitude was distinctly aggressive and, too late, Dickson must have realised that he had become involved in an interminable quarrel from which there was small hope of escape. But he was evidently not a man to be intimidated and he rushed into his tent for his rifle. On seeing this, one of the natives shot an arrow at him, but missed, after which they all hastily decamped.

Had Dickson left the matter at that all might have gone well, but he foolishly followed the natives into the forest. Whether he intended to do more than frighten them is impossible to tell, but on seeing one of the natives aim an arrow at him, he fired. The native fell dead with a bullet through the neck. The next instant Dickson was struck in the shoulder with a poisoned arrow, from the effects of which he died shortly afterwards. These were the events the runner had been sent to report to the Boma.

Bancock and I immediately prepared to set out for the scene of the tragedy, whilst the runner went on to the Boma to report the matter to the officer-in-charge.

When we arrived at the village, Gulu also furnished us with an account of the affair and it was corroborated by Dickson's headman. Gulu assured us that Dickson had willingly accompanied him on the expedition of vengeance, a statement I did not believe for a moment; but the headman could give us no information on the subject as he had not been present at the interview. He said that his master had only mentioned to him that they were all in a very critical position. There was nothing further to do but await the arrival of the police. In the meanwhile I ordered Gulu to return the nine loads of salt as well as six others which he had taken in excess of his due. He was inclined to dispute this command, but the position was reversed this time—we commanded twelve firearms—and I gave him the option of carrying out the order or facing the business end of an elephant gun. The salt was returned in due course.

Three days later a commissaire and a batch of askaris arrived on the scene. The details of the tragedy were explained to him and he asked us to accompany him to look for the culprits. On arriving at the murderers' village we found that they had disappeared. For two days we searched the neighbourhood but could find no trace of them.

The next morning the commissaire said he had to return to his post. He expressed his regret at our failure to locate the culprits; he did not think it worth while to go to further trouble in the matter and advised us to quit the neighbourhood as soon as possible. Whereupon he left us. We were not satisfied to leave the matter at that, and continued the search. That afternoon we returned to the village and there Dickson's headman recognised three of the culprits. They were sitting near a hut where I photographed them. They refused to accompany us to the Boma, and as the discussion progressed, many other natives gathered around. They were all armed with bows and arrows which we knew to be poisoned. Had we rounded up the guilty ones in the forest we might have been able to remove them by force, but in their own village this was not possible, and it would have been foolish to attempt it.

As soon as possible after this identification of the culprits we visited the ·Boma and I handed over the photographs to the officer who had come out to investigate the tragic event. But I might as well have saved myself the trouble, for although I remained in the vicinity for six months after that, hunting elephant, I heard no more about the matter. It is doubtful if anything further was ever done. One may pardon the officials, for they were well aware of the risks which attended an expedition into this savage country and they adopted the policy of letting sleeping dogs lie.

The death of Dickson· affected me deeply, for I felt that I had been an unwitting accessory to it. The tragedy was aggravated by the fact that he was the sole support of an aged mother.

Bancock and I gradually moved to the Sudan border, where we had a very successful season. At the end of our hunt we moved on to Amulah's village, over the border, where we waited for our porters to bring up the ivory and the rest of our belongings before returning South.

The Cannibals of Ubangi

Whilst waiting here I decided to make a hurried trip farther into the Sudan to examine the prospects of an elephant hunt at a future date. I left Bancock in charge to arrange for the reception and eventual expedition of our goods. My trip lasted three weeks and on my return I found my friend on the border-line of insanity. In order to humour the chief and enlist his support in the recruiting of porters to transport our goods, he had invited him to listen to a portable gramophone which we carried with us. That was Bancock's undoing. The least thing he required from Amulah after that had to be paid for with gramophone music. Only those who have travelled the wilds of Africa can realise to what extent one is dependent upon the village chiefs. In paying for favours with gramophone music and proving his hospitality in the same manner, Bancock declared that he had played the same record fifty thousand times; no other music appealed to Amulah, and for three weeks Bancock played that one tune incessantly night and day. No wonder he awaited my return with impatience!

The day following my return to Amulah's village we started on our journey South. Not expecting any trouble enroute, we went ahead of our porters and in the afternoon selected a suitable spot to camp for the night. By sunset all porters had arrived except two boys who had been with us since the beginning of the hunt and who did not belong to Amulah's tribe; they carried two metal boxes which contained some of our personal belongings. By midnight they had not appeared and we suspected foul play.

HORNED DEATH

Early the following morning we returned the way we had come. About two miles from Amulah's village we found the two natives; one was dead, whilst the other was in a dying condition. We went on to the village and asked Amulah the reason for this cowardly attack, pointing out that during the whole time our safari had stayed at his village he was daily supplied with large quantities of meat, and had availed himself of our hospitality. He replied that previous to our arrival some troops had been stationed near his village and they had greatly offended him and his people. He professed to know nothing of the attack on our porters, but attributed it to the grievance his people harboured against Europeans as a result of the behaviour of the troops. There was nothing to be gained by prolonging the discussion. We collected our boxes, which were still intact, and proceeded on our journey South with a feeling of satisfaction at leaving this inhospitable and savage country.

During this trip I had seen the very worst elements of African native life. Nearly forty years have elapsed since then, but those memories have not faded. Indelibly stamped on my mind are the savage rites at the death of the old chief and the lingering death of the cannibals' victims. Today, and not very far from where I witnessed these inhuman acts, the same customs are still being practised, but on a much smaller scale. The advance of civilisation is slowly changing all that, and I can only hope that this black page in the history of Africa will soon fall into the limbo of forgotten things

[264]

22: JOE DUBBIN, UNCROWNED KING

AFTER the boom following the arrival of the first train in Northern Rhodesia a period of calm set in. It was then that news began to circulate about impending activities in the Belgian Congo. At that time the hero of this story, Joe Dubbin, was conducting an indifferent cattle-trading business in Northern Rhodesia. Like many others, Joe became interested in the future prospects of the Congo, and early in 1908 he decided to try his luck in the new country. At that time there was no railway service to the Congo and Joe set out on a bicycle. He arrived at the Star Mine several days later, with an eye to business.

In those days it was no easy matter for a foreigner to obtain trading rights in the Congo. Although that country was known as the Congo FREE State, the difficulties in obtaining trading rights were so great that few, if any, foreigners ever attempted to secure licences. Joe could speak a little South African Dutch and in this respect he was lucky, as several of the Belgian officials were of Flemish origin and, owing to the similarity of the two languages, he found it easy to converse with them.

On arriving at the Star Mine, Dubbin immediately started to explore the possibilities of obtaining a trading right. He was informed that the nearest

[265]

administrative post was one hundred miles away, and to this post he forthwith proceeded on his bicycle. Arrived at the post, Joe informed the Administrator of the object of his visit. This official, in adhering to the established policy, immediately started to put all kinds of obstacles in the way, and finally informed the applicant that it would be necessary to present a proper map, clearly defining the area in which he intended to trade. Joe was practically illiterate and the only way he could have the map prepared was to return to the Star Mine and appeal to his friends there to assist him in the matter. On informing the official of his intentions, that worthy stated that he intended leaving his post two days later on a tour of inspection in the Lake Mwero district. As this was during the rainy season, his idea was to impress upon Joe the futility of returning to the post in the near future. Without flagrantly violating international law by openly refusing a trading right to a British subject, the official felt satisfied that he had, nevertheless, achieved his object. But in this he had underestimated the determination of the applicant, for Joe immediately remounted his bicycle and returned to the Star Mine where, late that night, the plans were prepared in accordance with the law.

At two p. m. the following day the administrator was amazed to see Joe back in his office with the required plans. The courage of a man who could accomplish a two-hundred-mile journey in two days in that part of the country, in the midst of the rainy season, made a favourable impression on the official, and after some discussion he granted Joe the first trading right ever issued to a foreigner in the Belgian Free State. Joe's intention was to establish himself as a trader and, at a later date, to try to enter a far more profitable enterprise, ivory and rubber trading, which was not covered by an ordinary trading licence such as he had now secured.

The ivory and rubber trade was at that time in the hands of a privileged few on whom Leopold II bestowed his favours. The Congo was his personal property and his method was to grant concessions to Belgian companies who, in turn, employed agents on a liberal commission basis. It was this system that was responsible for the abuses that inevitably crept in and later led to an inquiry into the slavery in the ivory and rubber trade in the Congo. That there were individual cases of excesses cannot be denied, and the conditions under which this trade was conducted influenced the situation to a very large extent. Certain it is that most of the reports of slavery and brutality were greatly exaggerated by people who were in no way competent to judge. Such excesses as did occur did not receive official sanction but were mostly the acts of unscrupulous agents plying a profitable trade.

When Leopold II died, in 1909, and Albert ascended the throne, a complete change came about. In May of the same year Albert, who was then Crown Prince, had visited the Congo and had left a very favourable impression on all those who were privileged to come in contact with him. Soon after his ascension rubber and ivory licences were granted to the general public without preference, and Joe Dubbin was the first to land an important consignment of these products at Elisabethville, which had by now assumed the proportions of an important town. When Joe landed his first consignment of rubber—a caravan of 1,000 porters—in Elisabethville he created a certain amount of jealousy amongst officials of the old school. His trading licences were in order legally, but the importance of his transactions served to create suspicion as to the methods he employed.

The rubber trade was confined almost exclusively to the Baluba country, in the Luabala district. The Balubas were at that time a very large and savage tribe but in some mysterious manner Joe had acquired an influence over them that was never equalled before or since. The natives looked upon him as a god and there was nothing he could not obtain from them for the sake of asking. On one occasion he actually persuaded the chief of a district to force his people to leave their homes in the agricultural plains and proceed to the mountainous country where the rubber vine grew, and stay there for several months to prepare rubber for him. Unlike many others who have exercised an influence over the savage tribes of Africa, Joe never resorted to brutality to attain his prestige. He was simply an opportunist who traded on the credulity and ignorance of the natives.

I was present on one occasion when two chiefs appealed to him to settle a feud which had endured for many years and which had reached alarming proportions. Joe was at that time at a native village where his assistance had been asked to dispose of a band of scavenger dogs amongst whom a virulent disease had broken out. As the feud affected a large number of natives in that district, Joe determined to take advantage of the situation and impress his power upon those concerned. He forthwith invited the two chiefs to present themselves at the village that afternoon. In the meantime he had arranged to have the dogs collected and tied to a tree. At the appointed hour the chiefs and their followers arrived on the scene. Meanwhile, unknown even to his personal servants, Joe had carefully prepared a piece of poisoned meat for each dog, and when all the followers of the two warring chiefs had arrived, Joe unobtrusively had a piece of poisoned meat served to each dog. The poison he employed for this purpose was strychnine, which, as everybody knows, is a slow killer. No sooner had the meat been served to the dogs than Joe started to explain to the natives that he was possessed of supernatural powers. Into a basin of clear water he had slyly placed a liberal supply of permanganate of potash; he then explained to his audience that he was going to change the water into blood. In a few seconds the miracle was an accomplished fact. But more miracles were to follow. From his pocket Joe produced a hypodermic syringe; he now told the awe-stricken natives that the "blood" contained magical qualities which would produce instantaneous death at his command. He then started spraying the liquid in the direction of the poisoned dogs, taking great care that none of the liquid should come into contact with the poisoned animals. He made a great ceremony of the proceedings and told the natives to watch results and be silent. A few seconds later the poison began to take effect and by the time the third dog had died not a native could be seen in the vicinity. Terror-stricken, they had fled from the neighbourhood.

The following day Joe sent his messengers to summon the two chiefs and their followers to his presence again. When they arrived, Joe immediately stated that it was his desire that there should be an end to the feud. He had various other wishes which he carefully outlined to them, at the same time strongly emphasizing his ability to dispense death at will, and that distance was no obstacle. At the end of his oration the two warring tribes dispersed. The feud was at an end. The effects of all this upon the imaginative minds of those superstitious natives can well be imagined. From that day onwards, Joe was known to the Baluba tribe as "Father." He became the uncrowned king of the Balubas—the biggest and most savage tribe of the Congo—and no power could diminish the respect in which he was held by them. At a later date even the organised efforts of the Belgian government failed to shake the confidence and fear which Joe had inspired in the minds of those natives.

For two years things went smoothly and Joe made a great name for himself as a hunter and trader. His procedure was to trade ivory and rubber in the outlying districts and send his stores to a central depot with a trained native in charge of the caravans. As time went on his caravans were subjected increasingly to interferences on the part of minor officials. Such meddling was all the more aggravating because redress could be obtained only by appealing to Elisabethville, many hundreds of kilometres to the south. Joe and his boon companion, Tim, finally decided that they would take the law into their own hands, regardless of head offices and consuls in Elisabethville. At this time they were stationed at one of their trading centres on Lake Mwero, a beauty spot of the Congo. Because of the numerous irritations they decided to shift nearer to their central depot, and with this object in view they sent off their personal belongings with native porters, their intention being to follow the caravan a few days later.

The following day the headman in charge of the caravan returned and reported that they had been held up. The porters had been beaten and the goods confiscated and sent to a Belgian administrative post in the vicinity. As the safari consisted exclusively of personal goods this interference was all the more annoying, and according to Joe, an unprovoked outrage. Joe and Tim immediately took up their rifles, armed a number of their most trustworthy natives and set off for the post. They had definitely decided to shoot the matter out with the erring official. Fortunately for all concerned, when they arrived at the post the official was absent. The other officials present were sympathetic and apologised for the inconvenience caused, but beyond that they were not prepared to go. They pleaded ignorance of the facts of the case and could do nothing in the absence of the administrator of the post, who was responsible for the interference. But this did not satisfy Joe, and he promptly ordered the Belgian askari who was in charge of the store to hand over the confiscated goods. The askari meekly obeyed; Joe and his companion signed a receipt and departed with the confiscated goods.

This incident was speedily related throughout the country and gave Joe an additional measure of notoriety. He was now considered superior even to the government and the law. But this fact remained— he had made armed entry into a police post and removed goods by threats. But Joe was still unsatisfied; he and Tim decided to go in search of the erring official and demand an apology. A short time later they met the administrator, who was accompanied by the chief medical officer of the territory. In the ensuing exchange of words the doctor explained that he had been present when Joe's caravan was held up and that the administrator had told him the caravan belonged to one of the most notorious bandits in the country. This was a libellous description of Joe, who had as exemplary a record as any European to be found in the country. This allegation merely helped to show that malice was responsible for the interference, and did not improve matters. Things were about to take an ugly turn when the doctor managed to restore calm, emphasizing that the official was anxious to make amends and apologise for the trouble he had caused. Joe insisted that he had come out to settle his grievance in a different manner, and if the official was not prepared to shoot it out he would have to apologise to him in the presence of the paramount chief and as many of his people as could be gathered to the spot for the occasion. In due course the official apology was made, in accordance with Joe's requirements. Whereupon Joe made a speech explaining the position to all present and announcing that he had decided to impose a fine of one hundred francs on the official. The threatening manner in which this announcement was made was apparent to everyone and the fine was paid promptly in the presence of the onlookers.

It was twelve months later, when the governor of the province made his annual tour, that the details of this incident were related to him and a warrant for Joe's arrest was issued immediately. Joe's popularity with the Baluba tribe, as well as his influence over them, had for a long time been a sore point with high government officials, and at the subsequent trial, which lasted over a month, evidence was produced to the effect that he was about to make an attempt to turn that part of the country into a republic which he intended to call the "Dubbinal Republic." Throughout the trial, which dealt not only with the incidents I have related but with many other thorny problems, there was a feeling that the matter would lead to international complications. Joe was finally fined one thousand francs for "forcing an armed entry into an administrative post"—the incident with the administrative official being overlooked. The fine was paid promptly, and immediately afterwards Joe was given a number of fantastic contracts, through government intervention, that helped to make him one of the wealthiest Europeans in the Congo.　　　[273]

There is much in the career of Dubbin that I have purposely omitted, it being unsuitable material for a book that deals with a much less explosive subject. Dubbin, as I have said, collected enormous wealth in the Congo, but he did not live long to enjoy it, as he died in Durban a few years later.

23: A ROUGH TIME IN THE RIFT VALLEY

Amongst the several employments into which I have been drawn was that of Field Officer on the Red Locust Staff. At this particular time—which I have not the slightest difficulty in recalling!—I was stationed in the Rift Valley. The campaign against the red locusts was in full swing and daily my crew of native porters had to transport several tons of bait from another camp some six miles away.* I had

---

* Editor's Note: Of more than passing interest is the author's off-record comment concerning his work with the Red Locust Staff. In a letter to his American friend, Elmer Keith of North Fork, Idaho, which was written from the field in Tanganyika, under the date of December 15, 1945, Mr. Burger states: ". . . I have finished my two months' hunting expedition and am now engaged on research work in locust destruction. From this you will be able to imagine the kind of country I am in—vast swamps, where the temperature soars to 125 degrees in the day and falls to zero at night. Here we are in the breeding haunts of the Red Locust, but mosquitoes and almost every other pest one can think of breed just as fast as any locust, and whilst I am busy destroying locusts the other pests get busy destroying me—the only difference is that I work on a larger and faster scale and I live in hopes that I shall be able to complete my job before they complete theirs!"

That American readers may appreciate the tremendous importance of the work done by the Locust Control, the South and East African Year Book and Guide (1947 Edition) offers the following facts: "It is estimated that, from 1927-31, locusts throughout Africa destroyed crops, etc., to the value of 6,000,000 pounds (sterling) and that preventive measures cost 1,000,000 pounds. The 1933-34 loss over Africa has been estimated at 7,000,000 pounds. As an instance of the vast dimensions a locust invasion may assume, a swarm that passed over the Red Sea in 1889 was estimated to weigh 42,850,000,000 tons. This swarm covered 2,000 sq. m."

The bait, referred to by the author, is maize bran or maize meal, poisoned with arsenate of soda. This bait is spread in the locusts' breeding grounds and kills the insects while they are still in the hopper stage. During 1944-45, the Union of South Africa expended 81,662 pounds (sterling) on locust destruction, and that amount included payments for domestic stock that accidentally ate locust poison.

put aside my rifles as the season was too far advanced for hunting and, in addition, I had experienced a great deal of trouble with a consignment of "dud" ammunition. The use of my heavy-calibre rifle had been marked by misfires and hang-fires (delayed actions) which, at best, made the hunting of dangerous game an unnecessarily risky occupation.

One afternoon the porters came to inform me that they had been chased by a buffalo bull, one of a herd of five, and asked me to go out and destroy the animal. I did not believe the story and saw in it only a ruse to get me out to shoot a bit more meat for their own benefit. But the next day several porters came rushing into camp minus their loads, which they said they had had to discard in order to escape from the same aggressive buffalo. Several hours later the rest of the convoy arrived in camp and corroborated the porters' story. This was a serious thing as, apart from the fact that supplies were urgently needed, there was the danger of a fatality should the buffalo run down any of the porters. The obvious thing to do was to go out and dispose of the troublesome animal before he could completely disorganise the work.

My old hunting natives were all in camp when the matter was discussed and I promised the porters that I would go out early next morning to see what could be done. I then returned to my tent to attend to some current work, whilst outside a heated discussion developed between my hunting boys and the porters, who were locally conscripted labourers. Their discussion continued for more than an hour and I could hear frequent references to "nyati" (buffalo) and "musito" (forest), but I took no particular notice, as natives— especially when they are of different tribes—will frequently argue for hours over mere trifles. But now I could hear Ndege say that he was "not going" and that he would refer the matter back to me. In the next moment my veteran tracker was at the tent door. "Ati Bwana, we have had a long discussion between ourselves and we have not been able to agree. We would like you to think this matter over again and decide what is best for us to do." "Yes, Ndege," I replied, "if I can help you I will do so, but I have not listened to the argument, so if you will tell me what it is all about I will help you if I can."

"You see, Bwana, tomorrow you want us to go after that buffalo and we think it is a bad business. I have been to that part several times and it is bad country. Long grass and plenty of trees, but the trees are full of long thorns, and if one had to climb one of them in a hurry one could not go far; the thorns are fully as long as my middle finger and sharp as needles. How could one possibly climb up such trees in a hurry in case of danger? You have heard it said that this buffalo is out for trouble. Better leave him alone, he is sure to go away from here in good time."

I countered, "But what do the local natives say about it, Ndege?"

"That is what the argument has been about, Bwana. They are not hunters, but only a lot of shenzies,* and they say that, thorns or no thorns, when

---

* Shenzie: a mongrel.

a buffalo chases one one does not think of such things, and if we have to run up one of those trees we will do so without any difficulty. I cannot see it their way and no more can the rest of our men. That is why I have come to ask your opinion."

• "My opinion, Ndege, is that far and away the best thing would be to avoid the necessity of having to run up those trees. But if it should so happen that one has to do so, I daresay the thorns won't be such a great obstacle. It is always easier, and better, to pull thorns out of your hide than to pull out buffalo horns. If the occasion should arise I can assure you that I will not let thorns stand in *my* way."

Ndege protested, "That is what these shenzies here say, Bwana, but I cannot see it that way. Those thorns . . ."

A week later Ndege came to me to announce that he had just rid himself of the last thorn in one of his legs! In going after that bull, the following day, we struck trouble early, for as soon as he had come under fire he hit back in no uncertain manner. Ndege, in spite of his age and doubts, ran up one of those thorn trees at an incredible speed, and most of the rest of my gang had followed suit. Ndege's dire prediction as to what the thorns would do was settled most convincingly, and for days the trackers, spotters, and porters found it difficult to move on account of the thorns that were embedded in various parts of their bodies. Also, there occurred something far more serious than injuries from thorns. On this outing one of the hunting natives came to grief and my otherwise excellent record, in so far as serious accidents are concerned, received a nasty stain.

As I have said, the season was too far advanced for buffalo hunting. The heavy rains had started some six weeks earlier and the Rift Valley was overgrown with long grass. That morning we had got onto the trail early and followed it into fairly dense clusters of bush. The trail was easy to follow as it had rained the night before and the ground was marshy. The tracks showed clearly that the herd consisted of five bulls, and after an hour or so of trailing we spotted the troublesome bull. The natives identified him readily as, unlike the four others of the group, he was of a rufous-brown colour. At the moment we saw him he was alone on the outside of a large cluster of thorn bush. From where I stood it was too difficult to shoot, owing to the long grass. We then started stalking him carefully until only about 120 yards separated us. The stalk in long grass had left me rather breathless, and before taking the shot I decided to wait for a few moments so as to recover fully from the effort. I was watching the bull closely when suddenly he turned and disappeared in the long grass. We maneuvered carefully to see what had happened to him. He had gone to lie down in a mud pool. In spite of the short distance separating us I found the target much too unsatisfactory. The far end of the cluster which afforded us cover stretched within a few feet from where the bull was lying, and a short stalk would bring me to the rear of him. From that position I could place a shot behind the head, always a safe shot on buffalo. All the situation needed now was careful and noiseless stalking. We were crawling around the edges of the cluster and all was going according to plan when there was a great crashing of branches right at my side. We had neglected to consider that the four other bulls might have taken shelter in the very cluster of bush we were encircling on our stomachs! We were within five yards of them before they became aware of us, and now they were rushing off at top speed across the plain. With them went the bull I was after.

I soundly berated myself for not chancing a shot when the bull was so close to me, but reproaches were not of much practical use, and all we could do was to follow the trail again. We set out and within fifteen minutes had again caught up with the herd. They were in the open plain and about 200 yards beyond the last clump of bush behind which we could take cover. From this distance I must shoot, as it would be useless to try to stalk the herd closer in open country.

In view of the trouble I had experienced with the ammunition for my heavy-calibre rifle, I now decided to use a medium .333 rifle for which I had a few good rounds of soft-nose ammunition. With this extremely accurate weapon I have shot many buffaloes and other big game, and at 200 yards I had no doubt I could place my shot where I wanted it. In this case, the bull's right shoulder was exposed to me. I fired and placed the shot successfully, but at that range the lighter rifle, with soft-nose ammunition, did not have the penetration to reach either the lung or the heart. I could distinctly see the bull "taking it," but instead of going down to the shot he rushed off with the herd. For a hundred yards or so he kept up with the others, but then abruptly his pace slackened and we saw him turn off to the right and make for a cluster of bush. Trotting slowly, he disappeared from view. As we advanced farther we could see that beyond the cluster of bush he had made for there was a larger and denser cluster. It was quite impossible to tell which cover he had made for, but it was certain that he had gone into hiding in one of them, as beyond the far cluster was open plain and we could see no sign of him.

Between the two clusters there were about 200 yards of open country. We had to ascertain now in which of these two clusters the bull was hiding. I suspected that he had gone to the far one as it was much the larger and denser of the two. The natives, however, were certain that he was so badly wounded that he would not go beyond the first cluster. After some discussion we agreed that we would circle around the far cluster at a safe distance and if the bull was not detected we would turn back; on our return we would pass midway between the two clusters, which would give us a safety margin of about one hundred yards in each direction. By following this course and looking for tracks we could easily determine whether he had gone as far as the second cluster.

We circled around the far cluster without seeing any sign of the buffalo, and the natives ahead of me had already entered the gap. All eyes were fixed on the first cluster, as up to now no tracks had been seen leading across the gap. I was keeping to the rear of the trackers as I felt that from this position I could cover both danger points. Although we had seen no trace of the buffalo in the larger cluster we had just passed, nor any tracks across the gap, I had a feeling that the bull was in there. That he had not shown up so far might be due to the fact that he was incapable of movement on account of his wound. Normally, had he been where I expected him he should have charged ere now. At that moment my attention was drawn to one of the natives ahead pointing towards the smaller cluster of bush. I naturally thought he had spotted the buffalo in hiding there and I started to walk quickly to take up a good position in the event of a charge. Our every movement and attention was focused on the smaller cluster. Just then we heard a commotion behind us. As I had suspected, the bull was hiding in the large cluster and had taken cover so skillfully that none of us had noticed him. He was now making his long overdue charge. Quickly I raised my rifle to fire, but before I could get the bull in my sights I was knocked spinning sideways. A fool native, in his panic, had rushed against me from the side. By the time I could regain a shooting position it was too late. The bull had already passed me and was in full pursuit of some eight fleeing natives. To fire at the bull from this position was too risky, as the natives were in the direct line of fire. The animal was gaining rapidly on the natives, and in a matter of seconds he had come within a few yards of them. The native nearest him stumbled and fell, but hardly had he touched the ground before the bull tossed him. As the native took off into space I fired at the bull. I could hear the thud of the bullet as it struck home, and then, without further ado, the bull left his victim and made off for forest country. Now he was running on three legs only, but he still maintained a fast pace as he disappeared from view in the long grass. By this time Ndege and the rest of the gang had found safety in the tree tops—amongst the thorns. (It was five days later before I discovered why this bull, with his victim at his mercy, had suddenly elected to call it a day. I aimed low deliberately, in order to avoid any possible accident, and my bullet had landed just above the hoof, smashing the ankle into fragments. The sheer pain of that wound had forced the bull to retire from the scene.)

The native who had been tossed was crying and groaning when we reached him, but I was soon satisfied that the damage was not nearly as bad as it might have been. The bull had hooked a horn into the fleshy part of the native's right thigh and had left a gaping five-inch wound. Fortunately no bones were fractured and there were no internal injuries. The man was suffering from severe shock, and serious as the injury undoubtedly was, I felt relieved that a major tragedy had been averted. The wounded man was promptly carried back to camp, some three miles away, on an improvised stretcher. On our arrival there I carefully dressed his wound.

That night I slept hardly at all, for I realised that now there was a badly wounded buffalo in an area where hundreds of natives had to pass daily in order to bring up stores. Such an animal could not be allowed to remain a menace to the entire community, for in his present condition he would certainly attack without provocation. I knew that bull had to be brought down once and for all, and at the earliest possible moment.

The accident left a bad impression on all the natives, and this, along with the injuries some of them had received in climbing the thorny trees, made it difficult for me to muster sufficient help to track the buffalo successfully on the next day. A couple of my old hunting crew helped in a half-hearted sort of way, but it was quite obvious that, whilst they were trailing, they were at the same time praying that we would never see this buffalo again. When the trail led into close forest they refused to go farther and I was compelled to return to camp. The next day I was down with a dose of fever which kept me in bed for two days. On both of those days I sent out scouts to see whether they could locate the bull and on each day they reported having spotted him from a distance. He was keeping close to the forest country and was in a truculent mood, having shown signs of aggressiveness as soon as he had picked up their scent. He had not moved more than 500 yards from the scene of the accident and when last seen he was quite close to the four other members of the group. No doubt he would join them again during the night.

The next day I felt better and early in the morning I set off again after the buffalo. I had only one round left for my .333 rifle and for the rest I would have to fall back on the defective ammunition for my heavy-calibre rifle. We soon were on the trail and in quick time we spotted the five bulls. The wounded one was grazing nearest to us, fully 300 yards away, and at too great a distance for the lighter rifle. Finally I managed to reduce the distance to about 200 yards, and from there I was obliged to fire, as farther out there was no cover and no trees to climb in case of emergency.

Perhaps the fact of having only one good round at my disposal made me over-careful and I missed the bull completely. All five bulls immediately rushed off towards a small creek where the grass was twelve feet high. Directly in front of us were several tall ant-heaps and the highest of these we now climbed in order to observe the herd's movements in the tall grass. But by the time we had mounted the steep ant-heap the buffaloes had disappeared completely. Two of the natives had mounted another ant-heap near by and whilst we were still looking out for a sign of the buffaloes one of these natives called out that the herd had emerged on the far side of the intervening swamp. I immediately went over to the next ant-heap and from there I could see the buffaloes distinctly. I could see only four animals, but the natives both assured me that all five had crossed over. A dark object which I could not distinguish properly was, they said, the wounded bull lying down. The four others remained standing in a group right next to this spot. I have excellent eyesight at long distances and was not at all satisfied that this dark object was indeed a buffalo.

But as they were fully a thousand yards away and the sky was heavily overcast, I finally agreed that the natives were probably right. They were certain that they had seen the wounded bull walk as far as the tree where this dark object was now visible. Quite close to that spot were several other trees, and with careful stalking and close attention to the wind, I felt certain I could reach those trees unobserved and, even with the poor ammunition, get close enough to account for the bull. With the definite assurance of the two natives I felt comparatively safe in following the trail. I took two trackers with me and left an observer on the ant-heap. In the long grass I soon advanced beyond sight of the two trackers, but the trail was easy to follow and I stuck to it for about 200 yards. Now I noticed that one set of tracks had turned off sharply at right angles and on examining those tracks I noticed fresh blood on the grass! This was a terrifying discovery, for I realised immediately that the wounded bull had gone into ambush in the long grass. At any moment now he could be expected to charge—either from the back, as they usually do, or from the side. That he had not charged up to now was due to the fact that he was allowing me to walk right into the trap he had set for me. Even were I to retrace my steps, I felt certain he would not allow me to go far. I had seen him do exactly the same thing a few days before when he thought the natives were getting beyond charging distance. This was an alarming position to be in. Here in the dense grass visibility was reduced to a few feet and I would have little or no time to shoot should he rush at me suddenly; also, my heavy-calibre ammunition had lately proved so defective that utter reliance upon it in close quarters was out of the question. The slightest movement on my part now, I felt certain, would bring about what I feared most, the charge from close quarters. Around me all was silent; there was no sign or sound of the two trackers at my rear. I had just made up my mind to get down flat on my stomach and crawl back to safety when the observer from the ant-heap shouted out. As I turned around I saw a pair of horns coming in my direction, about a hundred yards to my right. The bull had gone to a small embankment from where he could watch my movements, and I was just in time to see his horns disappear in the long grass. He was coming straight for me and I knew that the next time those horns appeared they would be at two or three yards range, when he would be ready to toss me. Here was a truly desperate position which allowed for no delay. Quickly I realised that if I could not see the buffalo whilst he was charging through the dense grass, he also could not see me. If I could manage to get out of his line of charge unobserved he would certainly carry on in a straight line for some distance beyond where he had last seen me. His speed would be reduced very considerably by the wound he had sustained in his front leg, but even at that there was not the slightest possibility of my outdistancing him in a race to the ant-heap. The long grass would give him no difficulty, whilst for me it would make movement extremely laborious. There was only one hope for me and that was to get out of the line of charge as quickly and silently as possible, and then to keep moving towards the direction where I had last seen the pair of horns. This would put the greatest possible distance between us in the quickest time, and it would also bring me nearer to the ant-heap, whilst the bull would be running farther away from it. The wind, fortunately, was in my favour. With my course of action decided, I sprinted off at right angles for a distance of about fifteen yards, then I turned to the left, and all with as little noise as possible. I now proceeded towards a point on the embankment which would be well to the right of where I had last seen the buffalo. These movements were made in a fraction of the time needed to describe them. Up to now I had seen or heard no more of the buffalo, and as the seconds went by I felt confident that my ruse had been successful. At last I reached a place on the embankment which was at least seventy yards to the right of the place where the bull had taken off. Now I felt safe enough to take a breather and try to locate him. The native on the ant-heap was shouting continually, but I could not hear what he said. As for the buffalo, there was no sign of him anywhere. For some minutes I stood there in suspense, waiting for the buffalo to show up. Now the shouting native was also pointing far down to his left, and as I looked there I saw those horns. The buffalo was fully 200 yards from where I had taken off; there he was circling, with his head well up, and trying to pick up my scent. So far he had not seen me, and I felt confident that, even were he to spot me now, he could not overtake me in a race to that ant-heap, which I knew would be too steep for him to mount without offering an easy target. I set off at full speed for the ant-heap, a hundred yards away. Although I put every ounce of strength into that effort, it seemed as though I would never reach safety. When I finally reached the ant-heap I fell exhausted at its foot and the natives were obliged to pull me to the top. (The two trackers who had followed me on the trail had taken no chances and kept far behind me. At the first sign of trouble they had rushed back to safety, with plenty of time to spare.)

From the top of the ant-heap we tried to locate the buffalo, for he had again disappeared from sight. For several minutes we could see no sign of him. Then one of the natives spotted him as he emerged on the far side of the swamp and rejoined his companions. And there I was quite content to leave him for the time being. I had been through one of the most nerve-racking experiences of my life, and I certainly did not feel equal to any further strain that day.

For half an hour we sat and watched the five bulls grazing peacefully. The dark object was still there—and there it remains, for that matter, for we eventually found it to be the burnt trunk of a palm tree! How those natives ever persuaded themselves to believe that they had actually seen the wounded buffalo in the first place is entirely beyond my comprehension. Their powers of imagination might easily have got me killed, as I would never have dreamt of entering the long grass had I entertained any further doubt as to the whereabouts of the wounded animal.

The bull, with their assistance, had scored heavily at my expense. That he was full of cunning was evident from the manner in which he had gone into ambush and then selected an elevated spot from which to watch our movements. The only fault in his technique was his tendency to charge from a distance of 100 yards or more; his time over such a long course had upset the effectiveness of both charges in which we were involved. The native who had watched and shouted information during the second charge told me that the bull had not slowed up, but had carried out the charge at full speed and in a straight line. He also said that at any moment he expected to see me being tossed, as he had lost sight of me when I ducked into the grass.

The buffalo was still very much alive and now a greater menace than before. The only hopeful feature was that, on account of his wound, he would not willingly move far away from where we had left him and it would be easy to trail him down the next day. And the next day it must be, for I was determined to settle the score with that brute, in spite of bad ammunition and a gang of panicky natives.

Ndege had not accompanied me on this outing as he was still suffering from the effects of the thorns. The other trackers were not of much use, as had been proved by their actions earlier in the day. On my return to camp I informed Ndege that, thorns or no thorns, he would have to accompany me the following morning, and after much talk I persuaded five other natives to come along. The place at which we had left the five bulls was comparatively good country, with several trees and short grass. Good tracking and spotting was what I needed mostly, and of this I was assured by having Ndege on the job.

We set out in the morning and had been on the trail only a short time when one of the natives noticed some white tick birds, and on closer investigation we found that they were busy de-ticking the buffaloes. All five bulls were lying down in the shade of a big thorn tree. The first thing for us to do was to look for a suitable tree within shooting range, and then to stir the herd in an effort to identify the wounded bull. Some fifty yards to our right was a tree that would answer our purpose, and in the immediate vicinity there were several other trees that would also offer safety in case of danger. Ndege and another native were at my side, whilst the four others kept in the background. As soon as we reached the tree, which was about 150 yards from the bulls, Ndege shouted at the top of his voice. Immediately four animals jumped up, whilst the wounded one was slow to rise. The four started off at a fast gallop and soon disappeared in the wooded country, but the wounded bull stood his ground. His attitude was truculence itself, his head swinging savagely from side to side— a sure sign that he was about to charge. I opened fire, but once again I had a bad hang-fire. The bullet splashed mud in front of the bull. That was the signal for fireworks, and out he came in full charge. By this time Ndege and the other native had taken to the nearby tree, but as the bull was still a good hundred yards away, I aimed and pressed the trigger again. Click ... BANG! ... a hang-fire; then, another click ... BANG! It was time for me to look for safety in the tree!

No sooner was I securely seated in the tree than the raging bull arrived at its base, and only a few feet below me; now, however bad the ammunition, I could not miss him at such short range. I still had two rounds left in my magazine, and they should be ample to dispose of this unpleasant business. The bull began to circle around the tree, frothing at the mouth and hooking a horn into the trunk. When once again he faced me I pressed the trigger, with the muzzle only two feet from his head. This time there was no report at all—the firing-pin thumped a dead primer. Quickly I extracted the dud cartridge; once again I pressed the trigger, and the last cartridge in the magazine refused to fire. Ndege was perched only a few feet above me, and now I asked him to pass down the ammunition bag he always carried for me. In that bag there were some twenty rounds. But once again the cards were stacked all wrong, for Ndege, whilst following the trail earlier, had handed the bag to one of the natives and given him instructions to keep close to me. This was quite a normal thing to do, as it is not unusual for a hunter to be separated from his trailer and Ndege had foreseen such an occurrence. But now this native was seated comfortably in the branches of another tree some thirty yards away, with my ammunition bag around his shoulders!

Still, the situation was not lost, for Ndege had

brought his antiquated muzzle-loader with him. At such short range it would be quite adequate in his expert hands. Dear old Ndege, always at hand in times of trouble! Once again he would come to my rescue; he would complete my humiliation by doing my shooting for me! The day before I had had to run for my life; today I sought safety in a tree; and now, in spite of my modern, seventy-five guinea heavy Express, Ndege, with his old blunderbuss, was about to destroy what little dignity I had left. Already he was preparing for the shot—my humiliation was complete. The next instant a terrific explosion rocked our tree and a fragment of iron screamed past my ear. I was almost knocked from the tree, whilst Ndege was blown off his perch, but luckily he grasped a branch and saved himself from falling headlong onto the buffalo's horns. His face was badly burnt and his right hand was bleeding profusely. The old muzzle-loader —or what was left of it, was wedged tightly in a fork of the tree. The barrel had split asunder; over the firing-chamber was a jagged hole six inches long. This, I soon learned, had been caused by an excessive charge of powder. Ndege, who was obviously no student of ballistics, had been so impressed by the danger of our mission that he had on that morning rammed a treble load down the barrel of his old fusil! Only by a miracle had we escaped being killed instantly when the explosion took place.

The commotion had, if possible, increased the buffalo's fury. There was nothing to do now but remain in the tree until hunger or thirst would induce the animal to leave the vicinity. During a long three hours he never got very far from the tree, and the smallest movement from any of us brought him back at full speed. Finally he wandered off far enough to allow the native with my ammunition bag sufficient time to reach us. He had a good start on the bull, and was safely installed in our tree before the brute was back menacing us again. He seemed to single me out for particular attention, and came so close to me that I could almost touch him with the muzzle of my rifle. As he stood swinging his head viciously, I placed a bullet between his eyes. And so came to an end one of the most difficult and exciting encounters I have ever had with a buffalo.

This gruelling affair proved, once again, how really determined a wounded buffalo can be in his quest for vengeance. As I had suspected, the rufous bull had been wounded some time previously by native hunters. We found a lead slug embedded in a festering sore in his side.

24: BUFFALO JONES IN AFRICA

W HEN NEWCOMERS to the hunting game suddenly find themselves possessed of a lively imagination and start to draw on that imagination for facts, the result, as a rule, is amusing. If the story they tell is a "tall one," as it generally is, the old-timer will sit and listen and his only comment will be a laconic "Oh yes!"

When the Buffalo Jones expedition came out to East Africa and informed all and sundry that the object of their visit was to lasso, and capture alive, every species of game they could catch up with, elephant alone excepted, the old-timers laid particular emphasis on the "oh yes," whilst others felt certain that, if the Americans had the nerve to try to put their plan into execution, there would speedily be three more fatal accidents to report in these parts, and there would not be much sympathy for them. That was *before* this trio started operations. Long before they had got halfway through their programme we had all changed our minds, and what was more, we readily admitted that their style of hunting had reached a standard of perfection that none of us of the old school could ever hope to attain, and the novelty of their methods was lost to none of us.

HORNED DEATH

Buffalo Jones*, the leader of the expedition, was a man of some sixty years of age, and was accompanied by two expert cowboys, a team of forty splendid ponies, and a number of trained hunting dogs—plus their hunting tackle, which consisted of saddles, bridles, lassos, nets, cages, etc., but no rifles. The trio soon gave evidence of their ability when, by way of getting acquainted with conditions, they confined their energies to lesser and harmless game, which they roped without effort. The tempo was quickly stepped up, and it was not long before they caught up with a monster crocodile sunning himself on the banks of a river. It was curiosity that led to the saurian's undoing, for as he lifted his head to see what was responsible for the rustling in the grass near him, a lasso suddenly closed around his neck, and a few minutes later he found himself securely tied to a tree. By that time he had lassos around each leg as well as around his tail.

Shortly after that the Jones party asked to be taken to lion country, and when one afternoon a particularly fine male was found near a tree, the dogs were set loose to keep him as near to the tree as possible, and to induce him to make a false move. The false move came when he struck out with a front paw at one of the dogs who had approached too near. A few seconds later the big fellow was being hauled off the ground by a lariat which had closed around the outstretched paw and had been passed quickly over an

---

* Buffalo Jones is the real-life, central figure of the book *The Last of the Plainsmen,* by Zane Grey. The author-sportsman hunted with Jones in 1907, in our American West, and the book is an absorbing record of that companionship. Here, too, Grey recounts some of the earlier activities of Buffalo Jones, "the last of the plainsmen."

over-hanging branch of the tree. Before he could get over his surprise he was safely trussed up in a net and deposited in a cage that had been brought along for the purpose.

Lions and crocodiles are dangerous animals, and to handle them with so little respect was something quite novel to us. But still, they do not belong to the "dreadnaught" class. "Wait until they start to play with the big fellows," was the general comment. The first big fellow to fall for their play was the hippo. The trio claimed afterwards that he was so clumsy "he just fell over his own feet as soon as we put the works on him." It was true, the hippo showed little fight, and, being a slow thinker, he had no plan of action ready to cope with the emergency. By the time he had thought up something there were so many ropes tied around him he did not think it worth while to resist the inevitable. There remained the buffalo and the rhino. It was then that we expected to see the fireworks, and in this we were not altogether wrong. The buffalo failed to run true to form. He was a big bull, selected from a running herd, and was not able to run fast enough to keep out of their way. He stumbled and came a nasty cropper as one of his front legs was jerked sideways violently whilst he was moving at top speed. Quickly more lariats closed around his legs and the team of ponies was set to work. An hour or so of violent struggling helped him to decide that it was not worth while to carry on the unequal struggle any further.

When finally the trio settled down to prepare for

the rhino, expectations ran high, and we were not disappointed. The first rhino was spotted soon after 7
o'clock in the morning, and the Americans decided to
rope him in. The three men were mounted on their
ponies, whilst close behind them followed the rest
of the team of riderless horses. As soon as the rhino
was maneuvered into a suitable position two lariats
closed around his front legs on either side, and then
began an amazing display of courage and skill. The
men dismounted immediately and left the two riderless
horses to start and "play" the rhino, whilst more ponies
were brought up from the rear. In a short time the
entire team was at work and, pull as the rhino would,
he never once succeeded in unbalancing either rider
or horse. As soon as he started a charge in one direction
the team on the other side would pull in the opposite
direction. In this manner the huge beast was played
out in much the same way as an angler will play out a
big catch. All day long this amazing struggle was
fought out, and at 5 o'clock in the afternoon the rhino
decided to call it a day. Heavy stakes were quickly
driven into the ground and to these the rhino was tied
with big chains. A few minutes later the leader of the
expedition came along with a red-hot iron and branded
the big fellow on his hind quarters. Later that evening
the trio held a consultation as to how they were to
release the rhino again. Their agreement provided
that no animal should be killed in the process of capture. It was either to be released or brought in alive.
Buffalo Jones was not in favour of traveling about the
country with a full-grown rhino as companion, and

whereas they had a well worked-out scheme for the capture of the beast, they found it difficult to work out a scheme for his release without danger to themselves. It was late that night before they finally decided on the plan they would follow the next day. But they might as well have saved themselves the trouble, for when they arrived on the scene the following morning the rhino had disappeared. After he had recovered from his fatigue he had pulled up the stakes and decamped with the chains.

If rhinos grow to the great age that is claimed for them, and if this one has not come to grief in the meanwhile, there is one disgruntled member of the species running about somewhere in the forest of Kenya with a chain around his neck, and a Buffalo Jones brand on his hind quarters! Knowing the vindictive nature of these animals, I would advise anyone who has the misfortune to meet him to shoot quickly and accurately, or to look for the largest tree in the vicinity and lose no time in finding out how high the topmost branches are from the ground.

The filming of the exploits of this amazing trio was left to the well known artist, Cherry Kearton, and required the greatest skill and nerve. In those days the cameraman operated with the aid of a black cloth, which covered his head and the camera. On more than one occasion the operator had hairbreadth escapes in filming the proceedings with the rhino. The closest call came when the big fellow charged, dragging the ponies and riders behind him, and made straight for the camera. It was a split second that separated the passing of the rhino and the removal of the camera.

Those of us who have made hunting our business for many years, and are referred to as "the old stagers," know just about all that is really worth knowing about the animals we hunt. We know their habits and traits; we know how to extricate ourselves from dangerous situations, and most of us can use the rifle with deadly effect—otherwise we could not survive for long. But the Buffalo Jones trio showed us something altogether new in the way of hunting. It is true, in their own country these men had a lifelong experience and training in their line of business, but although nearly forty years have elapsed since they showed us how it is done, none of us has attempted to emulate their feats. I have often wondered whether a second such trio could be recruited again—even in America.

At the time this expedition came out to Africa cinematography was still in its infancy, and the pictures of their exploits did not do justice to the enterprise. With the great improvements of the past thirty years, and the advent of sound and colour films, it is surprising that a second expedition on similar lines has not been organised. I pass the suggestion on for what it is worth—financially and otherwise. In comparison with their manner of capturing game, hunting with rifles is tame.

If this little group from America showed us points in the art of hunting, and provided us with food for reflection and cause for serious discussion, another group, somewhat more numerous, provided the comic element. During the East African campaign a friend of mine who is a well-known elephant hunter of Lado Enclave fame, and who acted also as guide for the Buffalo Jones expedition, was stationed at a post near Tsavo, where he was officer-in-charge of supplies and transport. One day a sergeant and a squad of men arrived at this post on their way out from England. They were due to leave for the front line, a hundred miles away, with the next convoy of supplies. As the convoy was not due to leave for two days they had to wait in camp, where there was nothing for them to do. In order to keep them occupied the O.C. decided to send them out on the road the next day to check up on a bridge some eight miles away, over which the trucks would have to pass. Instructions to this effect were given to the sergeant, a typical cockney, and early next morning the detachment left to carry out their instructions. Nothing further was thought about the matter until a few hours later when the sergeant came rushing into camp, almost speechless with excitement. As he approached the O.C. he came to the salute in his best parade ground style and bawled out at the top of his voice, "Gawd blimey, sir, we have gone and killed a blinking big elephant!" The sergeant was in such a state of excitement that it was difficult to obtain an intelligent account from him as to what had happened. After he had been given a tot of whiskey and ordered to sit down and calm himself, the O.C., who by now was rather worried about this unexpected turn of events and feared that an accident might have occurred, started to cross-question the sergeant. It seems that, whilst marching along the road, they had spotted an elephant asleep under a tree, some fifty yards from the road. In proper military style the sergeant had ordered his men to line-out and then gave the order to open fire on the elephant. The first volley had no visible effect, and a second volley was ordered. This had the desired result, for the elephant collapsed. After they had examined the elephant and found it to be quite dead, the sergeant had relegated the bridge to a place of secondary importance, and ordered his men to return to camp in order to report to headquarters the more important doings of the morning. After assuring himself that all the men had returned safely, the humour of the situation was readily appreciated by the O.C., who, as I have said, was himself an old elephant hunter. "And how many rounds of ammunition did you use, sergeant?" he queried. "I'm not quite sure, sir," replied the sergeant. "I ordered two rounds rapid, but I'll check up the ammunition and let you know." A few moments later the sergeant returned and announced that only sixty-three rounds of ammunition had been used!

No victory in battle could have inspired greater pride in that squad of men than did this unexpected adventure with the elephant. So proud was the sergeant of their achievement that he insisted the O.C. should accompany him to the scene of triumph and verify the facts for himself. An hour later the O.C., accompanied by the sergeant, left by car for the spot. On arriving there the elephant was found lying dead where it was shot. It was a fine big specimen with tusks weighing about one hundred pounds each. Of the sixty-three rounds of ammunition fired, only two had made contact—one in the head, which had fortunately penetrated the brain, and the other in the front foot. One is persuaded to excuse the bad shooting on the ground that their training did not include an elephant as target. But it is tempting to speculate on what would have happened if the elephant had only been stunned and had revived suddenly whilst the men were gathered around it to admire their handiwork.

25: A PRIZE TUSKER

I ARRIVED at Tabora, in Tanganyika Territory, on May 7, 1946, having just returned from a prolonged nine-month safari in the Great Rift Valley. I was on my way to the railway station to book passage South, when my attention was drawn to the imposing figure of a six-foot-four man walking on the opposite side of the street. His gait seemed familiar to me, and in the next instant I recognized my old friend Mickey Norton who, with over 4,000 dead elephants to his credit, must be considered the greatest elephant hunter of all time. He was still hale and hearty, in spite of his four-score years.

A year previously, Mickey had spent a fortnight with me in the Kigoma area. I was at that time preparing for my Rift Valley safari, and many were the adventures of earlier days we discussed during that memorable fortnight, and severe as ever were his strictures on my foolishness once again to set out on the buffalo trail—"a trail that will surely land you six feet under ground, and without profit to anyone." Mickey then proposed, "Why not get out after elephant? There, at least, you stand to make a few bob, and the risk is not so great. Why, I can put you on the trail of a pair of magnificent tuskers!" Mickey's advice had fallen on deaf ears, for two days later I was on my way to the Rift. Now, after nine months of intensive buffalo hunting, I was lucky to meet my old friend. Our latest meeting was the occasion for rejoicing and further reminiscing, and forthwith we repaired to the nearest hotel, where, before closing time, I obtained from him a rough map which would guide me to a spot where I could be sure of a pair of tusks exceeding 100 pounds each, and several other animals in the 70- to 80-pound class. A week later I bade goodbye to Mickey, and set out on this safari after the big tusker.

The spot to which my old friend directed me was not more than forty miles from where my buffalo safari had ended a couple of weeks earlier, and a good deal of the surrounding country was familiar to me. At the end of a five-day safari through rough country, I found myself at the large village indicated on Mickey's map, and here I knew I would find guides to take me to the hangout of the big tusker. The following day was spent in pitching camp and resting from the long walk.

At daybreak the next morning we were again on our way, accompanied by two guides from the village. The going was difficult, for this area, on the south side of Lake Rukwa, is covered by long grass and reeds. Numerous small streams, now little more than mud pools, added to our discomfort. By 10 o'clock there still was no sign or trace of an elephant, and the heat was becoming unbearable. Far out towards the west, below a ridge of hills which formed the edge of the escarpment, was close forest country, but between us and that ridge was a dense reed bed well over three miles in diameter. In this reed bed, the guides informed me, we could expect to meet with the herd of elephants which was sponsored by the big tusker—unpleasant country in which to have trouble with a wounded bull should I fail to bring him down with the first shot. The heaviest weapon in my armoury was a .404 rifle, which is ample for any elephant when one can indulge in "placing" shots; but in such close country shooting is more often done under difficult conditions and with little time for careful aim.

Deeper and deeper we waded through the long grass; apart from the little noise of the trackers behind me everything was quiet. Suddenly a violent commotion quite close at my side brought me sharply to the ready. In the direction from which the noise came I could see reeds being trampled down. This was no high-speed business, but the pace at which the trouble was advancing was fast enough to make me feel uncomfortable. I could not tell what kind of animal I would have to deal with, and as I have said, I was not looking forward to an encounter with the big bull at close quarters in such difficult country. As could be expected, the natives had scattered in all directions at the first sign of trouble. In the next instant the last few intervening reeds were trampled down and I found myself face to face with an old hippo cow! I was on the point of firing when she suddenly wheeled around and shot off in the opposite direction. Apart from the shock she had given me, I had no particular grievance to settle with her, and I allowed her to go her way.

A Prize Tusker

It was some time before the gang of natives could be brought together again and as soon as this was accomplished I instructed the guides to take the shortest cut that would lead us to more open country. The encounter with the old hippo showed plainly how difficult it would be to shoot one's way out of trouble should it start at close quarters. An hour later we had reached the foot of the escarpment, and here I decided to call a halt whilst the trackers looked for fresh tracks. My safari "boy" had just brought me a mug of tea, when two shots rang out in quick succession in the distance. As my trackers had struck out in the opposite direction, it was quite evident that they were not responsible for the shooting; either native hunters were busy shooting up the country, or some other European was on the trail of the big tusker. It did not take me long to dispose of the mug of boiling tea, and a few minutes later I set off in the direction of the shooting.

Near where I had camped was a small river, still trickling water, and as this stream ran in the general direction of the shots I had heard I decided to follow its course. There was always the chance that the bull might not have been killed outright and if he was badly wounded he would almost certainly make for water. The going was still difficult, for we were in close forest which contained many clusters of reeds and tall grass. We had just passed one of these large clusters when my attention was drawn to the rustling of grass some distance ahead. I was on an old elephant path and instinctively I knew that they were on the same track, and that we were heading for a meeting.

There was scarcely a breeze but several times during my slow advance I had tested the wind and now with the prospects of an imminent encounter, I moved off quickly to my left, where a forest giant offered cover and, if need be, protection.

From my position, under perfect cover, I had a clear view of the path a few yards at my right. Even then, I could hear approaching footsteps—those of elephants coming to water. In the next instant my rifle was raised in readiness for any eventuality. A few more seconds, and a raised trunk came into view. It was a cow elephant ahead of a group, and it was quite obvious that she was alarmed, for she kept turning her trunk from left to right, sniffing the air. Abruptly, she stopped at the very point where I had turned off. With ears spread wide open and trunk lifted high, she appeared every inch as dangerous as she actually was at that moment. I was watching her movements closely in anticipation of a charge, when suddenly three more forms came into view, and I was privileged now to witness one of the rare sights in elephant hunting. As the trio advanced, I could see that the one in the centre, a big bull, was in distress, and two cows, one on each side, were literally holding him up. His head was hanging low, and in the long grass it was quite impossible to get a good view of his tusks. The trio advanced a few more yards and came to a small clearing, where the leading cow halted. The bull was staggering and swaying from side to side, obviously dying, but his two companions were loyally supporting him. Suddenly, the leader turned in her tracks, and with great concern caressed the wounded bull with her trunk. She began to draw water from her stomach and spray it all over him with her trunk. But that bull was beyond all help, and in a few seconds he sank to his knees. The three cows were plainly distressed at the loss of their companion and kept circling around him for several minutes. I watched these proceedings closely, without making a move, for I had no desire to attract their attention and possibly find myself at the end of a charge. I was beginning to wonder whether I should have to spend the rest of the day under cover, when the leader of the quartette moved off and the two other cows promptly followed her.

As soon as I felt certain that the cows had got beyond earshot, I walked up to examine the carcass of the dead bull. As a tusker he was not worth a great deal, perhaps a fifty-pounder. This indicated that the shooting had not likely been done by Europeans. Close examination showed that two heavy slugs had entered the left side and penetrated the lungs. This was an extremely disappointing turn of events, for I felt certain that for several hours no elephants would approach the scene of the shooting; also, I would have to send a runner to report to the nearest Boma, as I did not wish to claim this inferior tusker on my license.

For the rest of the day I was compelled to remain where we were in order to allow the camp followers to attend to the ivory and load themselves with meat. Later in the day the trackers returned and brought me a negative report. They had encountered a couple of small herds, but of the big bull they had seen no trace. This was rather disappointing, and I decided to camp for the night. Before sunset that afternoon the first of the villagers from my previous camp began to arrive, and by nightfall only the bones of the big carcass remained.

Most of the villagers decided to return home with their meat, but amongst those who remained behind was an elderly man who came to me and asked why I was hunting elephants with "baby teeth" when big tuskers could be had so easily. Obviously, he was under the impression that I had killed this bull. The mention of big tuskers immediately set me off on a cross-examination, and I was soon certain that this native had that very morning seen the big bull I sought. He had seen him standing asleep under a tree, and from his description it was evident that here was indeed an outsize in tusks—so large and heavy were they that the bull actually used them as supports for his head whilst he slept. The spot where the old man had seen the big fellow was fully twelve miles from my camp, and further inquiries elicited the information that the bull frequently visited that particular area. Although he occasionally joined up with other herds, he would more often be by himself. After a good deal of discussion I persuaded my informant to accompany me to the spot next day, and early the following morning we set off on the trail of the big bull.

It was about 10 o'clock in the forenoon when we reached the spot where the bull had been seen the previous day, and in quick time I had the trackers and spotters out to look for any signs there might be of him. By 3 o'clock that afternoon we were still searching without success and I decided to call a halt for a while. We had been resting hardly five minutes when one of the spotters came running in to say that he had seen the bull. The animal was again standing asleep under a tree, with his head resting on his tusks. This was good news indeed. The spot was little more than a mile away, and unless something unexpected had happened I would find him there, still asleep. In that case the hunt would come to an end without excitement and with but little expenditure in the matter of fatigue. But in elephant hunting things do not always work out quite as easily as all that. When we arrived at the indicated spot there was no trace of the bull, and once again spotters and trackers were sent out in all directions to try to find him. Several hours were spent in fruitless search and then as the sun was about to dip one of the trackers passed the signal that he had spotted the bull. I was quickly on the scene, hoping to get the business settled before the fading light would make shooting impossible. It was difficult country, owing to the long grass, and matters were complicated further by the bull's being on the move. I watched him closely as he walked straight ahead. Every few minutes he would come to a stop and sniff the air. Obviously, he was suspicious and I could not afford to take chances. He was allowing me no opportunity for the brain shot I desired, for with the heavy .404 it would be a simple matter to dispose of him with a well-placed hit.

Twice more he came to a stop, but on each occasion I found myself unable to get in a head shot. By
now, the light was becoming distinctly bad, and I felt
that in waiting for the brain shot I might easily lose
my trophy. I decided that I would shoot for the heart,
should he come to a halt again and give me a suitable
chance. It was fully ten minutes later, with the light at
its worst, that the bull again came to a stop. As before,
he kept raising his trunk, and I simply could not get
my sight trained to his brain. But as he lowered his
trunk again and moved away slowly I pressed the
trigger. I had aimed for the heart—a raking shot
from behind—and hoped for the best. The range was
little less than one hundred yards, and as the bullet
made contact the bull whirled around. Once again,
his trunk was raised high and with huge ears fully
extended he rent the air with his screams. That bull
was out for trouble, and the slightest move to attract
his attention would be certain to draw a charge. The
light was fading rapidly, and for a moment things
looked awkward as he came forward in my direction
at a fast pace. Luckily, he had not yet detected me and
I crept as low down in the grass as I could whilst at
the same time keeping him under observation. Just
how much damage my bullet had done I could not tell,
for so far the effects were not apparent. Then, as he
changed direction, I fired a second shot for the heart.
This time I could see, as well as hear, the bull "take it,"
and as soon as the bullet made contact, he turned once
more and came straight for me. This was an unpleasant
business; the light was very bad and a head-on charge

An outsize bull shot in the Belgian Congo.

Natives dancing in welcome to a safari.

at close quarters is one of the most difficult situations to deal with in elephant hunting. The head, unlike that of the buffalo, is held high and its angle in relation to the hunter makes it almost impossible to attain the brain. Now he was barely twenty yards from me. There was only one thing left for me to do and that was to fire for the shoulder. If I could succeed in fracturing the limb the charge would come to a sudden stop. Up to now he had not slowed down as a result of my second shot and was squealing louder than before— a somewhat disconcerting spectacle, with trunk raised high and ears fully extended. There have not been many occasions in my life when I felt more insignificant than I did at that moment. Once again my Jeffery .404 spat fire, and this time the bull came to a sudden stop. I had fractured the left shoulder, and this made movement almost impossible for him. As he stood motionless, with his trunk aloft, I was about to fire a fourth shot when I noticed the trunk start to droop. The big fellow began sagging at the knees until finally he reached a kneeling position and thus he remained until I walked up and made death double-sure by placing a bullet in his brain.

My first shot proved to have been slightly high and missed the heart, but tore into the lungs; the second was placed squarely in the heart and left a tremendous cavity in that organ. The third bullet served only to break down the charge and prevent the bull from coming to grips with me before he finally collapsed. The whole business was over in something like two minutes from the time I had opened fire, but those two minutes were packed with thrills. The tusks fulfilled all my expectations, for they pulled the scales at 105 and 107 pounds, respectively. Two days later I caught up with another bull, but he proved to be a 75-pounder and provided no excitement. I had managed to stalk him to within twenty-five yards, from which range he shipped the full benefit of a 400-grain load in the brain.

My safari came to an end in less than half the time I had expected. It only remained for me to return to my home town, where Mickey Norton was to meet me and hear the full details of my hunt. Eight days later I arrived back home, late at night. Mickey was not there and there was a funereal atmosphere about the place. On the mantelpiece lay an opened telegram. I picked it up, and these words met my eyes: "Regret to inform you that Mickey Norton passed away this morning." Sadly I re-read the message. Yes, it was true; this was the end of yet another trail. But he who passed will forever fill a top niche in the history of elephant hunting. No man living knew more about elephants than Mickey, and I doubt seriously if any other man ever accounted for half as many, for at the time of his death his score had exceeded 4,200. In the late years of his life he gave up hunting entirely, but he never tired of telling of his early adventures.

A kindly and jovial soul, Mickey was ever ready to have a joke at some beginner's expense. One of his best efforts was at my expense, when one afternoon he asked me to shoot up some game for his camp requirements. Mickey handed me his favourite 8 mm. rifle, after carefully loading it, and gave me comprehensive instructions as to the sighting to be used at different ranges, to all of which I listened attentively. But I might as well have saved myself the trouble, for when, after a three-mile walk in the blistering sun, I came up with a herd of roan antelopes, I discovered to my dismay that Mickey had filled the magazine with five duds. So there it was, a six-mile walk for Mickey's amusement! I was in no mood for bantering on my return, but my remonstrances only brought the laconic reply: "Never let another man load your guns for you, my boy." Farewell, Mickey, my dear friend!

26: RIFLES - THEIR CAPACITIES AND LIMITATIONS

IN THE COURSE of an extended and pleasant correspondence with Mr. Elmer Keith, of North Fork, Idaho, U.S.A., much has passed between us concerning the rifles used on the game animals of our respective continents. And it is at the suggestion of this good American friend that I have here set down some observations on the rifles used on our African fauna. My views on this subject are those of a serious hunter who considers the weapon he carries to be the best tool for the job at hand. Therefore the words which follow are based on practical experience with certain weapons, along with some observations anent the natural and acquired abilities of the shooter himself.

What, then, are the best rifles one can use when following dangerous animals, such as buffalo, lion, elephant, rhino, etc.? There is no rifle that will meet *all* requirements; but there are rifles for which one will have a preference when facing awkward situations. In frequent discussions with others of the hunting fraternity, I have noted a marked tendency to vote for the heavyweights, such as the double .600 and the .450/500 Express D.B. To the uninitiated, it will doubtless appear sound logic that the heavier the rifle the better the results will be when one has to shoot it

[316]

out at close quarters with the "iron clads." However, my own experience has taught me that this is not always the case, and very early in my hunting career I decided to discard the double barrel heavies for a good heavy or medium magazine rifle.

It would be foolish to deny the fact that, against a charging buffalo at close quarters, one can expect quicker and better results from a D.B. heavy than from a medium or heavy magazine rifle. This, as a proposition, appears quite sound; but in actual practice, in my own case, it has not always worked out that way. My own contention is that by far and away the best manner to deal with a charge is to stop it before it gets under way, and the best way of doing this is to have at one's disposal the kind of rifle that is capable of bringing home the bacon immediately a vital spot is hit. It stands to reason, therefore, that velocity and energy in a rifle must be accompanied by accuracy, and it is in this latter respect that the double barrel heavies so frequently fail at longer ranges. In dealing with outsize bulls, charging from close quarters, I cannot remember a single instance where the results obtained by the super-heavies could not have been duplicated by a good medium or light heavy such as .375 or .404. There are surprisingly few spots on the huge carcass of a buffalo that will allow *immediate* killing results. These places are, notably, the brain, the spine, and the kidneys. Since it is almost impossible to place a kidney shot on any animal in a full head-on charge, there remain only the brain and spinal shots. I do not know of one modern medium or light-heavy rifle that would not be capable of bringing down any animal in existence, if the bullet were placed fairly in the brain or anywhere on the spinal column. A modern medium—the .333-calibre is representative—has all the velocity and penetration required to deal with any animal, provided the rifle is in the hands of a crack shot. The inferior marksman is not likely to fare any better with the cannons than he will with lighter weapons.

I freely admit that the super-heavies are capable of throwing almost any animal clean off its course, and will thereby give valuable time for a second shot, but I do not know of many instances where frontal shots have had this desirable result on buffalo. A shot fired from the side will invariably have this result—but buffaloes, elephants, and rhinos do not, as a rule, charge sideways! The double barrels have the advantage of a second shot which can be fired simultaneously with, or immediately after, the first shot, but against this ability one has to contend with the heavy recoil, which invariably affects the accuracy of the second *shot*. My remarks here are confined to the question of obtaining *immediate* results, not ultimate results. The cannons, with their greater penetration and proportionally greater destruction of tissue, will always have it over the lighter weapons, especially when safety, rather than a trophy, is the object desired. In the case of elephant and other outsize animals, where tissue destruction is of primary importance, the super-heavies are of inestimable value, and enjoy preference over the lighter weapons. But even in the case of the elephant, I am reminded of a notable incident where a good heavy magazine rifle would have given a far more satisfactory result.

Some years ago, a friend and I were out after elephant in the Belgian Congo, and the weapon he carried was a double .450/500. Late in the afternoon we caught up with a herd and my friend bagged a fine big bull, having fired the two rounds in rapid succession. In the next instant, a cow from the herd came out in full charge. My friend had not the time to reload, and if I had not been in a position to "cover" him with a heavy .425 magazine rifle, this episode would undoubtedly have ended on a tragic note.

I am convinced that modern hunting rifles of all calibres approach mechanical perfection, and it is unlikely that there will be any revolutionary improvements in their performance. Any likely improvement should be looked for in the ammunition itself, and I have often wondered why a type of delayed action, high-explosive bullet could not be perfected—something that would ensure a second and possibly more powerful shock than the primary contact. Such an innovation would likely be condemned by the armchair sportsman-critic; but since every true sportsman should desire immediate killing, without wounding and suffering, I fail to see on what grounds any effort in this direction should be classed as unsportsmanlike.

Having said so much about the heavies, mediums and super-heavies in their application to elephant, buffalo and rhino, we will consider the type of rifle that is the most satisfactory for general hunting out here in Africa. Here again there is a great diversity of opinion, as there are scarcely fewer varieties of rifles in use here than in America.

Since the hunting of antelopes, both large and small, does not involve the problems and risks encountered in dangerous hunting, one can get nearer to an answer as to which is the most satisfactory type of rifle to use. Here, as in the case of dangerous hunting, we are once again confronted with a variety of conflicting views. In the former case we had the partisans of the super-cannon, and in the present consideration we have those who are addicted to the use of the Magnum-accelerated-whatnot-express type of rifle. In this field I have had a long and varied experience, and I feel that I can speak with some little authority. The super-express has definitely come to stay, and its uses are manifold. Out on the open plains of Africa, where game has had a surfeit of man, approach is often very difficult, and extreme ranges have to be shot over. When these conditions apply, the efficacy of the express stands unchallenged.

At ranges of 300 to 600 yards, the flat trajectory of the express, as well as its penetration and velocity, bring something to the aid of the hunter that is, to all intents and purposes, indispensable. But conditions change; the open plain will give way to closely wooded country, and here the express can become an extremely undesirable weapon. Every hunter is aware that bullet-shock is as great a killer, if not greater, than tissue destruction, and when one takes into consideration the game animal's tenacity of life, it becomes apparent that higher bullet velocity at close quarters brings a

proportionate reduction of shocking power. The ultimate result of a well-placed shot from an express can
hardly be different from that of a medium, but from
the moment of contact to the moment of final collapse
there is often a great time-lag, and in closely wooded
country the animal is apt to be lost, because in such
places tracks are frequently all but impossible to
follow.

It must also be remembered that in close forest,
with animals on the alert, one has frequently to shoot
under difficulties and often with but little time for
careful aim. In connection with such conditions, I
once experienced what to me seemed an appalling display of bad marksmanship. I had acquired a superb
.275 Express, by one of the most renowned English
manufacturers, and in preliminary tests at ranges varying from 350 to 500 yards I had astonishing results.
Shortly afterwards, I had the occasion to empty a
magazine of five charges on as many buck at a range
of little more than 100 yards, and failed to see a single
result. I felt disposed to consign my acquisition to
the nearest foundry. None of these animals had
evinced the slightest sign of distress, nor could I hear
the bullets make contact, and I naturally felt disgusted
to have failed with five consecutive shots at such close
range. But further investigation turned my disgust
into delight. As I went in pursuit of my quarry, I
found five animals stretched out in a line over a distance of 1,000 to 1,500 yards. In this particular case,
I had scored five vital hits, but in each case the necessary shock was lacking. In closely wooded country

and without the aid of expert trackers, I might easily have lost all my trophies.

Far better were the results I achieved with a medium .333 Jeffery, which, to my mind, is one of the finest all-'round weapons and one capable of meeting any and every contingency when handled by an expert. Of my total score of over 1,000 buffaloes, at least 500 fell to this superb weapon, and what is more, I rarely had to contend with a charge when using it. My earlier axiom held good in most cases: Stop the charge before it gets under way.

For fear that I may have created the impression that lighter rifles are to be preferred when dealing with dangerous game, I would put the position clearly. The heavier rifle definitely has the advantage, having greater stopping powers; its energy and penetration ensure greater shock, with a more positive final result. But this very fact does not entitle any raw amateur to take the field against the "beef trusts" with a feeling that he has in his hands a panacea against all contingencies. When dealing with buffalo, wounded or otherwise, charges are generally unexpected, and as often as not from close quarters. What is required in such cases is a rifle, or a load, that will give *immediate* results. I know of no rifle that will have an immediate result on buffalo, elephant or rhino unless a vital motive organ is shattered. A fatal wound, inflicted in the heart or lungs, will bring about an ultimate collapse, but these intervening seconds, or minutes, often are sufficient to spell tragedy to the hunter. If an animal dies too late to be prevented from inflicting a casualty, or serious injury, it matters not whether he dies from the wound of a double .600 or from a minor wound of a .22. My preference for a good light-heavy or medium is due to the fact that with such rifles the standard of accuracy is so high that it is possible to place the bullet where it is wanted. And since it is the first shot that determines whether an animal is killed or wounded, I am in favour of the rifle that ensures the greatest accuracy. With such an important and vital requirement assured, the rest is up to the man who handles the gun. A poor marksman, or one of a nervous disposition, or who lacks the necessary experience, has no business to hunt the more dangerous animals. Without exception such hunters all come to a common end, if they are foolish enough to persist at it long enough, irrespective of the calibre or type of rifle they use.

We now move farther down the line, and consider the performance of the lighter rifle on game varying between the 50- and 150-pound weights. In this category, and in it alone, have I had the opportunity of testing out a first-class American firearm. I have no hesitation in saying that, in dealing with the lesser antelopes of Africa, I have found the little .22 Savage Hornet supreme. Not only have I tested it on antelopes in the 150-pound class, but in order to satisfy myself as to its capacity I have used it successfully on animals weighing up to 450 and 500 pounds, notably roan and sable antelopes, as well as zebra. Two of my closest friends in the hunting business have assured me that they have used it successfully on eland weighing up to 1,500 pounds. But here we are dealing with the cream of African hunters—men who not only can pick and place their shots, but who know all the tricks in the trade of stalking animals to within zero range. The Savage Hornet gave me all the answers where the smaller antelopes are concerned; its one deficiency is that at ranges beyond 100 yards there is a remarkable drop in performance. A better performer over the longer distances, where small game is concerned, is the .256 calibre. Its accuracy and penetration meet all requirements.

But it all comes back to the one established fact, and that is: The finest rifle is rendered impotent by the novice's lack of experience and poor marksmanship. Every hunter should know the habits and peculiarities of the animals he hunts and, knowing the limitations of the weapon he uses, he should take the necessary precautions and act in accordance. Thus, an inferior rifle, in the hands of an expert, will often give excellent results, whereas a superb weapon, in the hands of a novice, can lead to disaster. To my mind, a careful study of animals and their peculiarities, and a sound knowledge of their behaviour in general, are secondary only in importance to the weapons used in hunting. When dealing with buffalo and similarly aggressive animals, the smallest detail pertaining to their behaviour, especially under fire, should be carefully studied and remembered for future reference, and the more details the hunter can crowd into his repertoire the nearer he will get to taking the field on equal terms. I am definitely not one of those armchair critics who are forever harping about the chances being overwhelmingly in favour of the hunter in view of the perfection of the modern rifle. Hard experience has taught me that, in spite of being armed with the finest rifle money can buy, when one has to deal with an obstreperous buffalo in bad country, the chances will favour the buffalo by at least two to one.

To the young and inexperienced hunter who is climbing the ladder, my advice is: It is far better and safer to over-gun than to under-gun. Until you have reached the stage where you can get the last ounce of stopping-power out of the lighter rifles, it is sound policy to use as heavy a gun as you can handle conveniently and effectively.

27: THE SPOTTED CATS

B<small>Y</small> CONTINUAL observation and frequent contacts, one gets to know quite a lot about wild
animals and their habits. After a good many years,
during which time I have had innumerable opportunities to study them, I think I can claim to have more
than a nodding acquaintance with two important species of African fauna. They are the buffalo and the
leopard. Those who read the adventures I have related in connection with the buffalo will be able to
form their own conclusions as to the extent of my
acquaintance with him. Of the leopard I have written
much less, but he is the one animal I know better than
any other. My knowledge of the leopard is founded
on twenty years of association with them as pets and it
is only due to the difficulties in obtaining adequate and
regular meat supplies that I have not got one of the
big playful cats running about in my back yard at
this writing. So attached have I become to the spotted
cats that I have steadfastly refused to hunt them, and
during all of my wanderings in the bush I can remember only two occasions when I was compelled
to shoot one, and then not without regret that it was
necessary for me to do so.

Much that has been said about the leopard, to
his detriment, is true—only too true. That he is one
of the most dangerous animals one can encounter

anywhere no one will deny, and I, for one, consider that in many ways he is fully as dangerous as the buffalo or the lion. In natural cunning neither of them surpasses him, and often he is more aggressive and impetuous than either buffalo or lion. A wounded leopard will rarely try to escape, the moment he is hurt he will invariably charge and, when fangs are bared and the ears are pulled well back, only a bullet in the right spot will stop the charge. Only those who have had to resist those deadly claws and fangs can have any idea what it means to deal with this bundle of unbridled fury. It once fell to me to render first aid to a friend who had come to grief with a wounded leopard. He was a ghastly object. I doubt whether any other animal on earth could have inflicted so many wounds in such a short time. When the leopard attacks he uses his fangs and all four feet, and it is the hind claws that are the most dangerous, for with these he will disembowel his victim. My friend of the above-mentioned encounter did not survive for long. It is not necessary for me to give a description of the multiple wounds he received in that short encounter; I hope never to see the like again. I have always been puzzled as to why scratches inflicted by leopards in their wild state will invariably turn septic. Of many hundreds of scratches I have received whilst playing with the big cats not one has become infected. The feeding and manner of living, in both cases, are very much the same.

That the leopard can become a great nuisance once he has taken to raiding domestic animals is perfectly true, and in this respect he is often more destructive than other carnivora, for of all animals he is perhaps the only one who kills for the pleasure of killing. It frequently happens that on gaining entry to an enclosure where sheep, goats or fowls are kept, he will kill as many as time or opportunity will permit, after which he will satisfy his hunger with a small helping from one of the carcasses. Unlike the lion or the hyena, the leopard seldom gorges. He is a small eater and a very clean feeder; in fact, he is scrupulously clean in all his personal habits. The domestic cat can teach him nothing in this respect.

I have often been asked whether leopards ever turn man-eaters. One can not say definitely what any animal will, or will not, do. Personally, I have never come across an instance where the leopard has attacked a human being for food; as a general rule it may be said that he has no such tendencies. A lion will turn man-eater with a hundred times less inducement than will a leopard. It is, in fact, rare for a leopard to attack a human being at all. The notable exceptions are when they are wounded, or if one should approach too close to a female with cubs. In the latter case an attack is almost certain to result. Whereas a lioness with young may try to escape, with or without her cubs, the leopard will not do so. I know of a case where a leopardess with several cubs was disturbed by a car passing at a considerable distance; she immediately gave chase and followed the car for nearly a mile.

On the one occasion when I was forced to go gunning for "Spots" he had made himself a nuisance for fully three months. When the trouble started I had a baby vervet monkey, perhaps a month old. In the daytime this little fellow was allowed to roam about on the front verandah of my house, but at night he was kept in a back room, in a small box covered with heavy planks. To reach this back room it was necessary to cross the verandah, a dining room, and a lounge in which there were numerous stuffed specimens of lion, leopard and other animals on the floor. I was living in a lonely spot at the time and as there was no fear of intruders, the doors were generally left ajar at night. One night I was awakened by a scream from the room where the little vervet was kept, and this was followed by a commotion as the box and other articles in the room were overturned. By the time I had lit my lamp and was ready to investigate the disturbance, a couple of minutes had elapsed. Those two minutes saved me from a severe mauling, for had I gone out quicker I should have blocked the passage of a full-grown leopard with his victim in his jaws. That leopard had braved three rooms in order to pick up so small a morsel of food! After that he became a perfect nuisance, and during the next two months he deprived me of several more pet monkeys, a prize dog, and several chickens and ducks. By the time I decided to put an end to "Spots" he had developed such cunning that it took me a month before I could line him up in my sights. The trouble came to an end one night, when a nine-foot specimen lay stretched out in the backyard with my bullet in his brain.

HORNED DEATH

The other occasion when I had to gun for "Spots"
was when my friend, mentioned previously as being
fatally mauled, followed a leopard into long grass,
against my advice. A few moments later I heard the
report of his shot and that was followed almost immediately by loud screams. The leopard was accounted
for—too late.

Except for a minor compliment or two, I have
so far enumerated most of the unenviable traits of the
leopard. I would tell now why I have kept them as
pets and consider them, with one exception—the chimpanzee—the finest pets of all. I have successfully
raised five leopards, all caught young, and each grew
into a magnificent specimen. During all the years
I have kept them I know of no single occasion when
any one of them ever showed the least sign of aggressiveness or treachery. The worst that ever happened
to me was when, in playing and frolicking, they
became so excited that they forgot to retract their
claws, and minor scratches resulted. Actually, that
was not quite the worst that happened, for there were
other occasions when, in bouts of frolicking with the
big cats, I would have suits or shirts badly torn. Those
were the times when "Spots" really enjoyed the fun
and forgot that he had retractile claws! Then there
was the other memorable instance when "Spots" laid
my eyebrow open to the bone. For years I had made
it a habit never to pass this individual's cage at night
without entering and petting him. On that occasion
I was in a hurry and had not the time to devote to him,
but in passing I stopped for a moment and offered

[330]

him my face for a quick kiss and lick. But "Spots" was not satisfied with such stinted affection, and tried to pull me closer to him. Unfortunately he had hooked his claw in my eyebrow, and in the next instant blood was streaming down my face. It was at that moment that I decided to test the old theory that the leopard will revert to type and turn savage on tasting fresh blood. After I had entered the cage, I carefully closed the door behind me and took a seat on a big log. I then invited "Spots" to come and have a look at the damage he had done. My pet was undoubtedly sorry for what had happened, and in order to help soothe the pain he sat for thirty minutes licking the blood and the wound. That was first class treatment for the wound, as a week later only a faint scar remained to show where the claw had entered.

For years I made it a regular habit to spend at least an hour with "Spots" in his cage every afternoon. On those occasions he would be petted for a while, after which I would sit down and read. If the reading was alternated with stroking and petting, all went well. But if this affection was withheld for too long he would get restless, and if I did not make amends quickly the book would be knocked out of my hands and tossed into the air, after which it would be subjected to the kind of mauling only a leopard is capable of administering. "Spots" definitely would not accept a back seat in the matter of affection and attention.

Leopards, like domestic cats, are inclined to be lazy in the daytime, but I found that they took readily to the habit of following me about for strolls in the country. On these occasions we would have great fun, as "Spots" could never resist the temptation of getting out of sight and taking cover behind a bush or stone. There he would lie and wait for me to approach within inches before he would jump out, feet high, in my direction. In keeping with the spirit of the joke, I would pretend to be badly scared and run away. "Spots" never allowed me to get away very far. It was on such occasions that my clothing fared so badly. Leopards have a tremendous instinct for taking cover behind the smallest objects. "Spots" often appeared ludicrous when, in the absence of a more suitable object, he would go down flat on his stomach and try to hide behind a stone two or three inches high, or even a blade of grass!

In his playful moods I have found the leopard the most delightful of all pets. In his more serious moods he can be distinctly useful, and I consider him the finest "watchdog"* of all, as the following incident, one of many, will help to illustrate: I was at the time conducting a business in which considerable cash was accumulated after banking hours. On my arrival in the office one morning, I found that the place had been burgled and a determined effort had been made to force the safe. The matter was duly reported to the police and searching investigations were made, but

---

* The leopard is not noisy, as watchdogs frequently are; he makes no noise of any kind to scare intruders away. He will lie in wait until his victim is within range, and then only will he move. His faculties of scent and sight are keener than those of a dog, and he is much stronger physically. Native marauders will often brave the risk of facing a good watchdog, but when a leopard fills the role no native will approach within miles.

without result. Then during the next few weeks three more attempts were made to force the safe. A live electric cable, connected to doors and windows, provided no protection. It now occurred to me that "Spots" might be helpful, and that night he was smuggled into my office and tied there at the end of a long chain. From that night onwards the burglaries ceased abruptly! When I returned the next morning I found blood spattered all over the walls; the presence of a piece of black-skinned flesh showed that "Spots" had used his fangs as well as his claws. The numerous bits of tattered rags lying all over the floor indicated also that the intruder had had most of the clothing torn from his body. That robber was permanently cured of one of his bad habits, and how he managed to escape after the mauling he had received remains a mystery to me.

"Do you give them lots of beatings to make them so docile and afraid of you?" is a question I have been asked on hundreds of occasions by people who have witnessed the perfect understanding between the cats (to me they are always just cats) and myself. The answer is: I have never, at any time, or anywhere, beaten one of my cats. They are big, lovable, playful and affectionate creatures who know *only one* master, and to him they look, not for beatings, but for food, affection and understanding—and those needs they have always received from me.

28: ELEPHANT ETIQUETTE

THE MORNING was well begun, and already there was that stifling feeling in the air which presaged another of the scorching days for which the Usanga plain is famous. I scanned the vast expanse of earth with a pair of powerful binoculars. Out on the eastern horizon I could see a fast-moving cloud of dust. At moments, when a gentle breeze would disperse the dust for a second or two, I could identify a large herd of zebra. They were moving rapidly towards water. Farther along the skyline was another cloud of dust, also moving in the same direction. That herd, much smaller than the first, consisted of topi and kongoni. And there, away to the north emerging from the edge of a dense forest, was a third fast-moving billow of dust—a tremendous herd, that. So dense was the dust in that quarter that for some time it was impossible to identify the nature of the herd. The tracker at my elbow spoke. "They must be buffalo, making all that dust. It must be a very large herd; no other animals in these parts could stir up such a dust. Yes, they are buffaloes, Bwana, I am certain of it." A few minutes later I could see the herd plainly. The tracker was right, they were buffaloes, an immense herd of a thousand or more. But we were not after buffaloes; this day was to be different from other days.

ELEPHANT ETIQUETTE

Two days earlier we had camped at a small water hole in the open plain. I had still two elephants on my licence, and we had been brought to the area by the report of local natives, who stated that on several occasions during the past two weeks they had seen an outsize in tusks in the vicinity. On the morning preceding the one on which my narrative opens, Ndege and four scouts had struck out on a trail leading south, whilst I followed another trail which led to the north. By nightfall I had returned to camp hungry, thirsty and tired—and also disappointed. For by 3 p.m. I had caught up with the herd, the leader of which had left a trail of enormous footprints, but as a tusker he was not worth powder. By 10 o'clock that night Ndege had not returned and I began to feel uneasy on his account. Though he was too experienced a bushman to lose himself, even in unfamiliar country, I felt that some untoward incident might have prevented him from returning to camp. But I was utterly fatigued and soon dropped off to sleep.

Near midnight I was awakened by a jerking at my shoulder. Two of Ndege's scouts had returned, and they brought good news. Ndege had got on to a herd that was sponsored by a big bull with a tremendous pair of tusks. I was informed that he would stick to the herd until nightfall and that he wished me to come out immediately and follow the trail. That was cheerful news indeed. Now, since daylight, we had been following Ndege's trail.

(The scouts had warned me beforehand that the point where they had left Ndege was "mbali sani" (very far), with a special emphasis on the *very*. Under the circumstances I started off well provided with water and food, sufficient to enable me to remain out on the trail for at least three days. In this part of the plain, during the month of October, one can travel light. Bedding is not essential, as the abundant dry grass is an excellent substitute for a camp bed, and the night's clammy heat makes blankets a questionable comfort. An ample supply of water and rusks constituted the larder. Meat could be obtained at any time, as the plain is over-run with game, large and small.)

It was 9 a.m. as I scanned the plain with my binoculars, and we had come approximately ten miles. One of the scouts pointed towards the forest country— from which the great herd of buffaloes had just emerged—and explained that about three miles deeper in the forest was the spot where Ndege had come upon the herd of elephants. At a rough estimate, I judged the total remaining distance to be between twelve and fifteen miles, most of which we would have to cover during the hottest part of the day. This would be difficult going. Added to the heat was the discomfort of the dust, for in this part of the plain one frequently has to walk ankle-deep in fine, silty soil. During the day's hottest hours that soil becomes heated to such an extent as to make walking sheer agony. Great heat blisters form rapidly under one's feet and the resultant swelling frequently makes it necessary to slit the shoes in order to ease the pressure. This day would certainly bring all these discomforts, but the lure of a record-size tusker—with ivory at 20/- per pound—will induce one to suffer such inconveniences in a philosophic spirit!

The ten miles or so in the open plain was gruelling, for there was nothing more substantial than dry grass to offer protection from the sun. But we knew that once we entered the forest country the going would be much easier, and possibly the herd had not moved far from where it was first spotted. At midday only about a mile remained before we would reach the shelter of a giant tree at the edge of the forest. Even as I speculated on this welcome aspect of comfort, a runner emerged from the forest and came towards us at a fast pace. This would mean that Ndege was still sticking to the herd and the runner would lead me to him; or, perhaps there had been an accident. The former seemed the most likely explanation, but my optimism was soon dispelled. The runner announced that the big bull had killed Ndege a few hours earlier!

From the runner's account, Ndege had stuck to the herd all that morning. Against my advice, Ndege had gone on the trail accompanied by a mongrel dog of which he was very fond. The elephants had gone to rest and Ndege, relaxing for a moment, had failed to notice that the dog had gone in pursuit of the herd. The dog had barked at the big bull and excited its wrath, whereupon the elephant set out in pursuit of his tormenter. The dog ran straight towards his master and, before he could realize what had happened, Ndege himself was in the grip of the bull's trunk.

Twice he was tossed violently, and then the bull left him to pursue the dog, which he killed and trampled into a pulp. The runner, who had seen the whole affair from the safety of a high tree, went on to say that after the dog was thoroughly trampled, the bull returned to Ndege's corpse, rolled it over several times, and then proceeded to cover it carefully with large branches which he pulled from nearby trees. After the body was effectively concealed the bull spread his ears and cried in a loud voice, and then disappeared into the forest. Twice he returned, at short intervals, to make sure that his victim was still there. Finally, after two hours had elapsed since the bull's last appearance, the runner risked leaving his perch in order to bring me news of the tragedy.

So that was the end of my faithful servant and friend. An association of twenty years had come to an end on a tragic note—and on what was to have been our last safari together. How often in the past had Ndege saved me from a similar fate! Memories of other days now came to me in an endless stream. There was that fateful night when, over-fatigued, I had tried to settle an issue with a pride of lion. The male had gone down to my fourth shot and by the light of a glimmering torch I stood to face the female with only one round left in my magazine. Ndege knew the danger to which I was exposed and begged me to retreat, but it was too late. Already she was lowering her head for the charge. In the next instant Ndege was at my side to offer what protection he could, with a paltry little axe in hand. Neither of us knew just what the effect of my last shot would be, but in those fateful moments he would not desert me. When the big brute fell at my feet Ndege was there to attack it. Luckily his aid was not necessary for I had placed a vital shot and the danger was over. There were so many other occasions during our twenty years together when Ndege had stood by me in the face of danger and seen it through. But today, when dear old Ndege had needed my help, I had not been there to stand by him. I would find his body and pay my respects to his remains; but above all, I would find his slayer and level the score whatever the cost might be. In this spirit I followed the runner to the spot where the remains of my faithful friend lay buried beneath the branches.

We were following the elephant tracks through dense forest and the runner had just announced that the scene of the tragedy was only a few yards away, when my attention was drawn to a rustling sound in the long grass, a short distance ahead of me. In an instant I had leveled my rifle to deal with what I expected to be the charge of the big bull. Then, I looked upon the grinning face of Ndege! That meeting is best left to the imagination of the reader; before long we were both in tears, but they were tears of joy. For several minutes I listened to Ndege's story of what had happened. He concluded with the statement that the bull had tossed him so high he feared he would freeze to death—one of my old jokes with him when, on occasion, he had to find safety high in a tree. He assured me that after he had been tossed the first time, the elephant had subjected him to a close examination, during which he feigned death. Apparently dissatisfied with the result of his work, the bull had lifted him a second time and tossed him "many yards up into space." Again the bull had examined him closely, and had even placed his trunk to his nostrils in order to make sure there was no breath left in him. Ndege related, "For nearly an hour I never breathed as he kept his snout under my nose, and this must have convinced him that I was really dead. After that he buried me under the branches. I was too shaken to move for a long time, and it was perhaps as well, for that cunning devil returned twice after that to make sure I had not moved and that I was really dead. But his tusks, Bwana—I never saw such tusks before. Let us find him and the ivory will repay us handsomely for all the trouble he has given us."

The idea of cashing in on the ivory of this bull had been my least concern after I had received the startling news of the accident. But now, with Ndege safe, I was again aware that I had come out in search of ivory. In a few minutes we were on the trail—a trail not difficult to follow, as the herd had walked at leisure and pulled down many young trees. The wind sat in our favour, and after an hour's tracking I felt a light touch on my shoulder. Ndege was pointing to a large tree to my left where, less than fifty yards away, the monster bull stood peacefully asleep. In a second I had him aligned in my sights, but as I was about to press the trigger a feeling of remorse came over me. As much as I needed the ivory, I could not bring myself to kill an animal who would go to the trouble of burying the body of an enemy which he had had every right to kill. In a more vindictive spirit he could easily have pulverized Ndege as he had the dog, and who knows, perhaps he was not deceived by Ndege's trick of feigning death, but was merely determined to frighten him. I would give him the benefit of the doubt. He had spared Ndege's life when he had had him at his mercy. The tables were turned now, but I could not take the great bull's life. For fully two minutes I kept him covered in my sights and admired the enormous tusks. Then, lowering my rifle, I signaled to Ndege and the other trackers to return. "I'm not shooting today, Ndege," I remarked. "Another day . . . we will find other tuskers, there is plenty of time." The pitying look Ndege bestowed upon me made it clear that he firmly believed I had taken leave of my senses.

Once out of earshot of the bull, the incident became a lively topic for discussion. Ndege, as usual, had all the answers. He was convinced that, like so many other European hunters he had seen, I had lost my nerve. He said, "Perhaps it is well that Bwana did not shoot. He might easily have missed, and that big bull would not let me off so easily a second time. When their nerves go they will miss an elephant at five yards range." I did not bother to correct Ndege; his explanation was not the right one, but it would do. A week later he had ample evidence that it was not a question of nerves, for on that day I made amends and got two magnificent bulls whose tusks more than compensated for the loss of that other bull.

Another week passed and I was back at my main camp, where an unpleasant duty awaited me, for I had come to write "finis" to my adventures in Central Africa. One afternoon I bade farewell to Ndege and the many others of my hunting crew. As my truck pulled out and I looked back on the small group that had gathered to wish me Godspeed, the memories of the past crowded my mind and I felt sad to think that here, indeed, was the end of it all. I knew that I could never describe adequately the sense of comradeship that had grown amongst us in the wilds. Their loyalty and devotion to me had made my occupation a comparatively safe and easy business. But now I was returning to civilisation, for the first time in thirty years. Congo, Ubangi, Sudan, Uganda, Kenya, Tanganyika—they all belonged to the past. Any future telling of my adventures in those countries would lack campfires, to lend charm and romance to the occasion, and the drone of native voices discussing the day's adventures. The realities of the life I was leaving behind could be appreciated fully only by those who have themselves lived that life.

Farewell, Ndege; farewell my other faithful friends. Happy hunting wherever you may be; it is unlikely that I shall ever take part in your adventures again.